Becoming KCNA Certi

Build a strong foundation in cloud native and Kubernetes and pass the KCNA exam with ease

Dmitry Galkin

BIRMINGHAM—MUMBAI

Becoming KCNA Certified

Group Product Manager: Rahul Nair
Publishing Product Manager: Surbhi Suman
Senior Content Development Editor: Sayali Pingale
Technical Editor: Nithik Cheruvakodan
Copy Editor: Safis Editing
Project Manager: Sean Lobo
Proofreader: Safis Editing
Indexer: Hemangini Bari
Production Designer: Prashant Ghare
Senior Marketing Coordinator: Nimisha Dua

First published: February 2023
Production reference: 1130123

Published by Packt Publishing Ltd.
Livery Place
35 Livery Street
Birmingham
B3 2PB, UK.

ISBN 978-1-80461-339-9

www.packtpub.com

I would like to thank my beloved, Solongo, for her endless support, patience, and understanding throughout the 9-month-long journey of writing this book.

I would also like to thank my brother, German, who has been a great teacher and who inspired me to tie my life to IT at a very young age.

– Dmitry Galkin

Contributors

About the author

Dmitry Galkin is a cloud expert and a founder of Cloudification. For 12+ years, he has been working with cloud technologies, cloud-native solutions, DevOps, infrastructure, and service automation domains in a variety of roles. He has consulted international enterprises and supported small start-ups, mentored students, and developed IT certification programs for non-profit organizations as a subject matter expert.

Dmitry is an open source contributor, and he holds more than 10 professional certifications, including all four Kubernetes certifications from CNCF (namely, KCNA, CKA, CKAD, and CKS). He is based in Berlin and holds a master of science degree from the University of Bremen, Germany.

About the reviewers

Werner Dijkerman is a freelance cloud, Kubernetes (certified), and DevOps engineer. He's currently focused on, and working with, cloud-native solutions and tools, including AWS, Ansible, Kubernetes, and Terraform. He is also focused on infrastructure as code and monitoring the correct *thing*, with tools such as Zabbix, Prometheus, and the ELK stack, and has a passion for automating everything and avoiding doing anything that resembles manual work. He is an active reader of comics and non-fictional and IT-related books, and he is a technical reviewer for various books about DevOps, CI/CD, and Kubernetes.

Johann Gyger is a passionate software engineer living in Switzerland. He has over 20 years of industry experience working as a developer, architect, trainer, and consultant in various domains and for different customers and employers. Besides being a Cloud Native Ambassador, Johann is enthusiastic about the cloud-native movement and organizes the Swiss Cloud Native Day and the Cloud Native Bern Meetup. He strongly believes in open source software and vendor-neutral standards.

Table of Contents

Part 1: The Cloud Era

1

2

Part 2: Performing Container Orchestration

3

4

Part 3:
Learning Kubernetes Fundamentals

5

Assessments   261

Index   273

Other Books You May Enjoy   282

Preface

With more than 20 releases to date, Kubernetes is as hot as ever, even several years after its initial appearance in 2014. Kubernetes, along with other cloud-native technologies, is massively reshaping the IT landscapes in some of the most advanced and progressive companies around the world.

According to the **10th annual Open Source Jobs Report** by the **Linux Foundation**, cloud and containers are highlighted as the most demanded skills categories. Hence, having a strong command of Kubernetes and cloud-native skills is essential for advancing your career and working at some of the best organizations today. Becoming a certified Kubernetes and Cloud Native Associate helps you to stand out and prove your competence in the field.

This book will take you on a cloud-native journey from the very beginning and will teach you both the theoretical and practical aspects of Kubernetes. You'll learn how to build, configure, and run containers with Docker; how to bootstrap minimal Kubernetes clusters; how to deploy, configure, and manage containerized applications with Kubernetes; how to automate software delivery with CI/CD, and much more. You'll build a solid foundation to pass the KCNA exam on the first attempt and get a well-rounded view of today's industry standards.

The book is divided into five parts:

1. *The Cloud Era*
2. *Performing Container Orchestration*
3. *Learning Kubernetes Fundamentals*
4. *Exploring Cloud Native*
5. *KCNA Exam and Next Steps*

In the first part, you'll be introduced to cloud native computing, explaining how the industry evolved and why modern applications often run in containers. Next, you'll learn about Docker and get hands-on with running containers locally.

In *Part 3*, the largest part, you'll learn about Kubernetes: its features, architecture, API, and components. You'll find the best practices, recap questions, and lots of practical assignments to support your journey. In *Part 4*, we'll focus on cloud-native architectures and other technologies from the cloud-native ecosystem. We'll see how to monitor, observe, and deliver cloud-native applications. Finally, in *Part 5*, you'll find mock exams and tips on passing KCNA, as well as some advice on how to proceed after becoming certified.

Who this book is for

Kubernetes and Cloud Native Associate (KCNA) is a pre-professional certification designed for candidates interested in advancing to the professional level through a demonstrated understanding of Kubernetes foundational knowledge and skills.

A certified KCNA will confirm conceptual knowledge of the entire cloud native ecosystem, particularly focusing on Kubernetes. KCNA will demonstrate the candidate's basic knowledge of Kubernetes and cloud-native technologies, including how to deploy an application using basic **kubectl** commands, the architecture of Kubernetes, understanding the cloud native landscape and projects, and understanding the basics of cloud-native security.

Whether a fresh IT graduate, a developer, a system administrator, or a DevOps engineer, regardless of experience, anyone interested in learning about Kubernetes and cloud-native technologies will find this book practical and easy to follow. Familiarity with IT fundamentals (Git), operating systems, and command-line interfaces is required, but no prior knowledge of Kubernetes, Docker, or cloud-native technologies is needed to get started.

What this book covers

Chapter 1, From Cloud to Cloud Native and Kubernetes, shares how computing has evolved over the past 20+ years. It explains what the cloud is, how it appeared, and how IT landscapes have changed with the introduction of containers. You will learn about fundamentals such as IaaS, PaaS, SaaS, and FaaS, as well as take a first look at Kubernetes.

Chapter 2, Overview of CNCF and Kubernetes Certifications, introduces the Cloud Native Computing Foundation (CNCF) and its parent organization – the Linux Foundation. It will share what is behind those foundations, how they appeared, and which projects are curated in their ecosystems. This chapter will explain about the CNCF community, governance, cloud roles, and Kubernetes certification path.

Chapter 3, Getting Started with Containers, provides a closer look at containers, diving deeper into container technology and container ecosystem, and discovering commonly used Docker tooling. This chapter includes practical assignments.

Chapter 4, Exploring Container Runtimes, Interfaces, and Service Meshes, takes you further to explore container runtimes, networking, and interfaces, and learn about service meshes. You will learn how containers can communicate with each other over the network, which container interfaces exist in Kubernetes, and get to know what a service mesh is and its applications.

Chapter 5, Orchestrating Containers with Kubernetes, starts the coverage of the most important and perhaps the hardest part of KCNA certification – *Kubernetes Fundamentals*. You will learn about the features and the basics of Kubernetes architecture, its API, components, and the smallest deployable unit, called a Pod. The practical part includes the local installation of Kubernetes with the help of minikube.

Chapter 6, Deploying and Scaling Applications with Kubernetes, takes you further to explore the Kubernetes functionality and rich ecosystem. The chapter provides an overview of other Kubernetes resources and their purpose; it discusses how to implement self-healing and scaling of applications with Kubernetes, how to use Kubernetes service discovery, and how to run stateful workloads with Kubernetes. More practical Kubernetes exercises are an essential part of the chapter.

Chapter 7, Application Placement and Debugging with Kubernetes, demonstrates how to control the placement of workloads on Kubernetes, how its scheduler works, and how applications running on K8s can be debugged. The chapter covers aspects from the Kubernetes Fundamentals as well as Cloud Native Observability domains of the KCNA exam at the same time.

Chapter 8, Following Kubernetes Best Practices, talks about Kubernetes networking and network policies for traffic control, restricting access with Role-Based Access Control (RBAC), using Helm as a K8s package manager, and more. The final chapter of the Kubernetes part includes a few more hands-on exercises.

Chapter 9, Understanding Cloud Native Architectures, explores aspects of cloud native in more detail. The chapter shares core concepts that are a part of Cloud Native and Cloud Native architectures. This chapter covers further requirements of the Cloud Native Architecture domain of the KCNA exam.

Chapter 10, Implementing Telemetry and Observability in the Cloud, emphasizes the need to monitor and optimize Cloud Native applications based on observations for best performance with cost in mind. The chapter covers further requirements from the Cloud Native Observability domain of KCNA.

Chapter 11, Automating Cloud Native Application Delivery, talks about the Cloud Native application life cycle. You will learn about best practices for the development and delivery of Cloud Native apps and see how automation helps to develop better and ship faster.

Chapter 12, Practicing for the KCNA Exam with Mock Papers, shares a few tips on passing the exam and includes two mock exams to test the knowledge during final preparations.

Chapter 13, The Road Ahead, concludes the book with tips on how to advance and what to do next for a successful Cloud Native career.

To get the most out of this book

You'll install a number of tools; therefore, a system with administrative privileges will be needed.

Software/hardware covered in the book	Operating system requirements
Kubernetes	Windows, macOS, or Linux (macOS or Linux are recommended)
minikube	
Docker	
Prometheus	

If you are using the digital version of this book, we advise you to type the code yourself or access the code from the book's GitHub repository (a link is available in the next section). Doing so will help you avoid any potential errors related to the copying and pasting of code.

Download the example code files

You can download the example code files for this book from GitHub at `https://github.com/PacktPublishing/Becoming-KCNA-Certified`. If there's an update to the code, it will be updated in the GitHub repository.

We also have other code bundles from our rich catalog of books and videos available at `https://github.com/PacktPublishing/`. Check them out!

Download the color images

We also provide a PDF file that has color images of the screenshots and diagrams used in this book. You can download it here: `https://packt.link/OnZI3`.

Conventions used

There are a number of text conventions used throughout this book.

`Code in text`: Indicates code words in text, table names, folder names, filenames, file extensions, pathnames, dummy URLs, user input, and so on. Here is an example: "Let's delete the old `nginx-deployment` that we created at the beginning of this chapter."

A block of code is set as follows:

```
apiVersion: v1
kind: PersistentVolumeClaim
metadata:
```

```
    name: kcna-pv-claim
spec:
  storageClassName: standard
  accessModes:
    - ReadWriteOnce
  resources:
    requests:
      storage: 3Gi
```

When we wish to draw your attention to a particular part of a code block, the relevant lines or items are set in bold:

```
Normal    Scheduled  85s                    default-scheduler
  Successfully assigned kcna/liveness-exec to minikube
  Normal    Pulled     81s                  kubelet
    Successfully pulled image "k8s.gcr.io/busybox" in
3.4078911s
  Warning  Unhealthy  41s (x3 over 51s)  kubelet
    Liveness probe failed: cat: can't open '/tmp/healthy':
No such file or directory
  Normal    Killing    41s                  kubelet
    Container liveness failed liveness probe, will be restarted
  Normal    Pulling    11s (x2 over 85s)  kubelet
    Pulling image "k8s.gcr.io/busybox"
```

Bold: Indicates a term, an important word, or words. For instance, major points can appear in **bold**.

> **Tips or important notes**
> Appear like this

Get in touch

Feedback from our readers is always welcome.

General feedback: If you have questions about any aspect of this book, email us at customercare@ packtpub.com and mention the book title in the subject of your message.

Errata: Although we have taken every care to ensure the accuracy of our content, mistakes do happen. If you have found a mistake in this book, we would be grateful if you would report this to us. Please visit www.packtpub.com/support/errata and fill in the form.

Piracy: If you come across any illegal copies of our works in any form on the internet, we would be grateful if you would provide us with the location address or website name. Please contact us at copyright@packt.com with a link to the material.

If you are interested in becoming an author: If there is a topic that you have expertise in and you are interested in either writing or contributing to a book, please visit authors.packtpub.com.

Share Your Thoughts

Once you've read *Becoming KCNA Certified*, we'd love to hear your thoughts! Scan the QR code below to go straight to the Amazon review page for this book and share your feedback.

https://packt.link/r/1804613398

Your review is important to us and the tech community and will help us make sure we're delivering excellent quality content.

Download a free PDF copy of this book

Thanks for purchasing this book!

Do you like to read on the go but are unable to carry your print books everywhere? Is your eBook purchase not compatible with the device of your choice?

Don't worry, now with every Packt book you get a DRM-free PDF version of that book at no cost.

Read anywhere, any place, on any device. Search, copy, and paste code from your favorite technical books directly into your application.

The perks don't stop there, you can get exclusive access to discounts, newsletters, and great free content in your inbox daily

Follow these simple steps to get the benefits:

1. Scan the QR code or visit the link below

https://packt.link/free-ebook/9781804613399

2. Submit your proof of purchase

3. That's it! We'll send your free PDF and other benefits to your email directly

Part 1: The Cloud Era

In this part, you'll get a quick overview of how computing has evolved since the inception of the cloud, how traditional IT operated before, and what today's cloud native landscape looks like. We'll discuss the Cloud Native Computing Foundation, the Linux Foundation, and look at their projects and certifications.

This part contains the following chapters:

- *Chapter 1, From Cloud to Cloud Native and Kubernetes*
- *Chapter 2, Overview of CNCF and Kubernetes Certifications*

1

From Cloud to Cloud Native and Kubernetes

In this chapter, you'll see how computing has evolved over the past 20 or so years, what the **cloud** is and how it appeared, and how IT landscapes have changed with the introduction of containers. You'll learn about fundamentals such as **Infrastructure-as-a-Service (IaaS)**, **Platform-as-a-Service (PaaS)**, **Software-as-a-Service (SaaS)**, and **Function-as-a-Service (FaaS)**, as well as learning about the transition from monolithic to microservice architectures and getting a first glimpse at Kubernetes.

This chapter does not map directly to a specific KCNA exam objective, but these topics are crucial for anyone who'd like to tie their career to modern infrastructures. If you are already familiar with the basic terms, feel free to quickly verify your knowledge by going directly to the recap questions. If not, don't be surprised that things are not covered in great detail, as this is an introductory chapter, and we'll dive deeper into all of the topics in later chapters.

We're going to cover the following topics in this chapter:

- The cloud and **Before Cloud (B.C.)**
- Evolution of the cloud and cloud-native
- Containers and container orchestration
- Monolithic versus microservices applications
- Kubernetes and its origins

Let's get started!

The cloud and Before Cloud (B.C.)

The cloud has triggered a major revolution and accelerated innovation, but before we learn about the cloud, let's see how things were done before the era of the cloud.

In the times before the term *cloud computing* was used, one physical server would only be able to run a single **operating system** (**OS**) at a time. These systems would typically host a single application, meaning two things:

- If an application was not used, the computing resources of the server where it ran were wasted
- If an application was used very actively and needed a larger server or more servers, it would take days or even weeks to get new hardware procured, delivered, cabled, and installed

Moving on, let's have a look at an important aspect of computing – virtualization.

Virtualization

Virtualization technology and **virtual machines** (**VMs**) first appeared back in the 1960s, but it was not until the early 2000s that virtualization technologies such as XEN and **Kernel-based Virtual Machines** (**KVMs**) started to become mainstream.

Virtualization would allow us to run multiple VMs on a single physical server using hypervisors, where a hypervisor is a software that acts as an emulator of the hardware resources, such as the CPU and RAM. Effectively, it allows you to share the processor time and memory of the underlying physical server by slicing it between multiple VMs.

It means that each VM will be very similar to the physical server, but with a virtual CPU, memory, disks, and network cards instead of physical ones. Each VM will also have an OS on which you can install applications. The following figure demonstrates a virtualized deployment with two VMs running on the same physical server:

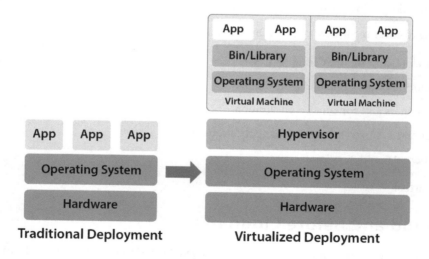

Figure 1.1 – Comparison of traditional and virtualized deployments

This concept of sharing hardware resources between the so-called *guest VMs* is what made it possible to utilize hardware more effectively and reduce any waste of computing resources. It means we might not need to purchase a whole new server in order to run another application.

The obvious benefits that came along with virtualization are as follows:

- Less physical hardware required
- Fewer data center personnel required
- Lower acquisition and maintenance costs
- Lower power consumption

Besides, provisioning a new VM would take minutes and not days or weeks of waiting for new hardware. However, to scale beyond the capacities of the hardware already installed in the corporate data center, we would still need to order, configure, and cable new physical servers and network equipment – and that has all changed with the introduction of cloud computing.

The cloud

At a very basic level, the cloud is virtualization on demand. It allows us to spawn VMs accessible over the network as a service, when requested by the customers.

> **Cloud computing**
> This is the delivery of computational resources as a service, where the actual hardware is owned and managed by the cloud provider rather than a corporate IT department.

The cloud has ignited a major revolution in computing. It became unnecessary to buy and manage your own hardware anymore to build and run applications and VMs. The cloud provider takes full care of hardware procurement, installation, and maintenance and ensures the efficient utilization of resources by serving hundreds and thousands of customers on shared hardware securely. Each customer will only pay for the resources they use. Today, it is common to distinguish the following three cloud types:

- **Public** – The most popular type. A public cloud is operated by a third-party company and available for use by any paying customer. Public clouds are typically used by thousands of organizations at the same time. Examples of public cloud providers include **Amazon Web Services (AWS)**, **Microsoft Azure**, and **Google Cloud Platform (GCP)**.

- **Private** – Used by one typically large organization or an enterprise. The operations and maintenance might be done by the organization itself or a private cloud provider. Examples include Rackspace Private Cloud and VMware Private Cloud.

- **Hybrid** – This is the combination of a public and private cloud, in a case where an organization has a private cloud but uses some of the services from a public cloud at the same time.

However, the cloud is not just VMs reachable over the network. There are tens and hundreds of services offered by cloud providers. Today, you can request and use network-attached storage, virtual network devices, firewalls, load balancers, VMs with GPUs or specialized hardware, managed databases, and more almost immediately.

Now, let's see in more detail how cloud services can be delivered and consumed.

Evolution of the cloud and cloud-native

Besides the huge variety of cloud services you can find today, there is also a difference in how the services are offered. It is common to distinguish between four cloud service delivery models that help meet different needs:

- **IaaS** – The most flexible model with the basic services provided: VMs, virtual routers, block devices, load balancers, and so on. This model also assumes the most customer responsibility. Users of IaaS have access to their VMs and must configure their OS, install updates, and set up, manage, and secure their applications. AWS **Elastic Compute Cloud (EC2)**, AWS **Elastic Block Store (EBS)**, and Google Compute Engine VMs are all examples of IaaS.

- **PaaS** – This helps to focus on the development and management of applications by taking away the need to install OS upgrades or do any lower-level maintenance. As a PaaS customer, you are still responsible for your data, identity and access, and your application life cycle. Examples include Heroku and Google App Engine.

- **SaaS** – Takes the responsibilities even further away from the customers. Typically, these are fully managed applications that *just work*, such as Slack or Gmail.

- **FaaS** – A newer delivery model that appeared around 2010. It is also known as **Serverless** today. A FaaS customer is responsible for defining the functions that are triggered by the events. Functions can be written in one of the popular programming languages and customers don't have to worry about server or OS management, deployment, or scaling. Examples of FaaS include AWS Lambda, Google Cloud Functions, and Microsoft Azure Functions.

These models might sound a bit complicated, so let's draw a simple analogy with cars and transportation.

On-premises, traditional data centers are like having your own car. You are buying it, and you are responsible for its insurance and maintenance, the replacement of broken parts, passing regular inspections, and so on.

IaaS is more like leasing a car for some period of time. You pay monthly lease payments, you drive it, you fill it with gas, and you wash it, but you don't actually own the car and you can give it back when you don't need it anymore.

PaaS can be compared with car-sharing. You don't own the car, you don't need to wash it, do any maintenance, or even refill it most of the time, but you still drive it yourself.

Following the analogy, *SaaS* is like calling a taxi. You don't need to own the car or even drive it.

Finally, *Serverless* or *FaaS* can be compared to a bus from a user perspective. You just hop on and ride to your destination – no maintenance, no driving, and no ownership.

Hopefully, this makes things clearer. The big difference between traditional on-premises setups where a company is solely responsible for the organization, hardware maintenance, data security, and more is that a so-called shared responsibility model applies in the cloud.

Shared responsibility model

Defines the obligations of the cloud provider and the cloud customer. These responsibilities depend on the service provided – in the case of an IaaS service, the customer has more responsibility compared to PaaS or SaaS. For example, the cloud provider is always responsible for preventing unauthorized access to data center facilities and the stability of the power supply and underlying network connectivity.

The following figure visually demonstrates the difference between the responsibilities:

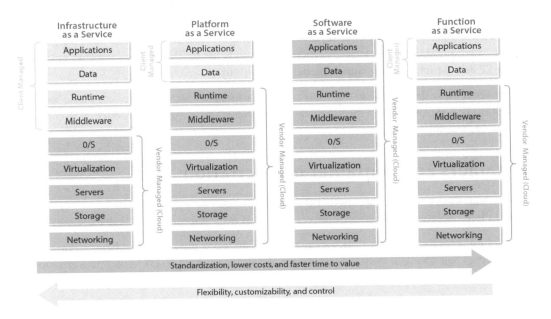

Figure 1.2 – Comparison of cloud delivery models

As cloud technologies and providers evolved over the past 20 years, so did the architectures of the applications that run on the cloud; a new term has emerged – **cloud-native**. Most of the time, it refers to the architectural approach, but you will often encounter cloud-native applications or cloud-native software as well.

> **Cloud-native**
>
> Is an approach to building and running applications on modern, dynamic infrastructures such as clouds. It is emphasizing application workloads with high resiliency, scalability, high degree of automation, ease of management, and observability.

Despite the presence of the word *cloud*, it does not mean that a cloud-native application must run strictly in a public, private, or hybrid cloud. You can develop a cloud-native application and run it on-premises with Kubernetes as an example.

Cloud-native should not be confused with **Cloud Service Providers** (**CSPs**), or simply cloud providers, and cloud-native is also not the same as cloud-first, so remember the following:

Cloud-native ≠ CSP ≠ cloud-first

For the sake of completeness, let's define the other two.

A CSP is a third-party company offering cloud computing services such as IaaS, PaaS, SaaS, or FaaS. Cloud-first simply stands for a strategy where the cloud is the default choice for either optimizing existing IT infrastructure or for launching new applications.

Don't worry if those definitions do not make total sense just yet – we will dedicate a whole section to cloud-native that explains all its aspects in detail. For now, let's have a quick introduction to containers and their orchestration.

Containers and container orchestration

At a very high level, containers are another form of lightweight virtualization, also known as **OS-level virtualization**. However, containers are different from VMs with their own advantages and disadvantages.

The major difference is that with VMs, we can slice and share one physical server between many VMs, each running their own OS. With containers, we can slice and share an OS kernel between multiple containers and each container will have its own virtual OS. Let's see this in more detail.

> **Containers**
>
> These are portable units of software that include application code with runtimes, dependencies, and system libraries. Containers share one OS kernel, but each container can have its own isolated OS environment with different packages, system libraries, tools, its own storage, networking, users, processes, and groups.

Portable is important and needs to be elaborated. An application packaged into a container image is guaranteed to run on another host because the container includes its own isolated environment. Starting a container on another host does not interfere with its environment or the application containerized.

A major advantage is also that containers are a lot more lightweight and efficient compared to VMs. They consume less resources (the CPU and RAM) than VMs and start almost instantly because they don't need to bootstrap a complete OS with a kernel. For example, if a physical server is capable of running 10 VMs, then the same physical server might be able to run 30, 40, or possibly even more containers, each with its own application (the exact number depends on many factors, including the type of workload, so those values are for demonstration purposes only and do not represent any formula).

Containers are also much smaller than VMs in disk size, because they don't package a full OS with thousands of libraries. Only applications with dependencies and a minimal set of OS packages are included in container images. That makes container images small, portable, and easy to download or share.

> **Container images**
>
> These are essentially templates of container OS environments that we can use to create multiple containers with the same application and environment. Every time we execute an image, a container is created.

Speaking in numbers, a container image of a popular Linux distribution such as *Ubuntu Server 20.04* weighs about 70 MB, whereas a KVM QCOW2 virtual machine image of the same Ubuntu Server will weigh roughly 500 MB. Specialized Linux container images such as *Alpine* can be as small as 5 to 10 MB and provide the bare minimum functionality to install and run applications.

Containers are also agnostic to where they run – whether on physical servers, on-premises VMs, or the cloud, containers can run in any of these locations with the help of container runtimes.

> **Container runtimes**
>
> A container runtime is a special software needed to run containers on a host OS. It is responsible for creating, starting, stopping, and deleting containers based on the container images it downloads. Examples of container runtimes include containerd, CRI-O, and Docker Engine.

Figure 1.3 demonstrates the differences between virtualized and containerized deployments:

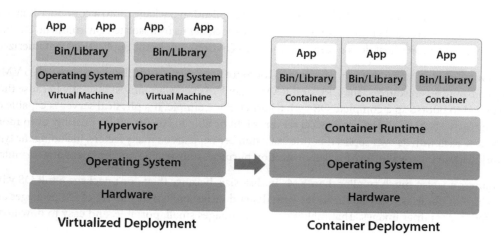

Figure 1.3 – Comparison of virtualized and container deployments

Now, a question you might be asking yourself is if containers are so great, why would anyone use VMs and why do cloud providers still offer so many VM types?

Here is the scenario where VMs have an advantage over containers: they provide better security due to stronger isolation because they don't directly share the same host kernel. That means if an application running in a container has been breached by a hacker, the chances that they can get to all the other containers on the same host are much higher than compared to regular VMs.

We will dive deeper into the technology behind OS-level virtualization and explore the low-level differences between VMs and containers in later chapters.

As containers gained momentum and received wider adoption over the years, it quickly became apparent that managing containers on a large scale can be quite a challenge. The industry needed tools to orchestrate and manage the life cycle of container-based applications.

This had to do with the increasing number of containers that companies and teams had to operate because as the infrastructure tools evolved, so did the application architectures too, transforming from large monolithic architectures into small, distributed, and loosely coupled microservices.

Monolithic versus microservices applications

To understand the difference between monolithic and microservice-based applications, let us reflect on a real-world example. Imagine that a company runs an online hotel booking business. All reservations are made and paid for by the customers via a corporate web service.

The traditional monolithic architecture for this kind of web application would have bundled all the functionality into one single, complex software that might have included the following:

- Customer dashboard

- Customer identity and access management

- Search engine for hotels based on criteria

- Billing and integration with payment providers

- Reservation system for hotels

- Ticketing and support chat

A monolithic application will be tightly coupled (bundled) with all the business and user logic and must be developed and updated at once. That means if a change to a billing code has to be made, the entire application will have to be updated with the changes. After that, it should be carefully tested and released to the production environment. Each (even a small) change could potentially break the whole application and impact business by making it unavailable for a longer time.

With a microservices architecture, this very same application could be split into several smaller pieces communicating with each other over the network and fulfilling its own purpose. Billing, for example, can be performed by four smaller services:

- Currency converter

- Credit card provider integration

- Bank wire transfer processing

- Refund processing

Essentially, microservices are a group of small applications where each is responsible for its own small task. These small applications communicate with each other over the network and work together as a part of a larger application.

The following figure demonstrates the differences between monolithic and microservice architectures:

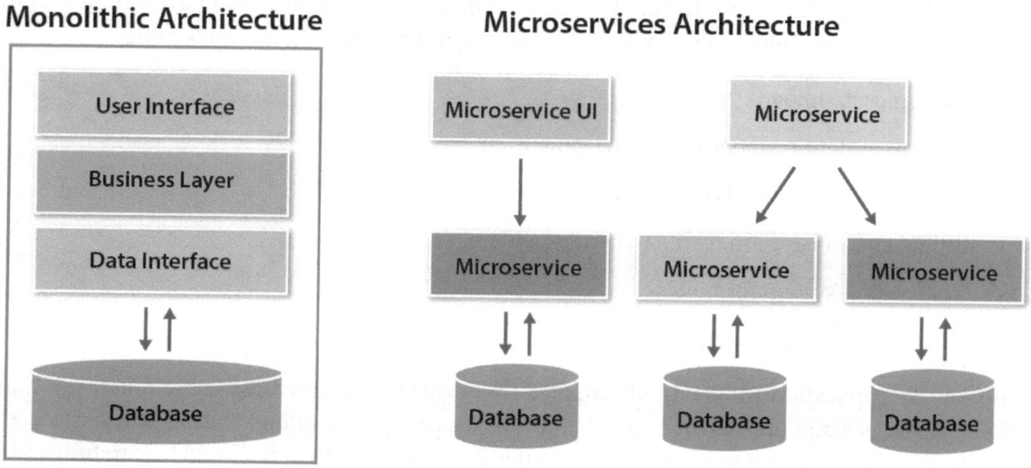

Monolithic Architecture

Microservices Architecture

User Interface

Business Layer

Data Interface

Database

Microservice UI

Microservice

Microservice

Microservice

Microservice

Microservice

Database

Database

Database

Figure 1.4 – Comparison of monolithic and microservice architectures

This way, all other parts of the web application can also be split into multiple smaller independent applications (microservices) communicating over the network. The advantages of this approach include the following:

- Each microservice can be developed by its own team

- Each microservice can be released and updated separately

- Each microservice can be deployed and scaled independently of others

- A single microservice outage will only impact a small part of the overall functionality of the app

Microservices are an important part of cloud-native architectures, and we will review in detail the benefits as well as the challenges associated with microservices in *Chapter 9, Understanding Cloud Native Architectures*. For the moment, let's get back to containers and why they need to be orchestrated.

When each microservice is packaged into a container, the total number of containers can easily reach tens or even hundreds for especially large and complex applications. In such a complex distributed environment, things can quickly get out of our control.

A container orchestration system is what helps us to keep control over a large number of containers. It simplifies the management of containers by grouping application containers into deployments and automating operations such as the following:

- Scaling microservices depending on the workload

- Releasing new versions of microservices and their updates

- Scheduling containers based on host utilizations and requirements
- Automatically restarting containers that fail or failing over the traffic

As of today, there are many container and workload orchestration systems available, including these:

- Kubernetes
- OpenShift (also known as **Open Kubernetes Distribution (OKD)**)
- Hashicorp Nomad
- Docker Swarm
- Apache Mesos

As you already know from the book title, we will only focus on Kubernetes and there won't be any sort of comparison made between these five. In fact, Kubernetes has overwhelmingly higher market shares and over the years, has become the de facto platform for orchestrating containers. With a high degree of confidence, you can concentrate on learning about Kubernetes and forget about the others, at least for the moment.

Kubernetes and its origins

Let's start with a brief history first. The name Kubernetes originates from Greek and means *pilot* or *helmsman* – a person steering a ship (that is why there is a steering wheel in the logo). The steering wheel has seven bars and the number seven has a special meaning for Kubernetes. The team originally working on Kubernetes called it *Project Seven* – named after seven of nine characters from the well-known TV series, *Star Trek*.

Figure 1.5 – The Kubernetes logo

Kubernetes was initially developed by Google and released as an open source project in 2014. Google has been a pioneer, having run its services in containers already for more than a decade by that time, and the release of Kubernetes triggered another small revolution in the industry. By that time, many businesses had realized the benefits of using containers and were in need of a solution that would simplify container orchestration at scale. Kubernetes turned out to be this solution, as we will see soon.

> **Kubernetes (K8s)**
>
> Kubernetes is an open source platform for container orchestration. Kubernetes features an extensible and declarative API that allows you to automatically reach the desired state of resources. It allows flexible scheduling, autoscaling, rolling update, and self-healing of container-based payloads.

(Online and in documentation, a shorter abbreviation, K8s, can often be encountered – where eight is the number of letters between "K" and "s".)

Kubernetes has inherited many of its features and best ideas from Borg – an internal container cluster management system powering thousands of different applications at Google. Many Borg engineers participated in the development of Kubernetes and were able to address relevant pain points based on their experience of operating a huge fleet of containers over the years.

Soon after its initial release, Kubernetes rapidly gained the attention of the open source community and attracted many talented contributors from all over the world. Today, Kubernetes is among the top three biggest open source projects on GitHub (https://github.com/kubernetes) with more than 80,000 stars and 3,000 contributors. It was also the first project to graduate from the **Cloud Native Computing Foundation** (**CNCF**), a non-profit organization that split off from the Linux Foundation created with the goal of advancing container and cloud-native technologies.

One of the most important features of Kubernetes is the concept of the desired state. Kubernetes operates in a way where we define the state of the application containers we want to have, and Kubernetes will automatically ensure the state is reached. Kubernetes constantly observes the state of all deployed containers and makes sure this state matches what we've requested.

Let's consider the following example. Imagine that we run a simple microservice-based application on Kubernetes cluster with three hosts. We define a specification that requires Kubernetes to run these:

- Two identical containers for the frontend
- Three identical containers for the backend
- Two containers with volumes serving the data persistence

Unexpectedly, one of the three hosts fails, and two containers running on the frontend and backend become unavailable. Kubernetes observes the changed number of hosts in the cluster and reduced number of containers responsible for the frontend and the backend. Kubernetes automatically starts one frontend and one backend container on the other two operational hosts to bring the system back to its desired state. This process is known as **self-healing**.

Kubernetes can do way more than scheduling and restarting failed containers – we can also define a Kubernetes specification that requires the number of microservice containers to automatically increase based on the current demand. For example, in the preceding example, we can specify that with an increased workload, we want to run five replicas of the frontend and five replicas of the backend.

Alternatively, in case of low application demand, we can automatically decrease the number of each microservice containers to two. This process is known as **autoscaling**.

This example demonstrates the basic capabilities of Kubernetes. In *Part 3*, we will explore more Kubernetes features and try some of them firsthand.

> **Important note**
> While being a container orchestrator, Kubernetes does not have its own container runtime. Instead, it has integration with popular container runtimes such as *containerd* and can work with multiple runtimes within a Kubernetes cluster.

You often see references to Kubernetes clusters because a typical Kubernetes installation will be used to manage hundreds of containers spread across multiple hosts. Single-host Kubernetes installations are only suitable for learning or local development, but not for production usage.

To sum up, Kubernetes has laid down the path for massive container adoption and is a thriving open source ecosystem that is still growing with new projects graduating from the CNCF every year. In this book, we will cover the Kubernetes API, components, resources, features, and operational aspects in depth, and learn more about projects that can be used with Kubernetes to extend its functionality.

Summary

In this chapter, we learned about the concepts of the cloud and containers, and the evolution of computing over the last 20 to 30 years. In the era before the cloud, traditional deployments with one or a few applications per physical server caused a lot of inefficiency and wasted resources with underutilized hardware and high costs of ownership.

When virtualization technologies came along, it became possible to run many applications per physical server using VMs. This addressed the pitfalls of traditional deployments and allowed us to deliver new applications more quickly and with significantly lower costs.

Virtualization paved the way for the cloud services that are delivered via four different models today: IaaS, PaaS, SaaS, and FaaS or Serverless. Customer responsibilities differ by cloud service and delivery model.

This progress never stopped – now, cloud-native as an approach to building and running applications has emerged. Cloud-native applications are designed and built with an emphasis on scalability, resilience, ease of management, and a high degree of automation.

Over recent years, container technology has developed and gained momentum. Containers use virtualization at the OS level and each container represents a virtual OS environment. Containers are faster, more efficient, and more portable compared to VMs.

Containers enabled us to develop and manage modern applications based on a microservices architecture. Microservices were a step ahead compared to traditional monoliths – *all-in-one, behemoth* applications.

While containers are one of the most efficient ways to run cloud-native applications, it becomes hard to manage large numbers of containers. Therefore, containers are best managed using an orchestrator such as Kubernetes.

Kubernetes is an open source container orchestration system that originated from Google and automates many operational aspects of containers. Kubernetes will schedule, start, stop, and restart containers and increase or decrease the number of containers based on the provided specification automatically. Kubernetes makes it possible to implement self-healing and autoscaling based on the current demand.

Questions

At the end of each chapter, you'll find recap questions that allow to test your understanding. Questions might have multiple correct answers. Correct answers can be found in the *Assessment* section of the *Appendix*:

1. Which of the following describes traditional deployments on physical servers (pick two)?

    A. Easy maintenance

    B. Underutilized hardware

    C. Low energy consumption

    D. High upfront costs

2. Which advantages do VMs have compared to containers?

    A. They are more reliable

    B. They are more portable

    C. They are more secure

    D. They are more lightweight

3. What describes the difference between VMs and containers (pick two)?

    A. VM images are small and container images are large

    B. VM images are large and container images are small

    C. VMs share the OS kernel and containers don't

    D. Containers share the OS kernel and VMs don't

4. At which level do containers operate?

    A. The orchestrator level

B. The hypervisor level

C. The programming language level

D. The OS level

5. What is typically included in a container image (pick two)?

A. An OS kernel

B. A minimal set of OS libraries and packages

C. A graphical desktop environment

D. A packaged microservice

6. Which advantages do containers have compared to VMs (pick multiple)?

A. They are more secure

B. They are more lightweight

C. They are more portable

D. They are faster to start

7. Which software is needed to start and run containers?

A. A container runtime

B. A hypervisor

C. Kubernetes

D. VirtualBox

8. Which of the following can be used to orchestrate containers?

A. containerd

B. CRI-O

C. Kubernetes

D. Serverless

9. Which of the following is a cloud service delivery model (pick multiple)?

A. IaaS, PaaS

B. SaaS, FaaS

C. DBaaS

D. Serverless

10. Which of the following statements about cloud-native is true?

   A.   It is an architectural approach

   B.   It is the same as a cloud provider

   C.   It is similar to cloud-first

   D.   It is software that only runs in the cloud

11. Which of the following descriptors applies to cloud-native applications (pick two)?

   A.   High degree of automation

   B.   High scalability and resiliency

   C.   Can only run in a private cloud

   D.   Can only run in a public cloud

12. Which of the following statements is true about monolithic applications?

   A.   They are easy to update

   B.   Their components communicate with each other over the network

   C.   They include all the business logic and interfaces

   D.   They can be scaled easily

13. Which of the following statements is true for microservices (pick multiple)?

   A.   They can only be used for the backend

   B.   They work together as a part of a bigger application

   C.   They can be developed by multiple teams

   D.   They can be deployed independently

14. Which of the following can be done with Kubernetes (pick multiple)?

   A.   Self-healing in case of failure

   B.   Autoscaling containers

   C.   Spawning VMs

   D.   Scheduling containers on different hosts

15. Which project served as an inspiration for Kubernetes?

    A. OpenStack

    B. Docker

    C. Borg

    D. OpenShift

2

Overview of CNCF and Kubernetes Certifications

In this chapter, you'll learn about **Cloud Native Computing Foundation** (**CNCF**) and its parent organization – the **Linux Foundation**. We will learn what is behind those foundations, how they appeared, and which projects are curated in their ecosystems. We will also talk about the CNCF community, governance, cloud roles, and the Kubernetes certification path.

While this is one of the least technical chapters of this book, the content you'll learn about makes up about half of the Cloud Native Architecture domain topics from the KCNA certification, so make sure that you answer all the recap questions at the end of this chapter.

In this chapter, we will cover the following topics:

- OSS and open standards
- Linux and CNCF
- CNCF community and governance
- Cloud roles and personas
- Kubernetes certification path

Let's get to it!

OSS and open standards

If you have ever worked in any IT position, there is a high chance that you've come across the term **open source software** (**OSS**), know what it means, and very likely already used some.

> **What is OSS?**
> OSS is when the source code of the software is publicly accessible and anyone can study, modify, and distribute it for any purpose.

Software cannot be considered open source simply because it can easily be found on the internet or can be downloaded from the *darknet*. Software is open source when it is released under one of the open source licenses, such as Apache 2.0 or GNU General Public License v3. Those licenses grant users the right to make modifications to the source code or even use it for commercial purposes. That's right – you can use OSS to build new software and sell it without paying any license fees to anyone. Alternatively, you can modify existing OSS, add new features, and sell it or offer related support services.

While the history of OSS goes back to the early days of computing, it was at the beginning of the 90s when one of the most successful OSS was created. Yes, you've guessed it – we are talking about Linux.

The Linux kernel, which was started in 1991 by *Linus Torvalds*, is one of the most prominent examples of open source. For three decades, the project has attracted volunteer and enthusiast programmers willing to contribute for no compensation at all. At the time of writing, more than 15,000 people have contributed their time, skills, and effort to create a core operating system that powers 100% of the world's supercomputers and about 95% of the world's servers.

There are plenty of successful open source projects – Kubernetes, OpenStack, Terraform, Ansible, Prometheus, and Django are all open source. Even companies with huge engineering resources such as Google realize the power of open source communities and how much the open source ecosystem can boost a project. This is what happened with Kubernetes.

Kubernetes has attracted many passionate engineers since the early days and became the first project incubated at CNCF. But before we move on and learn more about CNCF, let's touch on another important topic – open standards.

Open standards

In 2015, along with the establishment of CNCF, another important event occurred – the **Open Container Initiative (OCI)** was started.

> **OCI**
> OCI is an open governance structure whose purpose is to define open industry standards around container formats and runtimes.

OCI has a technical community within which industry participants may contribute to building container specifications that are vendor-neutral, portable, and open.

It also provides reference implementations and tools that deliver on the promise of containers for application portability. Those standards allow us to avoid vendor lock-ins (when a customer is forced to continue using a product or service because it is hard to switch to another vendor) and help ensure that different projects integrate and work well together. For example, as we learned in the previous chapter, container runtimes are not part of Kubernetes, so we need to make sure that different container runtimes and Kubernetes are fully compatible.

At the time of writing, OCI provides three important specifications for the container ecosystem:

- **Image specification** (image-spec) defines how to build and package an application into an OCI-compliant container image
- **Runtime specification** (runtime-spec) defines the container life cycle and execution environment
- **Distribution specification** (distribution-spec) defines the protocol to facilitate and standardize the distribution of container images using so-called registries

So, why are the OCI standards important?

Let's look at a simple analogy regarding transportation. Imagine that each car manufacturer has a way of attaching the wheels to the axle. Wheel manufacturers would have a hard time creating rims for each make and model if they haven't been standardized. But since everybody agreed to have certain wheel sizing parameters such as the width, diameter, number of bolt holes, and so on, it makes it possible for manufacturers to produce wheels that can fit any car model on the market. So, you can buy wheels based on your car's specifications and be confident that they fit your car.

Similar to containers, we have image, runtime, and distribution standards that allow anyone to develop 100% compatible software. The establishment of OCI standards has allowed further expansion of the container ecosystem with the new software. Before the OCI, there was only one way to build container images – using Docker. Today, there are projects such as **Kaniko**, **Podman**, **Buildah**, and others.

You don't need to know the exact differences at this point – just remember that OCI has marked an important point in the evolution of containers and the container ecosystem by providing open specifications. In the upcoming chapters, we will dive into Docker and some aspects of the OCI standards.

According to OCI, it does not seek to be a marketing organization or define a full stack or solution requirements – it strives to avoid standardizing technical areas undergoing innovation and debate (`https://github.com/opencontainers/tob/blob/main/CHARTER.md`). The organization that helped establish OCI and still plays a major role in its initiative is the Linux Foundation. Like with many open source projects, volunteers work in the field and would like to contribute their time to bring the technologies to the next level or bridge the gaps between existing projects.

We've already mentioned both CNCF and the Linux Foundation a few times here. Now, let's get to know them better.

Linux and CNCF

The Linux Foundation is a non-profit organization that appeared in 2000 as a merger between Open-Source Development Labs and the Free Standards Group. Foundation was initially created to standardize, promote, and support the adoption of Linux, but it has significantly expanded its role in the open source community since then.

Today, the supporting members of the Linux Foundation include many of the Fortune500 companies such as Google, IBM, Samsung, Meta, and more. Foundation hosts many projects besides the Linux kernel. These include **Automotive Grade Linux**, **Ceph** (storage), **XEN** (hypervisor), **Real-Time Linux**, the **OpenAPI Initiative** (**OAI**), and many others. Don't worry if you never heard of these projects before – you won't be questioned about them during the exam.

In recent years, the Linux Foundation has expanded its programs through conferences, certifications, training, and new initiatives. One such initiative is the **Cloud Native Computing Foundation** (**CNCF**), which was launched in 2015.

CNCF

July 21, 2015, became a remarkable date for the whole open source community – Kubernetes 1.0 was released. Along with its release, Google, as the key driving force and contributor behind K8s, partnered with the Linux Foundation to form CNCF. Kubernetes became the seed technology and the first incubating project of the new foundation. CNCF's mission was to advance container and cloud-native technologies and align the industry (`https://www.cncf.io/about/who-we-are/`):

> *"The Foundation's mission is to make cloud-native computing ubiquitous.*
>
> *Cloud-native technologies empower organizations to build and run scalable applications in modern, dynamic environments such as public, private, and hybrid clouds. Containers, service meshes, microservices, immutable infrastructure, and declarative APIs exemplify this approach.*
>
> *These techniques enable loosely coupled systems that are resilient, manageable, and observable. Combined with robust automation, they allow engineers to make high-impact changes frequently and predictably with minimal toil.*
>
> *The Cloud Native Computing Foundation seeks to drive the adoption of this paradigm by fostering and sustaining an ecosystem of open source, vendor-neutral projects. We democratize state-of-the-art patterns to make these innovations accessible for everyone."*

We touched on the basics of cloud computing, containers, and microservices in *Chapter 1, From Cloud to Cloud Native and Kubernetes*, and will dive deeper into those and other topics mentioned in the CNCF mission statement in the following chapters.

Today, CNCF is supported by more than 450 members and plays a major role in the cloud-native ecosystem. It provides governance and supports open source projects to make them mature and ensure they're in a production-ready state.

Speaking of maturity, there are three distinguished levels in CNCF:

- **Sandbox**: This is the entry point for early-stage projects that can add value to the CNCF mission. New projects might be aligned with existing projects if they complement them.

- **Incubating**: This is a project that is successfully used in production by the end users and has an ongoing flow of code commits and contributions, along with documentation, specifications, and a versioning scheme.

- **Graduated**: This is a project that has contributors from multiple organizations, maintains Core Infrastructure Initiative best practices, and has passed an independent third-party security audit. The project should also define governance and committer processes, as well prove to be in use by real users.

Every project hosted by CNCF has an associated maturity level. Projects increase their maturity levels by demonstrating that they received *end user adoption, a healthy rate of code changes, and committers from different organizations.*

In addition, all CNCF projects must adhere to the *IP Policy* and adopt the *Code of Conduct*. The Code of Conduct defines what behavior is acceptable and what is not to create a positive and emphatical collaborative environment. On the other hand, the IP Policy is concerned with intellectual property and determines which open source license shall be applied (typically, this is Apache 2.0 for the source code and Creative Commons Attribution 4.0 International for documentation and images).

CNCF community and governance

As open source projects such as Kubernetes gain momentum, they attract more contributors, which is always a good sign. However, larger communities may get out of control and quickly become a *mess* without adequate governance. While CNCF does not require its hosted projects to follow any specific governance model, for a project to graduate, an explicit governance and committer process must be defined. CNCF follows the principle of *Minimal Viable Governance*, which means the projects are self-governing and the CNCF bodies will only step in if asked for help or if things are going wrong.

Speaking about its structure, CNCF has three main bodies:

- **Governing Board (GB)**: Takes care of marketing, budget, and other business decisions for CNCF
- **Technical Oversight Committee (TOC)**: Responsible for defining and maintaining the technical vision, approving new projects, and aligning existing ones based on feedback
- **End User Community (EUC)**: Provides feedback from end users and organizations to improve the overall experience in the cloud-native ecosystem

TOC also determines if a project has reached another level of maturity. Projects can remain in an incubating stage indefinitely, but they are normally expected to graduate within 2 years.

As you already know, Kubernetes was the first project to be incubated in CNCF and the first to reach *Graduated* status in 2018. That's right – Kubernetes skipped the sandbox stage as it was first released at the same time CNCF was established. Since its inception, more than 10 other projects have graduated and about 100 projects are currently in the incubating or sandbox stage. In the next section, we'll explore the roles and personas that are common in cloud and cloud-native.

Cloud roles and personas

Cloud-native is not only about technologies and architectures, but also about people and efficient collaboration in working environments. Therefore, it is common to have certain positions and roles in organizations working with cloud infrastructures and the cloud-native ecosystem. It is also a KCNA exam requirement to understand which roles we are talking about and which responsibilities they assume.

The following roles can be encountered in modern organizations that are adopting the cloud and cloud-native:

- **Cloud Architect or Cloud Solutions Architect**
- **DevOps Engineer**
- **DevSecOps Engineer**
- **FinOps Engineer**
- **Site Reliability Engineer (SRE)**
- **Cloud Engineer**
- **Data Engineer**
- **Full Stack Developer**

This list is not exhaustive, and you may sometimes see variations of these roles, but this should give you a general idea. Now, let's make the differences between those roles and responsibilities clear:

- **Cloud (Solutions) Architect:** It comes as no surprise that an architect is responsible for designing the architecture of the cloud infrastructure and cloud-native applications. It must be highly resilient, observable, scalable, and have a high degree of automation.

  Cloud Architects are also often responsible for cloud strategy and selecting cloud providers (public, private, or hybrid) and suitable services (IaaS/PaaS/SaaS/serverless). Architect roles require broad knowledge from many technical and non-technical domains. For example, they must know the difference between **capital expenditure or upfront costs** (**CAPEX**) and **operational expenditures or simply speaking running costs** (**OPEX**). Traditional data centers are an example of high CAPEX, while the public cloud is an example of zero or almost zero CAPEX, with costs mostly being operational (OPEX).

- **DevOps Engineer: Dev** stands for **development**, while **Ops** stands for **operations**. A DevOps Engineer is somebody who can do both by bridging the gaps between developers and operationalists. Typically, a DevOps Engineer is somebody who has had previous experience as both a software developer and a system administrator or as an infrastructure engineer. This knowledge allows them to effectively automate infrastructure in the cloud and a whole application life cycle, including development, testing, and release. DevOps Engineers often need to know at least one programming language (for instance Python, Ruby, or Golang), as well as several tools for automation (such as Terraform, Ansible, Puppet, and so on) and **continuous integration and deployment/delivery (CI/CD)** systems. Nowadays, you'll also often see Kubernetes experience as one of the requirements for DevOps roles. DevOps, as a culture, emphasizes learning over blame and promotes shared responsibility and strong cross-team collaboration, along with continuous feedback loops.

- **DevSecOps Engineer**: This is very much like a DevOps Engineer, but with an extra focus on security. With DevSecOps, security is introduced at an early stage in application and infrastructure life cycles and requires tight collaboration with the security team.

- **FinOps Engineer**: **Fin** stands for **financial**, while **Ops** stands for **operations**. The FinOps engineer enables teams to track their budgets, provide transparency, and perform cost optimization in the cloud. This role requires a deep understanding of various pricing models and services in the cloud to find optimal and cost-efficient solutions.

- **Site Reliability Engineer (SRE)**: The responsibilities of the SRE include maintaining and optimizing cloud infrastructures and applications. SRE is, in a way, similar to DevOps but focuses more on the operational part and especially on meeting application availability requirements or objectives defined in **service-level agreements (SLAs)** or **service-level objectives (SLOs)**. SLA regulates the level of commitment between the service provider and clients regarding quality, availability, and responsibilities. SLOs are specific measurable characteristics of the SLA, such as availability or response time. SREs often participate in on-call rotation duties (that is, they are ready to react in case of incidents).

- **Cloud Engineer**: This is another role that's similar to DevOps but focuses on the cloud specifics or service offerings of a cloud provider. Typically, the DevOps Engineer role requires a broader skill set, whereas a Cloud Engineer needs deeper knowledge about particular public cloud services.

- **Data Engineer**: In this role, an engineer must deal with data protection, data storage, performance and availability requirements, and various tools for data classification, retention, and analysis. As enterprises accumulate more and more data, they need to make use of it. Therefore, Data Engineers are more in demand these days.

- **Full Stack Developer**: This is a broad role in which a developer needs to be able to take care of both the frontend, for example, the **user interface (UI)** and backend parts of an application. The backend is a generic term that describes software implementation that's not visible or accessible by end users. Sometimes, Full Stack developers can bring in some basic experience with cloud infrastructure and even DevOps tools.

While all these roles and personas are in extremely high demand all over the world, it may not be easy to get an offer for one of those if you are coming from a completely different background or if you've just graduated university or college and have no relevant working experience. Accomplished certifications always make your profile stand out and give you higher chances of getting an interview in one of the desired roles. You'll find a few pieces of career advice at the end of this book, but for now, let's see which Kubernetes certifications are offered by CNCF and what the certification path looks like.

Kubernetes certification path

At the time of writing, CNCF offers four Kubernetes certification exams:

- **Kubernetes and Cloud Native Associate (KCNA)**
- **Certified Kubernetes Application Developer (CKAD)**
- **Certified Kubernetes Administrator (CKA)**
- **Certified Kubernetes Security Specialist (CKS)**

CKA was the first exam to be launched in 2017 and was valid for 2 years, but later, the validity period was extended to 3 years. CKAD and KCNA also have a 3-year validity period; only the CKS exam is valid for 2 years after passing.

Out of all of the exams, CKS is the hardest and requires a candidate to hold a valid, non-expired CKA certification to demonstrate that they already possess sufficient K8s expertise. This means that while you can purchase CKS at any time, you won't be able to take it unless you first pass CKA. All the other exams can be attempted in any order; however, the recommended path is shown in the following diagram:

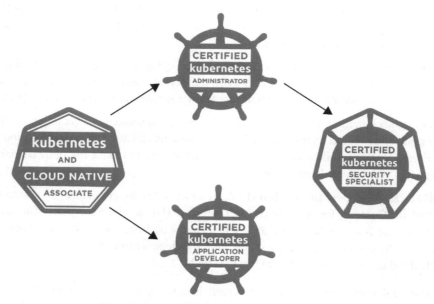

Figure 2.1 – CNCF Kubernetes certification path

KCNA is the easiest exam on the list and the only one that is hands-off – that is, it contains multiple-choice questions. The other certifications are all hands-on and require you to complete activities on multiple K8s clusters in a terminal.

But don't get your hopes up for a trivial KCNA exam. In fact, among entry-level certifications in the cloud field, it is a comparably hard certification. Even if you've worked in a relevant field for a few years, you are unlikely to pass it without any Kubernetes experience and some preparation. Make sure that you always answer all the recap questions and complete the mockup exam provided at the end of this book before attempting a real exam.

The following is some important information regarding the KCNA exam:

- 60 multiple choice questions
- 90 minutes to complete the exam
- A score of 75% or above is needed to pass
- The exam is scored automatically in around 24 hours
- Can be taken online from anywhere (webcam and microphone required)
- One free retake is included in the price

The following domains are tested in the KCNA exam:

- Kubernetes Fundamentals (46%)
- Container Orchestration (22%)
- Cloud-Native Architecture (16%)
- Cloud-Native Observability (8%)
- Cloud-Native Application Delivery (8%)

As you can see, Kubernetes makes up a major part of the exam. Therefore, the biggest part of this book (*Part 3, Learn Kubernetes Fundamentals*) is dedicated to K8s. Apart from that, the KCNA candidate should be able to confirm their conceptual knowledge of cloud-native and its landscape, projects, and practices. This includes high-level definitions from the previous chapter which might be questioned in KCNA.

The other three exams focus on different aspects of working with Kubernetes. The CKAD exam tests application deployment and management aspects, whereas CKA is more about setting up and managing Kubernetes itself. Nevertheless, these exams test many common domains and if you've passed one of those two, with a bit of extra preparation, you'll pass the other one as well. Finally, CKS focuses on security and requires significant experience working with Kubernetes.

Summary

In this chapter, we've learned about OSS and the importance of open standards in terms of OCI. OCI defines **image**, **runtime**, and **distribution** specifications that allow anyone to develop fully compatible container software. For instance, Kubernetes does not include its own container runtime; instead, it implements support for standardized runtime interfaces, allowing it to work with many container runtimes. Open, defined standards have paved the way for many new projects in the cloud-native ecosystem and CNCF.

Next, we covered the history behind CNCF and the Linux Foundation. CNCF was founded at the same time that the first version of Kubernetes was released and it became the first incubated project. CNCF distinguishes three levels of project maturity: **Sandbox**, **Incubating**, and **Graduated**.

CNCF has three major bodies: **Governing Board** (**GB**), **Technical Oversight Committee** (**TOC**), and **End User Community** (**EUC**). TOC makes decisions about the maturity of CNCF projects. One of the requirements for a project to reach graduation is that it must have governance and committer processes defined.

Cloud-native needs the right people to do the job and this is supported by a range of roles and personas you can find today in high demand on the market. We've looked at and compared the different roles to understand how the Cloud Architect's responsibilities are different from those of a DevOps Engineer or a Full Stack developer.

Finally, we looked at the Kubernetes certification path and looked closer at the KCNA exam that you are preparing for. Make sure that you answer all the recap questions before moving on to the next chapter, where we will look at Docker and run containers.

Questions

As we conclude, here is a list of questions for you to test your knowledge regarding this chapter's material. You will find the answers in the *Assessments* section of the *Appendix*:

1. Which of the following is a valid project maturity state in CNCF (pick multiple)?

    A. Sandbox

    B. Released

    C. Graduated

    D. Incubating

2. Which organization was started to establish industry standards for containers?

    A. Open Container Foundation

    B. Cloud Native Container Initiative

    C. Cloud Native Container Foundation

    D. Open Container Initiative

3. Which of the following requirements must a CNCF project meet to reach the Graduated state (pick multiple)?

    A. Have project development and maintenance plan for the next 3-5 years

    B. Have real users and defined governance and committer processes

    C. Have contributors from multiple organizations

    D. Follow Core Infrastructure Initiative best practices

4. Which of the following CNCF bodies determines if a project has reached another maturity level?

    A. End User Community (EUC)

    B. Governing Board (GB)

    C. Technical Oversight Committee (TOC)

    D. Technical Overview Committee (TOC)

5. Which of the following specifications is provided by the OCI (pick multiple)?

    A. Image specification

    B. Runtime specification

    C. Execution specification

    D. Distribution specification

6. Which of the following is required for a CNCF project at any maturity stage (pick two)?

    A. Acceptance of the CNCF Code of Conduct

    B. Acceptance of the CNCF IP Policy

    C. Acceptance of the GNU GPL v.3 license

    D. Acceptance of the Linux Foundation as the project owner

7. Which of the following does DevOps culture emphasize (pick multiple)?

    A. Shared responsibility

    B. Learning instead of blame

    C. Strong cross-team collaboration

    D. Developers should follow the Operations team

8. Which of the following organizations was founded with a mission to advance container and cloud-native technologies and align the industry?

   A. Linux Foundation

   B. Open Container Initiative

   C. Cloud Native Container Foundation

   D. Cloud Native Computing Foundation

9. Which of the following is likely to be among the Cloud Architect's responsibilities (pick two)?

   A. Selecting a cloud provider and suitable services

   B. Designing the cloud infrastructure architecture

   C. Deploying applications to production

   D. Maintaining applications in the cloud

10. What is the difference between DevOps and DevSecOps Engineers?

    A. DevOps only takes care of operations

    B. DevSecOps only takes care of security aspects

    C. DevSecOps is like DevOps, but with an extra focus on security

    D. DevSecOps must have security-related certifications

11. Which of the following describes SRE (pick two)?

    A. SRE needs to be present on-site with the cloud providers

    B. SRE does not participate in any operations

    C. SRE works on maintaining and optimizing infrastructure and apps

    D. SRE needs to ensure that the application's SLA and SLO are met

12. How are Cloud Engineers different from DevOps Engineers (pick two)?

    A. DevOps Engineers know nothing about the cloud

    B. Cloud Engineers have a deeper knowledge of cloud services

    C. DevOps Engineers often have a broader skill set

    D. DevOps Engineers need to do on-call duty, while Cloud Engineers don't

13. What are the benefits of having Full-Stack developers in a team?

    A. Full-Stack can tackle both frontend and backend work

    B. Full-Stack developers deploy applications to the cloud

    C. Full-Stack developers write code faster

    D. Full-Stack developers write cleaner code

14. Why is it important to have Open Standards (pick two)?

    A. They help us avoid vendor lock-in

    B. They allow different software to be compatible

    C. They ensure bug-free software

    D. They prevent earning profits with software

15. Which of the following technologies is a DevOps Engineer likely to work with (pick multiple)?

    A. Frontend technologies (for example, JavaScript, HTML, and CSS)

    B. Automation tools (for example, Terraform, Ansible, and Puppet)

    C. CI

    D. CD

Part 2: Performing Container Orchestration

In this part, you'll learn about the origin of containers, their practicality, and the reasons that led to their massive adoption across many organizations, from small start-ups to global enterprises. We will cover both theoretical and practical aspects, such as how to build and run containers, and why and when they need orchestration.

This part contains the following chapters:

- *Chapter 3, Getting Started with Containers*
- *Chapter 4, Exploring Container Runtimes, Interfaces, and Service Meshes*

3
Getting Started with Containers

In this chapter, we'll take a closer look at containers, dive deeper into container technology and the container ecosystem, and discover tooling that is commonly used.

An old Chinese proverb states, *"What I hear, I forget. What I see, I remember. What I do, I understand."*

Starting with this chapter, we will get our hands dirty and try building images and running containers to get a deeper understanding and first-hand practical experience. Even though KCNA is a multi-choice exam, it is very important to do things first-hand as this experience will help you in the future. **Don't just read the code snippets – make sure you execute them completely, especially if you have no previous experience with containers.** You'll need any computer running a recent version of Linux, Windows, or macOS and a working internet connection.

In this chapter, we will cover the following topics:

- Introducing Docker
- Exploring container technology
- Installing Docker and running containers
- Building container images

Technical requirements

All the example files and code snippets used in this chapter have been uploaded to this book's GitHub repository at `https://github.com/PacktPublishing/Becoming-KCNA-Certified`.

Introducing Docker

Docker has been around for quite a few years, so you may have heard about it before. For many people, the name *Docker* itself is synonymous with *container*. However, there are so many things called *Docker* that it is easy to get confused:

- **Docker Inc.**
- **Docker Engine**
- **dockerd (Docker daemon)**
- **Docker CLI**
- **Docker Hub**
- **Docker Registry**
- **Docker Swarm**
- **Docker Compose**
- **Docker Desktop**
- **Dockershim**

Let's clarify each one.

For starters, *Docker Inc.* (as a company) did not invent the technology behind containers, but it created easy-to-use tools from the list that helped kickstart broader container adoption. The company was founded in 2008 and was initially called dotCloud.

Docker Engine is an open source software bundle for building and containerizing applications. It is a piece of client-server software that consists of a daemon service known as **dockerd (Docker daemon)** that provides a REST API (for other programs to talk to it) and a **command-line interface (CLI)** that is simply called `docker`.

> **Containerization**
>
> Containerization is the process of packaging software application code with dependencies (libraries, frameworks, and more) in a container. Containers can be moved between environments independently of the infrastructure's operating system.

When you install a Docker engine, you essentially install two things – the `dockerd` service and the CLI. `dockerd` constantly runs and listens for commands to do any operations with containers such as starting new, stopping existing, restarting containers, and so on. Those commands might be issued using the `docker` CLI, or a common tool such as `curl`. We will be using the `docker` CLI in this chapter's examples.

Next on our list is *Docker Hub* (`https://hub.docker.com/`), a public container image registry. As you may recall, a container image is a predefined static template that we use as a base for starting new containers. Now, where do we get the images from? Docker Hub can be one such place. It is an online repository service offered by Docker Inc. where thousands of container images with different environments (**Ubuntu, Centos, Fedora,** and **Alpine Linux**) as well as popular software such as **Nginx, Postgres, MySQL, Redis,** and **Elasticsearch** are hosted. Docker Hub allows you to find, share, and store container images that can be easily pulled (downloaded) over the internet to the host where you need to create a new container. It's worth mentioning that Docker Hub is not the only such service – others include **Quay** (`https://quay.io/`), **Google Container Registry** (`https://cloud.google.com/container-registry`), and **Amazon Elastic Container Registry** (`https://aws.amazon.com/ecr/`).

Let's move on to *Docker Registry* which is today managed at CNCF as a project named *Distribution*. It is an open source server-side application that can be used for storing and distributing Docker images. The main difference compared to Docker Hub is that Docker Registry is a piece of software that you can just take, install, and run within your organization at no cost, whereas Docker Hub is a *registry as a service* with some additional paid features. Docker Registry can be used to store and serve container images with software that your *dev* teams are developing.

Docker Swarm is next on our list and its purpose is cluster management and container orchestration. Swarm is similar to Kubernetes; however, it is only compatible with Docker Engine (meaning no other container runtimes are supported) and has significantly fewer features and limited customizations compared to Kubernetes. That is the reason it did not receive such wide adoption as Kubernetes did.

Docker Compose is another Docker tool that allows you to define and share multi-container applications specifications. With Compose, you can define multiple containers that need to communicate with each other as a part of one application in a single **YAML** formatted file. For example, you can bootstrap a *Django* web application with a database running in two containers and define that the database has to start first, as well as expose certain ports of containers. Compose might be handy for some local development with Docker, but it is not compatible with Kubernetes, so we are not going to cover it in any more detail.

Docker Desktop is a combination of Docker Engine, the `docker` CLI, Docker Compose, Kubernetes, and some other tools for Windows/macOS that comes with its own **graphical user interface (GUI)**. That's right – Docker Desktop even packages Kubernetes and K8s clients for local development. Docker Desktop is free for non-commercial use but paid if used in organizations. There is also a beta version available for Ubuntu and Debian Linux.

Dockershim is a software compatibility layer that was created to allow Kubernetes (its *kubelet* component, to be precise) to communicate with `dockerd` (Docker daemon). As you might remember from the previous chapters, Kubernetes does not have its own container runtime (software for performing basic operations with containers such as starting, stopping, and deleting). In the early versions, Kubernetes only supported Docker to operate containers. As the container ecosystem evolved with **Open Container Initiative (OCI)**, support for new runtimes was added through structured and standardized interfaces.

Since `dockerd` did not have an OCI standardized interface, a translation layer between Kubernetes and `dockerd` called **Dockershim** was created. *Dockershim* has been deprecated since Kubernetes version 1.20 and with the 1.24 release, it has been completely removed from K8s.

Finally, we've reached the end of our list. Despite the number of alternatives that have appeared over the years, Docker Engine and the Docker tooling are still actively used by thousands of development teams and organizations across the globe. The following diagram demonstrates how, using the Docker CLI, we can communicate with the Docker daemon, which fetches the images from Docker Registry to create containers locally:

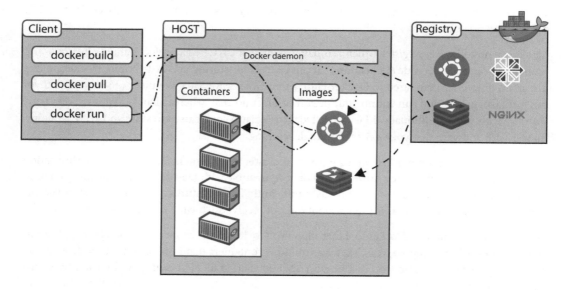

Figure 3.1 – Docker architecture

In the upcoming sections, we will install some of the Docker tools to see it in action and finally get our hands on containers.

Exploring container technology

Before we move on to the practical part, we still need to figure out the technology behind containers and who created it. The technology behind Linux containers was developed quite a long time ago and is based on two fundamental kernel features:

- **cgroups** (**control groups**)

- **Namespaces**

> **cgroups**
>
> cgroups is a mechanism that allows processes to be organized into hierarchical groups. How resources (CPU, memory, disk I/O throughput, and so on) are used by those groups can be limited, monitored, and controlled.

cgroups were initially developed by engineers at Google and first released in 2007. Since early 2008, cgroups functionality was merged into the Linux kernel and has been present ever since. In 2016, a revised version of cgroups was released and it is now known as cgroups version 2.

Even before cgroups, in 2002, the Linux namespaces feature was developed.

> **Linux kernel namespaces**
>
> This Linux feature allows you to partition kernel resources in such a way that one set of processes sees one set of resources while another set of processes sees a different set of resources. Linux namespaces are used to isolate processes from each other.

There are different types of namespaces, each with its own properties:

- **User namespace**: This allows a process to have its own user and group IDs. This makes it possible for a process to run as `root` (superuser) but be limited to its own namespace.

- **Process ID (PID) namespace**: This allows you to have a set of process IDs in one namespace that are independent of other namespaces. For example, multiple processes on the same host can have PID 1 thanks to namespaces.

- **Network namespace**: This allows you to run an independent network stack with its own routing table, IP addresses, connection tracking, and more for a set of processes.

- **Mount namespace**: This allows you to have independent mount points within a namespace. This means a process in a namespace can have different mounts without it affecting the host filesystem.

- **Interprocess communication (IPC)**: This allows you to isolate Linux interprocess communication mechanisms such as shared memory, semaphores, and message queues.

- **UNIX Time-Sharing (UTS)**: This allows you to have different hostnames and domain names for different processes.

This may sound complicated, but don't worry – namespaces and cgroups are not part of the KCNA exam, so you don't need to know about every namespace and what they do. However, since those are at the core of container technology, it is helpful to have an idea, plus you are always given bonus points if you can explain how containers work under the hood.

To summarize, *cgroups* and *namespaces* are the building blocks of containers. cgroups allow you to monitor and control computational resources for a process (or a set of processes), whereas namespaces isolate the processes at different system levels. Both functionalities can also be used without containers, and there's plenty of software that makes use of this functionality.

Enough theory – let's get some practice! In the next section, we will install Docker tooling and start our first container.

Installing Docker and running containers

If you are running Windows or macOS, you can download and install Docker Desktop from `https://docs.docker.com/desktop/`. If you are running a recent version of Ubuntu Linux, there is a version of Docker Desktop for you too. If you are running another Linux distribution, you'll have to install Docker Engine. You can find detailed instructions for your distribution at `https://docs.docker.com/engine/install/`. Please pick a *stable* release for installation.

If you restart your computer, make sure that Docker Desktop is running. On Linux, you might have to execute the following code in your Terminal:

```
$ sudo systemctl start docker
```

If you want it to start automatically in case of a system restart, you can run the following command:

```
$ sudo systemctl enable docker
```

Regardless of the OS or tooling that you've installed (Desktop or Engine), it will come with the Docker CLI that we will be using, which is simply called `docker`.

First, let's make sure that Docker was installed correctly and running by checking the version. Open the terminal and type the following:

```
$ docker --version
Docker version 20.10.10, build b485636
```

> **Important note**
>
> If you are on Linux and you have not added your user to the docker group after the installation, you'll have to call the Docker CLI with superuser privileges, so all docker commands should be prefixed with `sudo`. For the preceding example, the command will be `sudo docker --version`.

Your output might look slightly different – perhaps you'll have a newer version installed. If the preceding command did not work, but Docker is installed, make sure that Docker Desktop (if you're on macOS or Windows) or the Docker daemon (if you're on Linux) is running.

Now, let's start our first container with Ubuntu 22.04:

```
$ docker run -it ubuntu:22.04 bash
```

The output that you'll see should be similar to the following:

```
Unable to find image 'ubuntu:22.04' locally
22.04: Pulling from library/ubuntu
125a6e411906: Pull complete
Digest:
sha256:26c68657ccce2cb0a31b330cb0be2b5e108d467f641c62e13ab40cbe
c258c68d
Status: Downloaded newer image for ubuntu:22.04
root@d752b475a54e:/#
```

Wow! We are now running `bash` inside an Ubuntu container. It might take a few seconds for the image to be downloaded, but as soon as it is ready, you'll see the command-line prompt running as a `root` user inside a newly spawned container.

So, what exactly happened when we called `docker run`?

`docker run` executes a command inside a new container; it requires the name of the container image where the command will be executed (`ubuntu` in the preceding example), optionally the tag of the image (`22.04` here), and the command to be executed (simply `bash` here).

The `-i` argument is the same as `--interactive`, and it means we'd like to be running our command in interactive mode. `-t`, which is the same as `--tty`, will allocate a pseudo-TTY (emulated terminal).

As you may remember, images are templates for container environments. We have asked for an `ubuntu` environment tagged with version `22.04`. In the first few lines of output, we saw that the image was not found locally:

```
Unable to find image 'ubuntu:22.04' locally
22.04: Pulling from library/ubuntu
125a6e411906: Pull complete
```

If the requested image with a particular tag was not downloaded previously, it will be automatically downloaded (pulled) from the Docker Hub library and you should be able to see the download progress while it is happening.

Now, let's exit the container and try running it again. Simply type `exit` in the terminal:

```
root@d752b475a54e:/# exit
exit
```

Now, execute the same command we did previously:

```
$ docker run -it ubuntu:22.04 bash
root@e5d98a473adf:/#
```

Was it faster this time? Yes, because we already have the ubuntu:22.04 image cached locally, so we don't need to download it again. Therefore, the container was started immediately.

Did you notice that the hostname after root@ is different this time – e5d98a473adf versus d752b475a54e? *(Note: you will see your unique container names here.)* This is because we have started a new container that is based on the same ubuntu image. When we start a new container, we don't modify the read-only source image; instead, we create a new writable filesystem layer on top of the image. The following diagram shows such a layered approach:

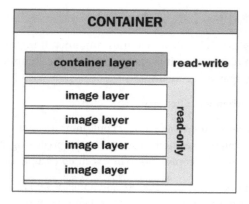

Figure 3.2 – Container layers

When we start a container, we add a new layer, which allows modifications to be made to the container image copy. This way, we can create any number of containers from the same base image without modifying the initial read-only image layer. The major benefit of this approach is that **in container layers, we only store the difference with the image layer**, which means significant disk space savings when used at scale.

The images can also consist of multiple layers, where one layer might be originating from another one. In the following section, we will learn how to build new images and include the software that we like inside.

Feel free to explore our container environment and exit it when you're done:

```
$ docker run -it ubuntu:22.04 bash
root@e5d98a473adf:/# echo "Hello World" > /root/test
root@e5d98a473adf:/# hostname
```

```
e5d98a473adf
root@e5d98a473adf:/# date
Sun May 1 13:40:01 UTC 2022
root@e5d98a473adf:/# exit
exit
```

When we called `exit` in the first container, it exited; later, when we called `docker run` again, a new container was created. Now that both containers have exited, we have an image layer stored on the disk, as well as two different container layers based on the `ubuntu:22.04` base.

Since the container layers only keep track of differences from the base image, we won't be able to remove the base image until all the container layers have been deleted. Let's get the list of images we have locally by running the following code:

```
$ docker images
REPOSITORY     TAG        IMAGE ID        CREATED        SIZE
ubuntu         22.04      d2e4e1f51132    39 hours ago   77.8MB
```

If we attempt to delete the `ubuntu:22.04` image with the `docker rmi` command, we'll get an error:

```
$ docker rmi ubuntu:22.04
Error response from daemon: conflict: unable to remove
repository reference "ubuntu:22.04" (must force) - container
e5d98a473adf is using its referenced image d2e4e1f51132
```

We can also execute the `docker ps` command to see all *running* containers:

```
$ docker ps
CONTAINER ID   IMAGE   COMMAND   CREATED   STATUS   PORTS   NAMES
```

An empty table means no containers are currently running.

Finally, we can execute `docker ps --all` to see all the containers on the local system, including those that have exited:

```
$ docker ps --all
CONTAINER ID     IMAGE        COMMAND     CREATED
                 STATUS                   PORTS      NAMES
e5d98a473adf     ubuntu:22.04    "bash"   8 minutes ago    Exited (0) 2
minutes ago vibrant_jenn
d752b475a54e     ubuntu:22.04    "bash"   18 minutes ago   Exited (0)
12 minutes ago   cool_perl
```

Try removing those exited containers with `docker rm CONTAINER ID`:

```
$ docker rm d752b475a54e
d752b475a54e
$ docker rm e5d98a473adf
e5d98a473adf
```

Now, the image should be deleted too:

```
$ docker rmi ubuntu:22.04
Untagged: ubuntu:22.04
Untagged: ubuntu@
sha256:26c68657ccce2cb0a31b330cb0be2b5e108d467f641c62e13ab40cbe
c258c68d
Deleted:
sha256:d2e4e1f511320dfb2d0baff2468fcf0526998b73fe10c8890b4684bb
7ef8290f
Deleted:
sha256:e59fc94956120a6c7629f085027578e6357b48061d45714107e79f04
a81a6f0c
```

`sha256` are the digests of image layers; they are unique and immutable identifiers. If we assign a different tag to our `ubuntu` image instead of `22.04` and try to pull (download) the same image from Docker Hub again, Docker will recognize that we already have an image with this digest and will do nothing except tag it again.

Let's try one more thing – pulling another Docker image without any tags. If you simply `pull` the image, no container is going to be started, but this will save download time the next time a new container is started from that image:

```
$ docker pull centos
Using default tag: latest
latest: Pulling from library/centos
a1d0c7532777: Pull complete
Digest:
sha256:a27fd8080b517143cbbbab9dfb7c8571c40d67d534bbdee55bd6c473
f432b177
Status: Downloaded newer image for centos:latest
docker.io/library/centos:latest
```

As you can see, if we don't specify the tag explicitly, `latest` will be taken by default.

In the upcoming section, we will learn more about the meaning of the `latest` tag, tagging in general, and building images with Docker.

Building container images

Now that we know how to start containers and pull images, we'll learn what should be done to create new container images. Since the image layer is immutable, you can create new images with the software of your choice to build an image by adding new layers on top of existing ones. There are two ways this can be done with Docker:

- Interactively
- Using Dockerfile

The interactive way is to create an image from an existing container. Let's say you start a container with the Ubuntu 22.04 environment, install additional packages, and expose port 80. To create a new image, we can use the `docker commit` command:

```
$ docker commit CONTAINER_ID [REPOSITORY[:TAG]]
```

The image name will be in the `REPOSITORY:TAG` format. If no tag is given, then `latest` will be added automatically. If no repository was specified, the image name will be a **unique identifier (UUID)**. The tag, as well as the name (which is the same as the image repository's name), can be changed or applied after the build.

While the interactive method is quick and easy, it should not be used under normal circumstances because it is a manual, error-prone process and the resulting images might be larger with many unnecessary layers.

The second, better option for building images is using Dockerfiles.

> **Dockerfile**
> A Dockerfile is a text file containing instructions for building an image. It supports running shell scripts, installing additional packages, adding and copying files, defining commands executed by default, exposing ports, and more.

Let's have a look at a simplistic Dockerfile:

```
FROM ubuntu:22.04
RUN apt-get update && apt-get install -y curl vim
LABEL description="My first Docker image"
```

As you've probably already guessed, the FROM instruction defines the base image with a tag for the image we are going to build. The base image can also be one of our previously built local images or an image from the registry. RUN instructs to execute apt-get update and then install curl and vim packages. LABEL is simply any metadata you'd like to add to the image. If you copy the preceding contents to a file called Dockerfile, you'll be able to build a new image by calling docker build in the same folder:

```
$ docker build . -t myubuntuimage
[+] Building 11.2s (6/6) FINISHED
 => [internal] load build definition from Dockerfile
                                             0.0s
 => => transferring dockerfile: 153B
                                                     0.0s
 => [internal] load .dockerignore
                                                     0.0s
 => => transferring context: 2B
                                                     0.0s
 => [internal] load metadata for docker.io/library/ubuntu:22.04
                                  0.0s
 => [1/2] FROM docker.io/library/ubuntu:22.04
                                             0.0s
 => [2/2] RUN apt-get update && apt-get install -y curl vim
                   9.9s
 => exporting to image
                                             1.1s
 => => exporting layers
                                             1.1s
 => => writing image sha256:ed53dcc2cb9fcf7394f8b03818c02e0ec4
5da57e89b550b68fe93c5fa9a74b53
                   0.0s
 => => naming to docker.io/library/myubuntuimage
                                       0.0s
```

With -t myubuntuimage, we have specified the name of the image without the actual tag. This means that the latest tag will be applied to the image by default:

```
$ docker images
REPOSITORY       TAG      IMAGE ID       CREATED         SIZE
myubuntuimage    latest   ed53dcc2cb9f   6 minutes ago   176MB
centos           latest   5d0da3dc9764   7 months ago    231MB
```

There are a few things we need to clarify about the latest tag, as it can be misleading:

- latest is applied by default if no tag is given during the build
- latest is pulled by default if no tag is given during image download or container run
- latest is not updated dynamically; you can tag any image as latest – even an older version of the same image

Therefore, the best practice is to tag images with something more descriptive rather than relying on latest. For instance, an incrementable version of the packaged application (v.0.32, v.1.7.1, and so on) can be used as a tag or even the build timestamp. The timestamp allows us to determine when the image was built without the need to inspect each image metadata.

Let's quickly go back to the instructions supported in Dockerfiles. We've already learned about FROM, RUN, and LABEL, but there are more:

- ADD: This is used to copy files and directories *into* the Docker image (from a build location or remote URLs).
- COPY: This is used to copy files *within* the Docker image.
- CMD: This is used to define the default executable of a Docker image (only the last CMD instruction will be respected). CMD can be easily overridden at container runtime.
- ENTRYPOINT: This is similar to CMD and allows us to define the executable of an image when a container is started. It can ban be used together with CMD.
- EXPOSE: This tells us that the application in an image will be listening on a particular network port at runtime.
- ENV: This is used to set any environment variables in the image.
- USER: This sets the username or **user ID** (**UID**) for any RUN, CMD, or ENTRYPOINT instructions.
- VOLUME: This is used to create a mount point with the given name and marks it for use with externally mounted volumes (for example, from the host where the container will be started).
- WORKDIR: This sets the working (current) directory for RUN, CMD, and ENTRYPOINT instructions.

A quick note about CMD and ENTRYPOINT: they are similar, yet not the same. We could specify either CMD, ENTRYPOINT, or both in our Dockerfile. If we specify both, then CMD acts as a parameter for ENTRYPOINT. Since CMD is a bit easier to override at runtime, then typically, ENTRYPOINT is the executable and CMD is the argument in such scenarios. For example, we could set ENTRYPOINT to /bin/cat and use CMD to give a path to a file we want to concatenate (/etc/hosts; /etc/group, and so on). For many public images from Docker Hub, ENTRYPOINT is set to /bin/sh -c by default.

This list is not meant to be a complete reference of instructions supported by Dockerfiles, but it mentions the most used instructions that cover 99% of scenarios. In addition, you don't often build containers on your laptop or local workstation; instead, you use a modern CI/CD system or an automated build from Docker Hub as an alternative.

Now, let's understand what a development workflow might look like when containers are in use:

1. Software developers write application code in their language of choice – for instance, **Python**, **Java**, **Ruby**, **Node.js**, **Golang**, or anything else.

> **Important note**
>
> There is no need to learn a new programming language – any software that runs in a Linux environment will run inside a container too.

2. The code is tested and pushed to a GitHub repository or other version control system. The CI/CD or a third-party solution is triggered when a change is made to the source code; the application is packaged inside a container image according to the defined Dockerfile.

3. Dockerfile instructions will be used to copy the code and run and install it inside the container image layer. These instructions vary, depending on the language and the OS environment that's chosen. For example, a Node.js application will likely require `yarn install` to run, whereas a Python application will be installed with the help of a `pip` command, and so on.

4. The image is built, tagged, and pushed (uploaded) to an image registry. This might be, for example, a private repository in Docker Hub, a repository offered by a cloud provider, or even your own registry maintained within the company.

5. At this point, the image can be downloaded and run by a container orchestrator such as Kubernetes, by a server with a container runtime, or simply by other team members with the Docker tooling they have installed.

As you may remember, one of the main features of containers is *portability* – a container running on one host will also run on another host. This means that you can have a container image with Alpine Linux and run it on both your laptop with Fedora Linux or on an Ubuntu-based Kubernetes cluster.

But wait – can we run Linux containers on Windows or vice versa? Not really. First, we need to distinguish between Linux containers and Windows containers.

> **Important note**
>
> Everything in this book and the KCNA exam itself is only about Linux containers.

Even if you are running Docker Desktop on Windows, it is using a minimal **Linuxkit** virtual machine in the background. Windows containers are different and might use one of the two distinct isolation modes (**WSL 2** or **Hyper-V**) available today in the Microsoft operating system. Docker Desktop allows you to switch between *Windows containers* and *Linux containers* if you are running on Windows. However, keep in mind that more than 90% of the servers in the world run Linux, so unless you are going to run Windows-only applications in containers, you are fine to only learn about and use Linux containers.

Summary

In this chapter, we gained experience with (Linux) containers and learned that the technology behind containers has existed for many years and is based on *cgroups* and kernel *namespaces*.

Docker has introduced tooling that's aimed at developers and engineers looking for a universal and simple way to package and share applications. Before containers, it has often been the case that an application could work in the development environment but fail in the production environment because of unmet dependencies or incorrect versions that have been installed. Containers have fixed this problem by bundling the application with all the dependencies and system packages in a template known as a container image.

Container images can be stored in registries that support private and public repositories and allow you to share them with different teams. **Docker Hub**, **Quay**, and **Google Container Registry** (**GCR**) are some of the most well-known container image registries today that can be reached over the internet. An image that's pushed (uploaded) to the registry can then be pulled (downloaded) by a container orchestrator such as Kubernetes or simply by a server with a container runtime over the internet.

Images are used to create containers, so a container is a running instance of an image. When a container is started with a writable filesystem, a layer is created on top of the immutable image layer. Containers and images can have multiple layers and we can start as many containers as we want from a single image. Containers are more lightweight compared to VMs and are very fast to start.

We also learned that to build a container image with Docker, we can leverage an interactive or Dockerfile method. With Dockerfile, we define a set of instructions that will be executed to build an image with our containerized application.

In the next chapter, we will continue exploring containers by learning about the runtimes and pluggable interfaces provided by Kubernetes.

Questions

As we conclude, here is a list of questions for you to test your knowledge regarding this chapter's material. You will find the answers in the *Assessments* section of the *Appendix*:

1. Which of the following features describes containers (pick two)?

    A. Portability between environments

    B. Large image size

    C. Small image size

    D. High security

2. Which of the following is true (pick two)?

    A. Applications are easy to package in containers

    B. Applications are easy to package in virtual machines

    C. Container images are easy to share

    D. VM images are easy to share

3. What programming language do developers have to learn to run their code in containers?

    A. Dockerlang

    B. Golang

    C. Python

    D. None – containers allow the same languages that are supported by the OS environment

4. Which of the following problems do containers address (pick two)?

    A. Unmet dependencies between environments

    B. Bugs in application code

    C. Need to test application code

    D. Long VM startup times

5. Which of the following is used by containers (pick two)?

    A. `cgroups`

    B. `hwmon`

    C. `acpi`

    D. `kernel namespaces`

6. Which of the following can be used to share container images (pick two)?

    A. Docker Hub
    B. Docker Swarm
    C. Docker Registry
    D. Docker Compose

7. Which of the following is true about container images (pick two)?

    A. They can only be built with Dockerfiles
    B. They include immutable filesystem layers
    C. The newest image is always tagged as the latest
    D. They can be built interactively

8. Which of the following applies when starting a new container (pick two)?

    A. A new writable filesystem layer is created
    B. The requested image is always pulled
    C. An image is pulled if the requested tag (SHA digest) is not found locally
    D. A new Linux kernel is loaded

9. Which of the following is true about container image tags (pick two)?

    A. Every image must have tags
    B. The latest tag is applied automatically on build, unless overridden
    C. The same image cannot have multiple tags
    D. The same image can have multiple names (repositories) and tags

10. How can a new container be created using Docker tooling?

    A. `docker run`
    B. `docker exec`
    C. `docker spawn`
    D. `docker launch`

Further reading

While this chapter provided an insight into the container ecosystem and the knowledge needed to pass the KCNA exam, it doesn't cover all the features of Docker tooling nor describes cgroups and namespaces in detail. If you'd like to go the extra mile, you are encouraged to check out the following resources:

- cgroups v1: `https://www.kernel.org/doc/Documentation/cgroup-v1/cgroups.txt`

- Namespaces: `https://man7.org/linux/man-pages/man7/namespaces.7.html`

- Getting started with Docker: `https://docs.docker.com/get-started/`

- Best practices for writing Dockerfiles: `https://docs.docker.com/develop/develop-images/dockerfile_best-practices/`

Exploring Container Runtimes, Interfaces, and Service Meshes

In this chapter, we'll go further into exploring container runtimes, networking, interfaces, and learning about service meshes. We will see which runtime implementations exist and the difference between them, learn how containers can communicate with each other over the network, which container interfaces exist in Kubernetes, and get to know what a service mesh is and its applications. We will also do a few more exercises using the Docker tooling we have previously installed to support our journey.

The contents of this chapter will cover topics from the *Container Orchestration* domain of the KCNA certification, which is the second biggest part of the exam, so make sure to answer all questions at the end of the chapter.

Here are the topics we're going to cover:

- Container runtimes
- Container networking
- Container storage
- Container security
- Introducing service meshes

Let's get started!

Container runtimes

As you know from the previous chapters, containers can run on virtual machines, in the cloud, on-premise, on bare-metal servers, or simply on your laptop. The software responsible for basic operations such as downloading images from the registry and creating, starting, stopping, or deleting containers is called the **container runtime**. We've already learned about Docker tooling and runtime, but there are more runtimes that exist, including the following:

- **Containerd**
- **CRI-O**
- **kata**
- **gVisor**

Before going into runtime specifics, we need to understand what a **Container Runtime Interface (CRI)** is.

> **CRI**
>
> The CRI is a plugin interface that allows Kubernetes to use different container runtimes. In the first releases of Kubernetes before the CRI was introduced, it was only possible to use Docker as a runtime.

As you might remember, Kubernetes does not have its own runtime to do basic container operations, so it needs a runtime to manage containers and this runtime has to be CRI compatible. For example, Docker Engine does not support the CRI, but most of the other runtimes, including *containerd* or *CRI-O*, do. Essentially, the CRI defines the protocol for communication between Kubernetes and the runtime of choice using **gRPC** (the high-performance **Remote Procedure Call** framework), as shown in *Figure 4.1*:

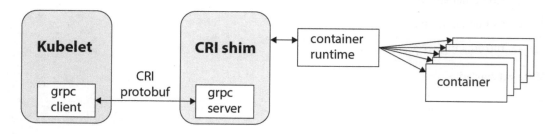

Figure 4.1 – Container runtime integration with CRI

Initially, there was no CRI implementation in Kubernetes, but as new container runtimes were developed, it became increasingly hard to incorporate all of them into Kubernetes, so the solution was to define a standard interface that would allow compatibility with any runtime. The introduction of the CRI in Kubernetes version 1.5 allowed the use of multiple container runtimes within a single K8s cluster and also made it easier to develop compatible runtimes. Today, *containerd* is the most used runtime with newer versions of Kubernetes.

But why would you need to run a mix of different runtimes in the same cluster? This is a rather advanced scenario and the main reason behind it is that some runtimes can provide better security for more sensitive container workloads. Therefore, when we talk about containers and their runtimes, we need to distinguish three main types:

- **Namespaced** – The fastest and most used type that is based on Linux kernel *cgroups* and *namespaces* functionality we covered in the previous chapter. This type shares the same kernel to run multiple containers and thus is considered the least secure out of all container types. Examples include *Docker, containerd*, and *CRI-O*.

- **Virtualized** – The slowest type of container, which in fact requires a hypervisor as virtual machines do. Each container is started inside its own lightweight VM with its own dedicated kernel. This type is considered the most secure as it provides maximum isolation for container workloads. Virtualized containers are still faster to start than VMs and their advantage over traditional VMs is their easy integration with container orchestration systems such as Kubernetes. The *Kata* project is an example of virtualized containers.

- **Sandboxed** – This is a container type in-between the other two, providing better security than namespaced containers and being faster than virtualized containers. Better security is achieved with another layer of isolation that intercepts the system calls coming from the container workload. *gVisor* is an open source project from Google that allows the creation of sandboxed containers.

While this might sound very complicated, for the scope of the KCNA exam, you don't really need to know all the details about container runtimes. This knowledge will be needed if you ever go for a CKS exam or have a special use case for using *sandboxed* or *virtualized* containers. For now, make sure to remember which container runtimes exist and the fact that in most scenarios, *namespaced* containers are used. Also, don't confuse *CRI* with *OCI*, which we covered in *Chapter 2, Overview of CNCF and Kubernetes Certifications*.

Important note

The **Open Container Initiative (OCI)** provides the industry specifications for containers (image, runtime, and distribution specs) while CRI is a part of Kubernetes that makes it possible to use different runtimes with K8s in a pluggable way.

In practice, you do not interact with container runtimes directly but instead use orchestration systems such as Kubernetes or Docker Swarm. We can also use a CLI to talk to container runtimes as we did with the Docker CLI or as you can with the `ctr` or `nerdctl` CLI when using the *containerd* runtime.

Moving on, in the following section, we are going to learn more about container networking.

Container networking

We have only tried creating individual containers so far, however, in the real world, we would need to deal with tens and often hundreds of containers. As the microservice architectures gained wider adoption, the applications were split into multiple smaller parts that communicate with each other over the network. One application could be represented by the frontend part, several backend services, and the database layer, where end-user requests hitting the frontend will trigger communication with the backend, and the backend will talk with the database. When each component is running in its own container across multiple servers, it is important to understand how they can all talk with each other. Networking is a large part of containers and Kubernetes, and it can be really challenging to understand how things work. For the moment, we are only going to touch the surface of container-to-container communication and continue with more details such as exposing containers and K8s specifics in the later chapters.

Let's get back to the Docker tooling we installed in the previous chapter and try starting another Ubuntu container.

> **Important note**
> Make sure that Docker Desktop is running before attempting to spawn containers. If you have not enabled auto-start previously, you might need to start it manually. On Linux with Docker Engine, you might need to execute $ `sudo systemctl start docker`.

Open the terminal and run the following:

```
$ docker run -it ubuntu:22.04 bash
```

Because the image is stripped down to the minimum to save space, there are no preinstalled basic packages such as `net-tools`. Let's install those inside our container by calling `apt update` and `apt install`:

```
root@5919bb5d37e3:/# apt update; apt -y install net-tools
... SOME OUTPUT OMITTED ...
Reading state information... Done
The following NEW packages will be installed:
  net-tools
```

```
... SOME OUTPUT OMITTED ...
Unpacking net-tools (1.60+git20181103.0eebece-1ubuntu5) ...
Setting up net-tools (1.60+git20181103.0eebece-1ubuntu5) ...
root@5919bb5d37e3:/#
```

Now that we have net-tools installed, we can use the ifconfig tool inside the container. The output you'll see should be similar to this:

```
root@5919bb5d37e3:/# ifconfig
eth0: flags=4163<UP,BROADCAST,RUNNING,MULTICAST>  mtu 1500
        inet 172.17.0.2  netmask 255.255.0.0  broadcast
172.17.255.255
        ether 02:42:ac:11:00:02  txqueuelen 0  (Ethernet)
        RX packets 14602  bytes 21879526 (21.8 MB)
        RX errors 0  dropped 0  overruns 0  frame 0
        TX packets 3127  bytes 174099 (174.0 KB)
        TX errors 0  dropped 0 overruns 0  carrier
0  collisions 0

lo: flags=73<UP,LOOPBACK,RUNNING>  mtu 65536
        inet 127.0.0.1  netmask 255.0.0.0
        loop  txqueuelen 1000  (Local Loopback)
        RX packets 5  bytes 448 (448.0 B)
        RX errors 0  dropped 0  overruns 0  frame 0
        TX packets 5  bytes 448 (448.0 B)
        TX errors 0  dropped 0 overruns 0  carrier
0  collisions 0
```

We can also see the container's routing table by calling the route tool inside the container. The output will be similar to the following:

```
root@9fd192b5897d:/# route
Kernel IP routing table
Destination     Gateway          Genmask          Flags Metric
Ref
    Use Iface
default         172.17.0.1       0.0.0.0          UG    0        0
            0 eth0
172.17.0.0      0.0.0.0          255.255.0.0      U     0        0
            0 eth0
```

As we can see, our container has an `eth0` interface with the `172.17.0.2` IP address. In your case, the address might be different, but the important part is that our containers, by default, will have their own isolated networking stack with their own (virtual) interfaces, routing table, default gateway, and so on.

If we now open another terminal window and execute `docker network ls`, we will see which network types are supported using which drivers. The output will be similar to the following:

```
$ docker network ls
NETWORK ID      NAME      DRIVER     SCOPE
c82a29c5280e    bridge    bridge     local
83de399192b0    host      host       local
d4c7b1acbc0d    none      null       local
```

There are three basic network types:

- `bridge` – This is the default type and driver for Docker containers we create. It allows containers connected to the same bridge network on the host to communicate with each other and provides isolation from other containers (that can also be attached to their own bridge network). Communication with the *outside world* is possible with the help of **Network Address Translation (NAT)** done via the **IPtables** of the host.

- `host` – This is a type that is used when we want to create containers without network isolation. A container spawned with a host network won't be isolated from the network of the host system where it was created. For example, you can start a container with the Apache web server listening on port `80` and it will be reachable from any other hosts on the same network right away unless protected by a firewall.

- `none` – This is a rarely used option that means all networking will be disabled for the container.

Pay attention that those types in the output of `docker network ls` have the `local` scope, meaning that they can be used on individual hosts where we spawn containers with Docker. But they won't allow containers created on one server to communicate with containers created on another server directly (unless host networking is used, which is similar to running applications directly on the host when no containers are involved).

In order to establish networking between multiple hosts where we spawn containers communicating with each other, we need a so-called *overlay* network. Overlay networks connect multiple servers together, allowing communication between containers located on different hosts.

> **Overlay network**
>
> An overlay network is a virtual network running on top of another network, typically using packet encapsulation – an overlay network packet resides inside another packet that is forwarded to a particular host.

Whether you are running Kubernetes, Docker Swarm, or another solution to orchestrate containers, in the real world, you'll always run multiple hosts for your workloads, and containers running on those hosts need to talk with each other using overlay networks.

When it comes to Kubernetes, similar to the CRI, it implements a **Container Network Interface** (**CNI**) that allows the usage of different overlay networks in a pluggable manner.

> **CNI**
> A CNI is an interface that allows Kubernetes to use different overlay networking plugins for containers.

The introduction of the CNI has allowed third parties to develop their own solutions that are compatible with Kubernetes and offer their own unique features, such as traffic encryption or network policies (firewall rules) in container networks.

Some of the CNI network plugins used with Kubernetes today are **flannel**, **Cilium**, **Calico**, and **Weave**, just to name a few. Kubernetes also makes it possible to use multiple plugins at the same time with **Multus** (a Multi-Network Plugin); however, this is an advanced topic that is out of scope for the KCNA exam. In *Part 3*, *Learn Kubernetes Fundamentals*, of the book, we will have another closer look at networking in Kubernetes, but now it is time to look further into container storage.

Container storage

Containers are lightweight by design and, as we saw earlier, often even the basic tools such as `ifconfig` and `ping` might not be included in container images. That is because containers represent a minimal version of the OS environment where we only install an application we are going to containerize with its dependencies. You don't usually need many packages or tools pre-installed inside container images except for those required for your application to run.

Containers also don't keep the state by default, meaning that if you've placed some files inside the container filesystem while it was running and deleted the container after, all those files will be completely gone. Therefore, it is common to call containers **stateless** and the on-disk files in containers **ephemeral**.

That does not mean we cannot use containers for important data that we need to persist in case a container fails or an application exits.

> **Note**
> In case the application running inside the container fails, crashes, or simply terminates, the container also stops by default.

It is possible to keep the important data from the container by using *external* storage systems.

External storage can be a block volume attached to the container with a protocol such as **iSCSI** or it could be a **Network File System** (**NFS**) mount, for example. Or, external could also simply be a *local* directory on your container host. There are many options out there, but we commonly refer to external container storage as *volumes*.

One container can have multiple volumes attached and those volumes can be backed by different technologies, protocols, and hardware. Volumes can also be shared between containers or detached from one container and attached to another container. Volume content exists outside of the container life cycle, allowing us to decouple container and application data. Volumes allow us to run **stateful** applications in containers that need to write to disk, whether it is a database, application, or any other files.

Let's get back to our computer with Docker tooling and try to run the following in the terminal:

```
$ docker run -it --name mycontainer --mount
source=myvolume,target=/app ubuntu:22.04 bash
```

As we run it and attach *tty* to a container, we should be able to see our new `myvolume` mounted inside container at `/app`:

```
root@e642a068d4f4:/# df -h
Filesystem      Size  Used Avail Use% Mounted on
overlay         126G  7.9G  112G   7% /
tmpfs            64M     0   64M   0% /dev
tmpfs           3.0G     0  3.0G   0% /sys/fs/cgroup
shm              64M     0   64M   0% /dev/shm
/dev/vda1       126G  7.9G  112G   7% /app
tmpfs           3.0G     0  3.0G   0% /proc/acpi
tmpfs           3.0G     0  3.0G   0% /sys/firmware
root@e642a068d4f4:/# cd /app/
root@e642a068d4f4:/app#
```

What happened is that Docker automatically created and attached a `local` volume for our container at the start. Local means the volume is backed by a directory on the host where the container was started.

> **Important note**
> Local storage can be used for testing or some development, but by no means is it suitable for production workloads and business-critical data!

If we now write any files to /app, they will persist:

```
root@e642a068d4f4:/app# echo test > hello_world
root@e642a068d4f4:/app# cat hello_world
test
root@e642a068d4f4:/app# exit
exit
```

Even if we remove the container by calling docker rm:

```
$ docker rm mycontainer
mycontainer
```

By calling docker volume ls, we are able to see which volumes currently exist on our host:

```
$ docker volume ls
DRIVER      VOLUME NAME
local       myvolume
```

To find more details about the volume, we can use the docker volume inspect command:

```
$ docker volume inspect myvolume
[
    {
        "CreatedAt": "2022-05-15T18:00:06Z",
        "Driver": "local",
        "Labels": null,
        "Mountpoint": "/var/lib/docker/volumes/myvolume/_data",
        "Name": "myvolume",
        "Options": null,
        "Scope": "local"
    }
]
```

Feel free to experiment more with volumes yourself at this point. For example, you could create a new container and attach the existing volume to make sure the data is still there:

```
$ docker run -it --name mycontainer2 --mount
source=myvolume,target=/newapp ubuntu:22.04 bash
root@fc1075366787:/# ls /newapp/
hello_world
```

```
root@fc1075366787:/# cat /newapp/hello_world
test
```

Now, when it comes to Kubernetes, you've probably already guessed it – similar to the CRI and the CNI, K8s implements the **Container Storage Interface** (**CSI**).

> **CSI**
>
> The CSI allows using pluggable storage layers. External storage systems can be integrated for use in Kubernetes in a standardized way with the CSI.

The CSI allows vendors and cloud providers to implement support for their storage services or hardware appliances. For example, there is an **Amazon Elastic Block Store** (**EBS**) CSI driver that allows you to fully manage the life cycle of EBS volumes in the AWS cloud via Kubernetes. There is a **NetApp Trident** CSI project, which supports a variety of NetApp storage filers that can be used by containers in Kubernetes. And plenty of other CSI-compatible storage solutions available today.

Kubernetes is very powerful when it comes to managing storage; it can automatically provision, attach, and re-attach volumes between hosts and containers in the cluster. We will learn in more detail about Kubernetes features for stateful applications in *Chapter 6, Deploying and Scaling Applications with Kubernetes*, and now let's move on to learn about container security.

Container security

Container security is an advanced and complex topic and yet even for an entry-level KCNA certification, you are expected to know a few basics. As we've learned, *Namespaced* containers are the most commonly used containers and they share the kernel of an underlying OS. That means a process running in a container cannot see other processes running in other containers or processes running on the host. However, all processes running on one host still use the same kernel. If one of the containers gets compromised, there is a chance of the host and all other containers being compromised as well.

Let's get back to our Docker setup for a quick demonstration. Start an Ubuntu container as we did before and run the uname -r command to see which kernel version is used:

```
$ docker run -it ubuntu:22.04 bash
root@4a3db7a03ccf:/# uname -r
5.10.47-linuxkit
```

The output you'll see depends on your host OS and kernel version. Don't get surprised if you see another version. For example, you might see this:

```
5.13.0-39-generic
```

Now exit the container and start another one with an older version of Ubuntu:16.04:

```
$ docker run -it ubuntu:16.04 bash
Unable to find image 'ubuntu:16.04' locally
16.04: Pulling from library/ubuntu
58690f9b18fc: Pull complete
b51569e7c507: Pull complete
da8ef40b9eca: Pull complete
fb15d46c38dc: Pull complete
Digest: sha256:20858ebbc96215d6c3c574f781133ebffdc7c18d98af
4f294cc4c04871a6fe61
Status: Downloaded newer image for ubuntu:16.04
root@049e8a43181f:/# uname -r
5.10.47-linuxkit
root@049e8a43181f:/#
```

See? We took an Ubuntu:16.04 image that is more than 5 years old by now, but the kernel version used is exactly the same as in the first container. Even if you take a different flavor of Linux, the kernel version of your host OS will be used.

So, how can we protect the kernel of our host where we run *Namespaced* containers? Perhaps the two most well-known technologies are **AppArmor** for Ubuntu and **Security-Enchanced Linux** (**SELinux**) for Red Hat and the CentOS Linux family. Essentially, those projects allow you to enforce access control policies for all user applications and system services. Access to specific files or network resources can also be restricted. There is also a special tool for SELinux that helps to generate security profiles specifically for applications running in containers (https://github.com/containers/udica). Kubernetes has integration with both AppArmor and SELinux that allows you to apply profiles and policies to containers managed with K8s.

Moving on, it is considered a bad practice and a security risk to run containers as a root user. In Linux, a root user is a user with an ID of 0 and a group ID of 0 (UID=0, GID=0). In all our hands-on exercises, we've used a root user inside containers:

```
root@4a3db7a03ccf:/#
root@4a3db7a03ccf:/# id -u
0
```

In a real production environment, you should consider running applications as a non-root user because `root` is essentially a super-admin that can do anything in the system. Now comes the interesting part – a `root` user inside a container can also be a `root` user on the host where the container is running *(very bad practice!)*. Or, thanks to the Namespace functionality of the Linux kernel, the `root` user inside the container can be mapped to a different user ID on the host OS (such as `UID=1001`, for example). This is still not perfect, but in case a container is compromised, `root` inside the container won't automatically gain `root` privileges on the host OS.

> **Note**
>
> It is possible to specify which user and group to use for the application packaged in the container during the image build process. You can simply add the `USER mynewuser` instruction to a `Dockerfile` to define which user to use. You might need to first create this user by adding one more instruction above it. For example: `RUN useradd -r -u 1001 mynewuser`

Last but not least, keep in mind which container images you are using in your environments. If you go to Docker Hub (`https://hub.docker.com/`) or any other online container registry, you'll find lots and lots of third-party images that anybody can download and run. You might encounter an image that does exactly what you need. For example, an image might package a tool or an application you wanted to try (e.g., to monitor the database you are running). But it may well package malicious code inside. Therefore, make sure to run trusted code in your containers.

It is also better to build the image yourself and store it in your own repository because third-party public image repositories are completely out of your control. Their owner might simply delete or replace the image at any given point in time or make the repository private. You won't notice that immediately and this might cause an incident when the image isn't available for download. Finally, there are a number of tools available today that perform container image scanning for security vulnerabilities (**Clair**, **Dagda**, and **Anchore**, to name a few). Those tools can be integrated into the image build process to reduce the risks of using outdated packages or installing software with known security exposures.

Now that we know more about container security and networking, we will look into *service meshes* – a rather new technology for managing traffic and securing cloud-native applications.

Introducing service meshes

Before jumping into the definition of the service mesh, let's reiterate quickly what we've learned previously about the architecture of cloud-native applications.

Modern cloud-native applications rely on microservices that work together as a part of bigger applications and communicate with each other over a network. Those microservices are packaged as container images and run with the help of an orchestration system such as Kubernetes. The nature of cloud-native applications is highly dynamic, and the number of running containers varies a lot depending on the current load and infrastructure events or outages.

Consider a situation where you are responsible for running an application your company has developed that consists of 20 different microservices. You have implemented autoscaling for all services and in the peak load times, the number of running containers goes well over a hundred (e.g., several container replicas for each service spread across multiple cloud instances). Even if using Kubernetes to effectively orchestrate that fleet, you still want to make sure your application runs reliably, infrastructure is secure, and if any problem occurs, you're able to detect it and act fast. This is where a service mesh comes into play.

> **Service mesh**
>
> A service mesh is a dedicated infrastructure layer for making communication between services safe, observable, and reliable.

A service mesh is a special layer for handling service-to-service communication. The service here is typically a microservice running in a container orchestrated by Kubernetes. Technically, a service mesh can be used without Kubernetes and even containers, but in practice, most of the time, a service mesh is used together with containers orchestrated by Kubernetes. Examples of service meshes include the following:

- **Linkerd**
- **Istio**
- **Open Service Mesh (OSM)**
- **Consul Connect Service Mesh**

The first three in the list are in fact open source CNCF projects, although of different maturity levels.

Now, what does *safe communication* mean in the context of a service mesh?

In the preceding part, we covered the basics of container security, but we have not looked further into securing network communication *between* containers. Securing network communication is often a part of the so-called **Zero Trust** security approach.

> **Zero Trust**
>
> Zero Trust is an approach where no one is trusted by default from within the network or outside of the network. Verification is required to gain access to services connected to the network.

The traditional network security approach is based on securing the perimeter of the infrastructure, that is, it is hard to obtain access to the network from the *outside*, but *inside* the network everyone is trusted by default. Obviously, if an attacker can breach perimeter security and access internal networks, they are very likely to gain access everywhere else, including confidential data. This is the reason why more and more enterprises are implementing the Zero Trust approach, and this is where a service mesh is very helpful.

One of the major advantages of a service mesh is that you do not need any changes in the application code to use a service mesh and its features. A service mesh is implemented *on the platform layer*, meaning that, once installed on the platform, all the applications (e.g., microservices in containers) can benefit from its features. With a service mesh, all traffic between containers can be automatically encrypted and decrypted and the applications running inside *won't require a single line of code change*.

The traditional approach to accomplishing this without a service mesh would require managing SSL certificates, requesting and renewing them on expiration, and potentially making further changes to the application or the infrastructure levels.

In fact, all service meshes from the aforementioned list offer **mutually-authenticated Transport Layer Security (mTLS)** for all TCP traffic between containers connected to the mesh. It is similar to regular *TLS* when the server identity is presented with a certificate, with the difference that in the case of *mTLS*, both sides have to identify themselves to start communicating. That means the client also needs to present a certificate that the server will verify. In our example, the client and server are two services in containers connected to the service mesh. And again, mTLS can be enabled completely automatically with no extra work required on the application part.

Before exploring other features, let's first understand better how a service mesh works. The service mesh layer is interfaced with microservices through an array of lightweight network proxies and all traffic between microservices is routed via those proxies in their own infrastructure layer. Typically, proxies run alongside each service in so-called *sidecar* containers, and altogether, those sidecar proxies form a service mesh network, as depicted in *Figure 4.2*.

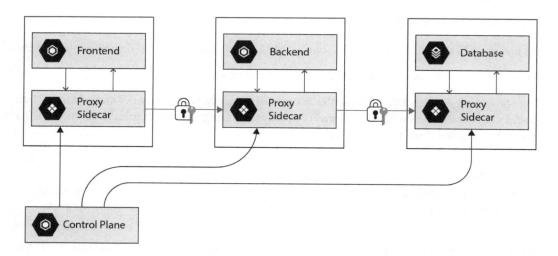

Figure 4.2 – Service mesh overview

The service mesh is usually made up of two parts:

- **Data plane** – This consists of network proxies that run next to containers with microservices. For example, in the case of the *Linkerd* service mesh, a *linkerd-proxy* is used, and in the case of *Istio*, an extended version of the *Envoy* proxy is used.

- **Control plane** – This consists of multiple components responsible for configuring network proxies, service discovery, certificate management, and other features.

For a service mesh to work with Kubernetes, it has to be compatible with the K8s **Service Mesh Interface (SMI)**.

SMI

This is a specification defining a standard, common, and portable set of APIs for smooth service mesh integration in a vendor-agnostic way. *SMI* serves the same purpose as *CRI*, *CNI*, and *CSI*, but for service meshes.

When it comes to observability, a service mesh offers detailed telemetry for all communications happening within the mesh. Automatically collected metrics from all proxies allow operators and engineers to troubleshoot, maintain, and optimize their applications. With a service mesh, we can trace the calls and service dependencies as well as inspecting traffic flows and individual requests. This information is extremely helpful to audit service behavior and response times, and to detect abnormalities in complex distributed systems.

Finally, a service mesh offers traffic management and reliability features. The exact functionality might vary from project to project, therefore some features provided by one service mesh might not be offered by another one. For the sake of example, let's see what a *Linkerd* mesh has to offer:

- **Load balancing** – This is used for **HTTP, HTTP/2**, and **gRPC** requests as well as **TCP** connections. A service mesh can also automatically detect the fastest service endpoints and send requests there.

- **Automatic retry and timeouts** – This allows you to gracefully handle transient service failures by transparently doing retries.

- **Traffic splitting** – This allows you to dynamically shift a portion of service traffic from one service to another to implement complex rollout strategies for new service versions.

- **Fault injection** – This allows you to artificially introduce errors and faults to test the impact on the system or connected services.

All in all, a service mesh is a complex and advanced topic and we have only scratched the surface to learn the minimum required for passing the KCNA exam. If you are interested in knowing more, it is recommended to check the *Further reading* section.

One question you might be asking yourself at this point is *what's the difference between overlay networks and service meshes and why do we need both?*

The short answer is that most overlay networks operate on the lower layer of the **Open Systems Interconnection (OSI)** model (Network layer 3) whereas a service mesh operates on layer 7 of the OSI model, focusing on services and high-level application protocols (if you're not familiar with the OSI model, check the *Further reading* section). The functionality of one is not a replacement for the other, and service meshes are still gaining momentum meaning, that not every microservice-based or containerized application running on Kubernetes will use a service mesh. Technically, we are also not obligated to always use overlay networks with containers, as we saw in our exercises with Docker, but in the upcoming chapters, we'll see why it is favorable.

Summary

In this chapter, we've learned a lot about container runtimes, container interfaces, and service meshes. A container runtime is low-level software that manages basic container operations such as image downloading and the start or deletion of containers. Kubernetes does not have its own runtime, but it provides interfaces that allow you to use different runtimes, different network plugins, different storage solutions, and different service meshes. Those interfaces are called CRI, CNI, CSI, and SMI respectively and their introduction allowed a lot of flexibility when using K8s.

We've also learned about container runtime types and their differences. *Namespaced* containers are the most popular and lightweight, however, they are not as secure as other types. *Virtualized* containers are the slowest, but they provide maximum security as each container uses an individual Linux kernel. *Sandboxed* containers fill the gap between the other two – they are more secure than namespaced ones and faster than virtualized ones.

When it comes to container networking, there are many options. For container-to-container communication in a cluster, we would typically use an overlay network. Kubernetes supports third-party network plugins through CNI, and those plugins provide a different set of features and capabilities. It is also possible to run containers in a non-isolated network environment, for example, directly in the network namespace of the host where the container is started.

Containers are *stateless* by design, meaning that they don't preserve the data on the disk by default. To run a *stateful* application in a container, we need to attach external storage volumes that can be anything ranging from an iSCSI block device to a specific vendor or cloud provider solution or even a simple local disk. Kubernetes with a pluggable CSI allows a lot of flexibility when it comes to integrating external storage to containers orchestrated by K8s.

We additionally touched on the basics of container security. *Namespaced* containers share the same kernel, which is why it is important to make sure that no container gets compromised. There are security extensions such as *AppArmor* and *SELinux* that add an extra kernel protection layer with configurable profiles and there are best practices that help to minimize the risks.

One of the practices is to use regular *(non-root)* user accounts in containers and another one is to ensure that you execute trusted code in a container. It is recommended to build your own images and keep them in your own registries, rather than using images from unknown third-party repositories. Additionally, you could implement automatic vulnerability scanning as a part of the image build process.

Finally, we learned about the service mesh – a special infrastructure layer that allows securing network communication between services without any changes to the application code. A service mesh also provides a rich set of features for observability and traffic management and even allows you to automatically retry requests and split traffic.

In the upcoming chapter, we will get to a major part of the KCNA exam and this book – namely, Kubernetes for container orchestration. Now make sure to answer all of the following recap questions to test your knowledge.

Questions

As we conclude, here is a list of questions for you to test your knowledge regarding this chapter's material. You will find the answers in the *Assessments* section of the *Appendix*:

1. Which of the following is software responsible for starting and stopping containers?

    A. Container hypervisor

    B. Container daemon

    C. Kubernetes

    D. Container runtime

2. Which of the following are valid types of containers (pick multiple)?

    A. Hyperspaced

    B. Sandboxed

    C. Namespaced

    D. Virtualized

3. Which of the following is an example of sandboxed containers?

    A. Kata

    B. gVisor

    C. Docker

    D. containerd

4.   Which of the following is an example of virtualized containers?

   A.   Docker

   B.   containerd

   C.   gVisor

   D.   Kata

5.   Which of the following allows you to use different container runtimes with Kubernetes?

   A.   CSI

   B.   SMI

   C.   CNI

   D.   CRI

6.   Which of the following allows you to use different service meshes with Kubernetes?

   A.   CRI

   B.   SMI

   C.   CNI

   D.   CSI

7.   Why are Namespaced containers considered less secure?

   A.   They use old kernel features

   B.   They need Kubernetes to run

   C.   They share a host kernel

   D.   They share a host network

8.   Which container type is considered the most lightweight and fast?

   A.   Virtualized

   B.   Sandboxed

   C.   Namespaced

   D.   Hyperspaced

9. Which of the following storage solutions can be used with Kubernetes?

    A. Any that supports NFS v4.1

    B. Any that is CSI compatible

    C. Any that is CNI compatible

    D. Any third-party cloud provider storage

10. What has to be changed in the application code for the service mesh to work?

    A. The application has to be rewritten in Golang

    B. The application needs to expose the SMI

    C. The application has to be stateless

    D. No application changes needed

11. Which of the following is a feature of a service mesh (pick multiple)?

    A. mTLS

    B. Traffic management

    C. Observability

    D. Traffic compression

12. Which component does the service mesh data plane include?

    A. Lightweight network firewall

    B. Lightweight network proxy

    C. Lightweight load balancer

    D. Lightweight web server

13. Which of the following is a service mesh (pick multiple)?

    A. Istio

    B. Prometheus

    C. Falco

    D. Linkerd

14. Which of the following is considered best practice when it comes to container security (pick multiple)?

    A. Run the application as `UID=0`

    B. Scan container images for vulnerabilities

    C. Run the application as non-root

    D. Run containers with Kubernetes

15. Which of the following technologies can be used to improve container security (pick multiple)?

    A. AppArmor

    B. Ansible

    C. SELinux

    D. Firewalld

16. Which potential problems can you encounter when using public container registries (pick multiple)?

    A. Third-party images might be deleted at any time

    B. Third-party images might fail to download due to rate limiting

    C. Third-party images might contain malware

    D. Third-party images might work in development but fail in production

17. Which containers can Kubernetes spawn?

    A. Namespaced containers

    B. K8s does not spawn containers; the runtime does

    C. Virtualized containers

    D. Sandboxed containers

18. What is typically used for multi-host container networking?

    A. IPtables

    B. CNI

    C. Service mesh

    D. Overlay network

Further reading

To learn more about the topics that were covered in this chapter, take a look at the following resources:

- Zero Trust: `https://www.beyondcorp.com/`
- Linkerd overview: `https://linkerd.io/2.12/overview/`
- About Istio: `https://istio.io/latest/about/service-mesh/`
- Open Systems Interconnection (OSI): `https://en.wikipedia.org/wiki/OSI_model`

Part 3: Learning Kubernetes Fundamentals

In this part, you'll learn about Kubernetes from the basics: the architecture, resources and components, features, and use cases. You will install Kubernetes and get practical experience with it using minikube. You will learn how to run stateless and stateful workloads, debug applications, and follow best practices with Kubernetes.

This part contains the following chapters:

- *Chapter 5, Orchestrating Containers with Kubernetes*
- *Chapter 6, Deploying and Scaling Applications with Kubernetes*
- *Chapter 7, Application Placement and Debugging with Kubernetes*
- *Chapter 8, Following Kubernetes Best Practices*

5
Orchestrating Containers with Kubernetes

In this and the following few chapters, we will cover the most important and perhaps the hardest part of the KCNA certification – *Kubernetes Fundamentals*. It makes up almost half (46%) of the total exam questions, so it's crucial to understand all the details. We'll take it one step at a time, and we'll also get practical experience with Kubernetes that will help you to memorize everything you need to pass the exam.

In this chapter, we'll learn about the features and the basics of the K8s architecture, its API, components, and the smallest deployable unit called a **Pod**. We will install and run Kubernetes locally with the help of the **minikube** project to support us along the way.

The topics we're going to cover are as follows:

- Kubernetes architecture
- Kubernetes API
- K8s – the Swiss Army knife of container orchestration
- Installing and exploring Kubernetes with minikube

Let's get started!

Kubernetes architecture

As you already know, Kubernetes is used to orchestrate fleets of containers that run on multiple servers that make up a Kubernetes cluster. Those servers are often called *nodes*, and nodes can be virtual machines running on-premises, in the cloud, or bare-metal servers. You can even combine different nodes in one Kubernetes cluster (for example, several nodes represented by VMs plus a few others as bare-metal servers).

There are two distinguished node types in Kubernetes:

- *Control plane* nodes (sometimes also called *master* nodes)
- *Worker* nodes

It is the *worker* nodes where the containerized applications run, and it is the *control plane* nodes where the K8s cluster management components run. We can see this in more detail in *Figure 5.1.*

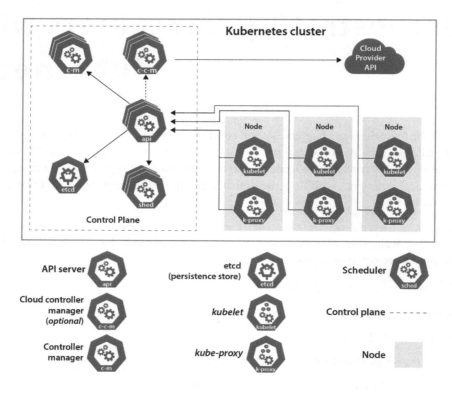

Figure 5.1 – Kubernetes components

Control plane nodes run several specialized K8s services and make global decisions about the Kubernetes cluster, such as scheduling containerized applications. Control plane nodes are also responsible for managing worker nodes in the cluster.

The following five services run on control plane nodes:

- *API server* (**kube-apiserver**): The core service that exposes the Kubernetes HTTP API for internal and external cluster communication. All operations within the cluster are performed through an API server – for example, when you query the state of the cluster or a particular application or start a new container.

- *Cluster data store* (**etcd**): A place where all information about the Kubernetes cluster state and configuration is kept. *etcd* is an open source, distributed key-value store used for this purpose and it is the only stateful component.

- *Scheduler* (**kube-scheduler**): A component that picks where, and on which worker node, the application containers will run in the cluster. The factors that can affect scheduling decisions include individual application requirements, load on the nodes, hardware or policy constraints, and more.

- *Controller manager* (**kube-controller-manager**): A component that runs various controller processes, such as *Node*, *Job*, or *Deployment* controllers. Those controllers watch the current state of respective resources in the cluster and take action if the current state differs from the desired state.

- An optional *Cloud controller manager* (**cloud-controller-manager**): A component that lets you integrate the Kubernetes cluster with a cloud provider by running controller processes specific to your provider. For example, it allows you to create load balancers for containerized applications or determine if a worker node cloud instance has been deleted. *Cloud controller manager* is a component that you do not need when K8s is running on-premises.

Let's move on to the components of worker nodes:

- **Kubelet**: An agent that ensures that containers assigned to the node are running and healthy. Kubelet also reports the status to the API server.

- **Proxy** (**kube-proxy**): This is a network proxy that helps to implement Kubernetes *Service* functionality. Proxy maintains network rules on nodes to allow container communication from inside or outside of your K8s cluster.

- **Container runtime**: This is a piece of software that's responsible for basic container operations. Thanks to *CRI*, Kubernetes can use different container runtimes. One of the most popular runtimes today is *containerd*.

> **Note**
> Kubelet does not manage containers that were not created via the Kubernetes API. For example, containers created by other means on the worker nodes won't be known to Kubernetes.

Today, the worker node components **also run on the control plane nodes**. That's right – on the Kubernetes control plane, you'll have not just the *scheduler, kube-apiserver, etcd*, and *kube-controller-manager*, but also *kubelet, kube-proxy*, and a *runtime*. This means that worker components are run on all Kubernetes nodes in the cluster.

Why is that? The reason is that control plane components are deployed in containers themselves and therefore can be managed by Kubernetes with so-called static **pods**. Alternatively, control plane components can be started and managed with **systemd**, but this approach is becoming less popular today.

> **What is a pod?**
>
> A pod is the smallest deployable unit that can be created in Kubernetes. A pod is a group of one or multiple containers that share storage, network, and a specification of how to run containers within the pod.

You can think of a pod as a Kubernetes wrapper for containers, and you'll always deal with pods when deploying any application in a K8s cluster. Even if you need to run a small simple application consisting of only one container, you'll need to define a pod with that single container. In other words, **it is not possible to run containers on Kubernetes without a pod wrapper**.

It is also rather common to have two or more containers in one pod where the second or third container in the pod acts as a *helper* to the *main* container. This happens when multiple containers need to work together and share resources. Such *helper* containers are called *sidecars*. In the previous chapter, we learned about the *Service Mesh*, which utilizes sidecars to deploy a proxy together with the application containers. Another example where you might run multiple containers in one pod is to collect monitoring metrics from the application running in the main container. A sidecar container may also be used for log aggregation – for example, a sidecar container might collect and ship logs for long-term storage from the main application in the same pod, as shown in *Figure 5.2*:

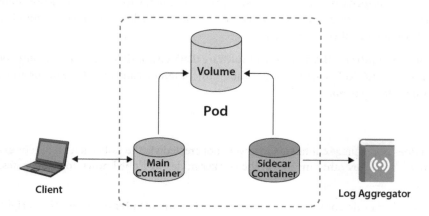

Figure 5.2 – Pod example with two containers

> **Note**
>
> Containers of one pod are always co-located and co-scheduled on the same node.

Other than the *sidecar*, there is yet another type called **Init Containers**. They are handy for running setup scripts and initialization utilities that are needed for the containerized application.

> **initContainers**
>
> These are containers that are executed in order before the other containers in the pod are started. Until all `initContainers` have finished, no other containers are going to start and initContainers will run every time a pod starts.

Besides allowing you to run co-located and individual containers on Kubernetes, pods have more features, including the following:

- **Shared storage**: All the containers in a pod can access shared volumes, allowing containers to share data.

- **Shared networking**: All the containers in a Pod share the *network namespace* with an IP address and network ports. Containers don't have individual IP addresses, but the pod does, and containers in one pod can communicate with each other simply via *localhost*. Also, because of shared networking, two containers in one pod cannot listen on the same network port.

- **Shared memory**: Containers in a pod can use standard Linux inter-process communication such as **SystemV semaphores** or **POSIX shared memory**.

Now, we've already mentioned Kubernetes *clusters* many times, meaning that we need at least two nodes. Technically, you could run Kubernetes on a single node while combining both the control plane and worker node functionality at the same time. **However, you should never do this for production environments. This is only acceptable for learning or development purposes**.

In real-life scenarios, we would run at least three control plane nodes with several worker nodes. The nodes should be spread across multiple **failure domains** (typically called **availability zones** by cloud providers) that might be represented by individual data centers interconnected with high bandwidth networks. In the case of an outage of a single server or an availability zone, such a Kubernetes cluster will remain operational.

Having just one control plane node in the cluster is not sufficient for production environments because, in the case of an outage, you won't able to query the state of your cluster and applications, start new pods with containers, or make any changes. Also, you don't want to lose your *etcd* data store, which keeps all the information about your cluster.

Therefore, like with many clustered systems, the best practice is **to run an odd number of control plane nodes**; for example, three or five. Having an odd number helps to prevent *split-brain* scenarios where, in the event of a network failure, two parts of the cluster won't be able to establish a majority (for example, four nodes split into two parts can lead to inconsistencies or an inoperable state).

> **Note**
> This practice does not apply to worker nodes, and it is fine to run two, four, seven, or even 200 worker nodes in a cluster.

I know this is a lot to digest, but when we get our hands on Kubernetes and deploy our first few pods, things will become much clearer and easier. Later in this chapter, we will have a closer look at the pod specification, but for now, let's learn more about the Kubernetes API and how we can use it.

The Kubernetes API

As we learned previously, the Kubernetes API server is the main gateway for all cluster operations. When we want to know the state of the cluster, the number of nodes or pods or other resources, and their state, we need to use the Kubernetes API. The same is valid for all operations, such as creating new pods or making changes in the specifications of other resources. In a nutshell, the API server is the *brain* of K8s.

There are multiple ways to interact with the Kubernetes API:

- **Kubectl**: A command-line interface tool available for all common platforms, including Linux, Windows, and macOS. Operators very often use kubectl to interact with K8s clusters and manage or debug applications running in Kubernetes.

- **dashboard (kube-dashboard)**: A popular web-based graphical user interface. It allows you to view, create, and modify resources, as well as troubleshoot applications running in K8s. dashboard, however, does not support all functionality that kubectl does.

- **Client libraries**: Available in many programming languages, including *Golang, Java, Python, JavaScript*, and more. They allow you to write software that uses the Kubernetes API and helps handle common tasks such as authentication.

- **HTTP REST calls**: Using any common HTTP client such as curl or wget, you can directly access the Kubernetes API. This is not a very commonly used method but it can be helpful sometimes.

This list is not exhaustive, and today, you can find many other tools (**Lens, Octant**) developed by third parties that allow you to use the Kubernetes API. However, they are outside the scope of this book and the KCNA exam. To successfully pass the exam, you only need to have experience with kubectl.

In the previous chapters, we mentioned that the Kubernetes API is **declarative**.

> **Declarative API**
> A declarative API means you declare the *desired state* of your Kubernetes resources and Kubernetes controllers, constantly ensuring that the current state of Kubernetes objects (for example, the number of pods for a certain app) is in sync with the declared desired state.

Thus, the Kubernetes API is different from an imperative approach where you instruct the server on what to do. After you have defined the desired state via the API, Kubernetes, using its *kube-controller-manager*, will instruct the controllers running in infinite control loops to check the resource state to be the same as the desired state and *reconcile* if not. For example, we have instructed K8s to run our application with three replicas and one of the replicas eventually crashed. Kubernetes will automatically detect that only two replicas are running and will spawn one new pod with our application:

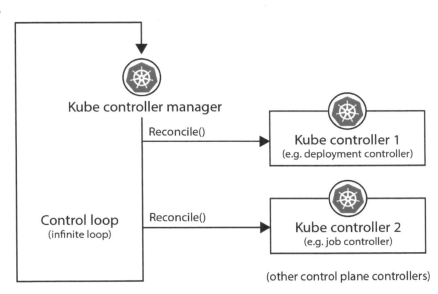

Figure 5.3 – Kubernetes control loops

> **Note**
> The infinite control loops of controller managers are sometimes also called reconciliation loops.

Because Kubernetes is developed at high velocity, its APIs are constantly evolving. New API resources can be added frequently, and old resources or fields are removed over several release cycles following Kubernetes's depreciation policy. To make it easier to make such changes, K8s supports multiple API versions and API grouping and maintains compatibility with existing API clients for an extended period. For example, there can be two API versions for the same resource: `v1` and `v1beta1`. You may have first created a resource using its `v1beta1` version, but you'll still be able to make changes to this resource using either the `v1` or `v1beta1` API version for a few releases.

Each new feature of Kubernetes follows a defined life cycle and the respective API evolves from alpha to beta to the generally available state over several K8s releases, as shown in *Figure 5.4*:

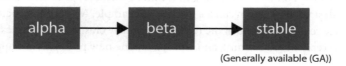

Figure 5.4 – Kubernetes feature life cycle

It's worth mentioning that the alpha features of Kubernetes are usually *disabled*. However, you can enable them by setting so-called **feature gates**. Beta and stable Kubernetes features are enabled by default.

The implementation of new and major changes to existing features in Kubernetes typically starts with **Kubernetes Enhancement Proposal (KEP)**. Those are detailed specification documents that outline the motivation, goals, and design of the changes. You can find existing KEPs in Kubernetes GitHub repositories (`https://github.com/kubernetes/enhancements/tree/master/keps`).

Because Kubernetes is a complex project with many components, it has multiple operational areas, including storage, networking, scaling, and more. Those areas are typically covered by Kubernetes **Special Interest Groups (SIGs)**. SIGs are smaller communities of developers that focus on particular parts of K8s. Since K8s is an open source project, anybody can become a part of SIG to fix issues, review code, and make enhancement proposals.

Last, but not least, the Kubernetes API is highly extensible in one of two ways:

- With **Custom Resource Definitions (CRDs)**: A method that does not require any programming
- With **aggregation layers**: A method that requires programming but allows you to have more control over the API behavior

Both methods allow you to add extra functionality to Kubernetes, beyond what is offered by the standard Kubernetes APIs. You don't need to know many details for the scope of the KCNA exam, but as you gain more hands-on experience, you'll see that the extensible API is a very powerful feature of Kubernetes that allows us to add unique features without the need to know or modify existing K8s source code.

Now that we've learned about the Kubernetes API, let's understand more about the features of Kubernetes that made it the number one orchestrator of containers.

K8s – the Swiss Army knife of container orchestration

We've mentioned a few times that Kubernetes is great for running cloud-native applications that consist of many microservices packaged in containers. But why exactly?

Kubernetes offers many features that enormously simplify the operation of large container fleets. We already know that it is possible to automatically scale the number of containers with Kubernetes or restart failing containers. What about the other features Kubernetes has to offer?

- **Automated rollouts and rollbacks**: Allows you to deploy new versions and changes of your application (or its configuration) in a controlled way, monitoring the application's health status and ensuring it is always running. K8s also allows you to roll back to the previous versions of the application, its image, or its configuration if something goes wrong.

- **Service discovery and load balancing**: Allows different microservices in a cluster to easily find each other. In a set of pods representing the same microservice, each pod will have an IP address, but the set will have a single DNS name, allowing simple service discovery and load distribution.

- **Secret and configuration management**: Allows you to handle microservice configuration and secrets without the need to rebuild container images or expose sensitive credentials – for example, when a service needs to access a database or has many configuration parameters that change.

- **Self-healing**: Allows you to automatically restart containers that fail for any reason, automatically reschedule containers to another node if a worker node stops responding, restart containers that fail predefined health checks, and route requests to containers when only the applications inside are fully started and ready to serve.

- **Horizontal scaling**: Allows you to scale a containerized application up or down by adding or reducing the number of pods running the application. This can be done manually or automatically, for example, based on CPU usage.

- **Batch execution**: Allows you to schedule the execution of containers and flexibly manage batch processing or CI workloads.

- **Automatic bin packing**: Allows you to automatically determine the best worker node to start the container based on requested resources, current cluster utilization, or other requirements. It also allows you to define workload priorities to handle different critical and non-critical applications.

- **Storage orchestration**: Allows you to integrate and manage storage systems of your choice. Kubernetes can automatically provision and mount storage volumes when a pod is spawned and re-mount volumes to different nodes as needed.

This is a long list and yet not 100% complete. In the previous section, we saw that it is possible to extend the Kubernetes API to add new features. Today, Kubernetes has a rich ecosystem with numerous projects that extend Kubernetes and even allow you to manage other workloads besides containers. That's right – Kubernetes can be used to orchestrate not just containers. There are several projects we should mention:

- **KubeVirt**: A project that's used to provision and manage virtual machines with Kubernetes alongside containers. This is used for cases when a workload cannot be easily containerized or for an ongoing process of application containerization where some applications still run in VMs.

- **Kubeless**: A serverless computing framework that runs on top of Kubernetes. It adds FaaS capabilities to your K8s cluster and can serve as an alternative to cloud provider FaaS offerings.

- **Knative**: Another serverless computing framework for Kubernetes that has recently been accepted to the CNCF. It was originally founded by Google and has been actively developed since 2018.

- **OpenFaas**: Another serverless framework that can be used with Kubernetes or without in a standalone mode. Like the other two serverless frameworks, it supports many programming languages that can be used to write functions, including *Golang*, *Java*, *Python*, *Ruby*, *C#*, and others.

You don't need to know further details about those projects for the KCNA exam or any other Kubernetes certification from CNCF. Just remember that it is possible to orchestrate VMs with the help of KubeVirt and offer FaaS on top of Kubernetes with projects such as Knative. If you'd like to learn more about these projects, you'll find links in the *Further reading* section at the end of this chapter.

> **Note**
>
> Even though it is possible to manage VMs with the help of Kubernetes, it is still primarily used to orchestrate containers most of the time.

Before we jump into installing Kubernetes and trying its numerous features out, let's look at an example of how K8s can be a part of the development workflow, as shown in *Figure 5.5*:

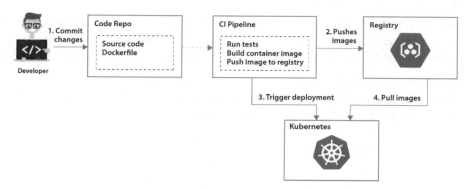

Figure 5.5 – Simple development workflow example with Kubernetes

The simplified workflow may look like this:

1. A developer writes code for a new microservice and commits it to a GitHub repository. As you may recall, developers don't need to learn a new programming language to run applications in containers.

2. There should be a `Dockerfile` that defines the steps needed to package the application into a container image. Before the container image is built, automated tests are executed in the CI pipeline. If the tests are successful, a Docker image is built and pushed into the image registry.

3. Next, the deployment of the container is triggered in the Kubernetes cluster. To run containers on Kubernetes, we need a pod spec definition in either **YAML** or **JSON** format. The easiest way to apply a spec is simply by using the `kubectl` tool, which must be configured to work with our K8s cluster.

4. As the spec is applied, Kubernetes will take care of finding a suitable worker node to download the container image from the registry and start the pod with our containerized application. We can define it to run multiple replicas of applications for high availability requirements and to balance the load.

5. This process can be repeated many times and Kubernetes can handle deploying the new image with a new application version in a rolling update manner where, for instance, only one replica will be replaced at a time.

A pod is just one example of a Kubernetes object, and it is the smallest deployable unit. In the next chapter, we'll get to know other, more advanced resources that use Kubernetes controllers and provide more advanced features.

> **Kubernetes objects**
>
> Kubernetes objects are persistent entries that represent the state of the cluster, including information about which containerized applications run and on which nodes, resources available to these applications, and their associated policies (for example, restart policies, scheduling requirements, and so on).

Kubernetes objects are created the moment we apply a spec definition, and they are essentially a *record of intent*. Once the object has been created, Kubernetes will work to ensure that the object exists and is in the *desired state*. The time it might take to reach the desired state depends on many factors and might take as little as a second or as much as several minutes if, for instance, the container image that's downloaded from the image registry is large and the network performance is poor.

> **Note**
>
> Kubernetes spec definition files are also known as Kubernetes manifests. It is a specification of API objects in JSON or YAML format.

Now that we are familiar with some of the basics, let's try things out ourselves. In the next section, we are going to install a single node Kubernetes to gain hands-on experience.

Installing and exploring K8s with minikube

Today, many projects allow you to quickly bootstrap a simple K8s cluster or a single node Kubernetes for learning or local development purposes. We will be using **minikube**, a project supported by an official Kubernetes SIG that focuses on cluster deployment and its life cycle. Other projects let you get similar results, such as **Kind** and **CRC**.

> **Important note**
>
> miniKube, Kind, and some other projects are not designed to set up production-ready Kubernetes clusters. Do not use these setups to run important workloads!

Quickly make sure that your system meets *minikube's* requirements:

- A recent version of Linux, macOS, or Windows
- 2+ CPU cores
- 2+ GB of free RAM
- 20+ GB of free disk space
- Internet connection
- Administrator/superuser privileges
- Container or VM manager (our Docker Engine installation from previous chapters can be used)

First, open the minikube start documentation (`https://minikube.sigs.k8s.io/docs/start/`) in your browser and select your operating system under the *Installation* section. Make sure that you select the *Stable* release type and the correct CPU architecture if you're running on macOS or Linux.

> **Note**
>
> If you don't have the `curl` tool installed, you can also simply copy the URL from the documentation, paste it into a new browser tab, and save it to your computer, just like any other downloadable. In such a case, the `installation` command should be executed in the same path where the `minikube` binary was saved.

Open your Terminal and execute the command for your OS, and enter the password if requested. For example, on macOS with an x86-64 CPU, the output might look like this:

```
$ curl -LO https://storage.googleapis.com/minikube/releases/
latest/minikube-darwin-amd64
  % Total     % Received % Xferd  Average Speed   Time
    Time        Time  Current
                                  Dload  Upload   Total
    Spent     Left  Speed
100 68.6M  100 68.6M    0     0  38.5M      0  0:00:01
    0:00:01 --:--:--:-- 38.7M
$ sudo install minikube-darwin-amd64 /usr/local/bin/minikube
Password:
```

At this point, we are ready to start our local Kubernetes with the help of the `minikube start` command:

```
$ minikube start
😄   minikube v1.25.2 on Darwin 12.4
✨   Automatically selected the docker driver. Other choices:
hyperkit, ssh
👍   Starting control plane node minikube in cluster minikube
🚜   Pulling base image ...
💾   Downloading Kubernetes v1.23.3 preload ...
    > preloaded-images-k8s-v17-v1...: 505.68 MiB / 505.68
MiB  100.00% 40.26 Mi
    > gcr.io/k8s-minikube/kicbase: 379.06 MiB / 379.06
MiB  100.00% 14.81 MiB p
🔥   Creating docker container (CPUs=2, Memory=4000MB) ...
🐳   Preparing Kubernetes v1.23.3 on Docker 20.10.12 ...
    • kubelet.housekeeping-interval=5m
    • Generating certificates and keys ...
    • Booting up control plane ...
    • Configuring RBAC rules ...
🌟   Enabled addons: storage-provisioner, default-storageclass
🏄   Done! kubectl is now configured to use "minikube" cluster
and "default" namespace by default
```

> **Note**
>
> You might have a newer version of Kubernetes and a slightly different output from `minikube`
> `start`. If you encounter an error, there likely will be a link to a related issue in the output
> that should help you to resolve the problem. If you are using another system than in the
> previous chapters, you'll need to install Docker Engine first. Refer to *Chapter 3, Getting Started*
> *with Containers*, for details and the drivers' documentation page of minikube (`https://`
> `minikube.sigs.k8s.io/docs/drivers/`). For other problems, check the minikube
> troubleshooting guide linked in the *Further reading* section of this chapter.

Now that we have Kubernetes up and running, we should be able to access its API using the `kubectl`
CLI tool. You can go and download `kubectl` yourself, but minikube can do this for you. It is
recommended to let `minikube` do this as it will automatically pick the correct version. All you
need to do is run any command with `kubectl` for the first time – for example, a command to list
all Kubernetes nodes in the cluster:

```
$ minikube kubectl get nodes
    > kubectl.sha256: 64 B / 64 B [--------------------------]
100.00% ? p/s 0s
    > kubectl: 50.65 MiB / 50.65 MiB [-------------] 100.00%
54.17 MiB p/s 1.1s
NAME        STATUS      ROLES                   AGE     VERSION
minikube    Ready       control-plane,master    18m     v1.23.3
```

Minikube has downloaded the K8s CLI for us and ran the command. At no surprise, we only have
one node that is called `minikube` and has roles of `control-plane` and `master`.

Let's see what is currently running in Kubernetes. You can list the pods using the `kubectl get`
`pods` command:

```
$ minikube kubectl get pods
No resources found in default namespace.
```

As we can see, nothing is running at the moment because we've just bootstrapped a new cluster. Let's
run the same command with an extra option – that is, `--all-namespaces` (mind the two extra
dashes between `kubectl` and `get`; they are needed to separate the `kubectl` from `minikube`
arguments since both have their own sets of arguments):

```
$ minikube kubectl -- get pods --all-namespaces
NAMESPACE       NAME
READY   STATUS      RESTARTS    AGE
kube-system     coredns-64897985d-x28hm
1/1     Running     0           31m
```

```
kube-system    etcd-minikube
1/1       Running    0           32m
kube-system    kube-apiserver-minikube
1/1       Running    0           32m
kube-system    kube-controller-manager-minikube
1/1       Running    0           32m
kube-system    kube-proxy-hwv2p
1/1       Running    0           32m
kube-system    kube-scheduler-
minikube             1/1       Running    0           32m
kube-system    storage-
provisioner               1/1       Running    0           32m
```

The output has changed quite a bit and we can now see all those components of Kubernetes that we learned about at the beginning of this chapter: kube-apiserver, kube-controller-manager, kube-proxy, kube-scheduler, etcd, and a couple of other running in individual pods in the kube-system namespace.

Kubernetes namespaces

Kubernetes namespaces provide a grouping mechanism to separate Kubernetes objects within a cluster. It is common to use Kubernetes namespaces to group workloads per team, project, or application. The kube-system namespace is reserved for Kubernetes's components.

Now, let's see which namespaces we have in our new shiny Kubernetes:

```
$ minikube kubectl -- get namespaces
NAME             STATUS     AGE
default          Active     56m
kube-node-lease  Active     56m
kube-public      Active     56m
kube-system      Active     56m
```

The default namespace, as its name suggests, is simply a standard namespace where container workloads will be created by default. kube-node-lease is another reserved Kubernetes namespace for node heartbeats (checks that determine that the node is running) and kube-public is an automatically created namespace for public resources such as those required for cluster discovery.

Normal practice is to create new namespaces either per application, group of microservices working together, or per team. Let's create a new namespace and call it `kcna` by executing `kubectl -- create namespace kcna`:

```
$ minikube kubectl -- create namespace kcna
namespace/kcna created
```

> **Note**
> You can also set up an alias for `minikube kubectl`, as suggested in the minikube documentation (`$ alias kubectl="minikube kubectl --"`) to skip writing `minikube` every time. (Make sure that you remove it when you're not using `minikube` anymore.)

Now, let's deploy a containerized *Nginx* web server into our new `kcna` namespace. We can always set the namespace where we want to execute the `kubectl` command by adding the `--namespace` argument:

```
$ minikube kubectl -- create -f https://k8s.io/examples/pods/
simple-pod.yaml --namespace kcna
pod/nginx created
```

Here, we provided a pod spec file that is located in the examples shown on the `https://k8s.io/` web page. The Kubernetes CLI is smart enough to download the file, validate the spec, and apply it to create the objects it defines – in this case, a single pod with Nginx. If we were to write this simple pod specification ourselves in YAML format, it would look like this:

```
$ cat simple-pod.yaml
apiVersion: v1
kind: Pod
metadata:
  name: nginx
spec:
  containers:
  - name: nginx
    image: nginx:1.14.2
    ports:
    - containerPort: 80
```

Let's see what each line of this spec file means.

apiVersion: v1 defines which version of the Kubernetes API we are using to create this object. As you know, Kubernetes APIs evolve from alpha to beta to stable versions. v1 is the stable version in this example:

- kind: Pod – Defines the kind of object we are describing.

- metadata: – Defines metadata for the object, such as name or further annotations.

- name: nginx – Defines the name of the pod.

- spec: – Defines the block where we describe the desired state of the object.

- containers: – Defines the list of containers that are part of this pod.

- - name: nginx – The name of the first container in the Pod. Multiple containers can run together in one pod.

- image: nginx:1.14.2 – The name of the image (nginx) that can be optionally preceded by the image registry URL and followed by the image tag (1.14.2). If you run multiple containers in one pod, you'll need to define the image and name for each one.

- ports: – This is an optional informational block that tells us about which ports are to be exposed. Those are the ports where the process in the container is listening on. However, not specifying this block does not prevent ports from being exposed.

- - containerPort: 80 – This is port 80 in this example.

> **Note**
>
> The indentation is very important in YAML format and one missing space or an extra space can make it invalid. kubectl will complain if there are parsing errors when applying a specification. It is recommended to copy example files from this book's GitHub repository to avoid typos and formatting mistakes.

Alright, so, what happened with our Nginx pod?

```
$ minikube kubectl -- get pods --namespace kcna
NAME    READY   STATUS    RESTARTS    AGE
nginx   1/1     Running   0           10m
```

It is in a Running status and 1/1 (one out of one) containers in the pod are ready. There are several statuses the pod might be in:

- Pending: The specification has been accepted by Kubernetes and, currently, the pod is waiting to be scheduled or for a requested container image to be downloaded from the image registry.

- Running: The pod is assigned to a certain node and all containers in the pod have been created. At least one container is running.

- `Succeeded`: All the containers in the pod have successfully finished/exited with a *good* exit code (for example zero). This happens when, for example, an application in a container has gracefully shut down.

- `Failed`: All the containers in the pod terminated and at least one has failed; for example, it has exited with a non-zero exit code.

- `Unknown`: The state of the pod cannot be obtained. This might happen when a node where the pod should be running is unreachable, for example, due to network issues.

- `ErrImagePull`: The image specified in the manifest cannot be retrieved (pulled). This might be due to a wrong image name or wrong tag that does not exist in the registry.

Additionally, you might encounter a `ContainerCreating` or `Terminating` status describing the startup or termination phase of pod containers, respectively.

Currently, our Nginx pod does nothing; it does not serve any applications or content except for its default static page. In the next chapter, we will learn how to expose and access applications in Kubernetes with the **Service** concept. For now, try to get more details about our `nginx` pod using the `kubectl describe` command:

```
$ minikube kubectl -- describe pods nginx --namespace kcna
```

You'll find a lot of information about the pod, such as the node where it runs, its start time, IP address, environment variables, recent events, and much more. This information is very helpful for cases when we need to debug failing pods or applications.

Now that we have used `kubectl` a bit, let's try the Kubernetes dashboard as well. Minikube offers a convenient one-command dashboard installation with `minikube dashboard`:

```
$ minikube dashboard
🔑    Enabling dashboard ...
   ▪ Using image kubernetesui/dashboard:v2.3.1
   ▪ Using image kubernetesui/metrics-scraper:v1.0.7
😀  Verifying dashboard health ...
🚀  Launching proxy ...
😀  Verifying proxy health ...
🎉  Opening http://127.0.0.1:55089/api/v1/namespaces/
kubernetes-dashboard/services/http:kubernetes-dashboard:/proxy/
in your default browser...
```

At this point, the dashboard will be installed into a new `kubernetes-dashboard` namespace and your browser should automatically open it in a new tab (in case it did not, try executing `minikube dashboard --url` to get the URL of the dashboard). You'll need to switch to another namespace in the top-left corner drop-down menu as there is nothing currently running in the `default` namespace. If you switch to the `kcna` namespace, you'll be able to see our `nginx` pod, whereas if you switch to `kube-system`, you'll see the Kubernetes control plane components that we described previously in this chapter. You may notice that, besides pods, there are **Deployment**, **Daemon Set** and **Replica Set** workloads. Those will be the topic of the next chapter, where we will see how these can be used to create pods and learn about the features of those K8s resources.

Feel free to explore the dashboard a little more by yourself; when you're done, delete our Nginx pod using the dashboard or via the `kubectl delete` command. To interrupt `minikube dashboard`, you can use *Ctrl + C* shortcut:

```
$ minikube kubectl -- delete pods nginx --namespace kcna
pod "nginx" deleted
```

> **Note**
> `kubectl` is a user-friendly tool that allows you to type pod, pods, or simply po, all of which mean the same thing. It also has a lot of convenient short names, such as ns, for namespaces. To list all short names, run `minikube kubectl api-resources`.

If you are about to shut down your workstation before moving on to the next chapter, you can also temporarily stop your Kubernetes node by executing the `minikube stop` command:

```
$ minikube stop
   Stopping node "minikube"  ...
   Powering off "minikube" via SSH ...
   1 node stopped.
```

This has been a long and very intense chapter, so congrats on making it this far! Take a break before moving on to the next chapter and make sure you answer the questions provided.

Summary

In this chapter, we finally got our hands on Kubernetes. We learned a lot about its architecture, components, and API. Kubernetes clusters consist of control plane (also known as the master) and worker nodes, where control plane nodes run K8s management components and worker nodes run the actual containerized applications with the help of *kubelet*, *container runtime*, and *kube-proxy*. Among the master node components, there's *kube-apiserver*, *etcd*, *kube-scheduler*, *kube-controller-manager*, and, optionally, *cloud-controller-manager*.

We saw that a *pod* is the smallest deployable unit of Kubernetes and that it allows us to run individual containers as well as multiple containers together on K8s. Containers inside one pod are coupled and can share storage, network, and memory. The secondary container in the pod is typically called the *sidecar* and can help the container run the main application by doing log aggregation, for example.

The Kubernetes API is *declarative*. When we work with K8s, we describe the desired state of resources in the cluster; Kubernetes ensures that the current state reaches the desired state after object creation. Due to rapid development, Kubernetes APIs are grouped and multi-versioned, and by default only enable *beta* and *stable* (GA) features. There are several ways to access the Kubernetes API, with the *kubectl* CLI and *dashboard* being the most popular ones. One of the specialties of K8s is its ability to extend its APIs through CRDs and aggregation layers.

When it comes to features, Kubernetes has a lot to offer, ranging from automatic rollouts, service discovery, and secret management to auto-scaling, self-healing, and even storage orchestration. We will try many of those features in practice in the next few chapters. It is also possible to use Kubernetes to manage virtual machines or provide FaaS with the help of separate projects such as *KubeVirt* and *Knative*.

In the last section, we installed a simple one-node Kubernetes deployment using the *minikube* project and learned about the concept of Kubernetes *namespaces* for resource separation and grouping. We also created a pod with a single Nginx container and explored the minimal pod spec definition in YAML format.

In the next chapter, we will learn about other Kubernetes resources and their usage. We will learn how to configure and scale multi-container applications with Kubernetes, how to run stateful workloads with Kubernetes, and learn about exposing applications running in K8s.

Questions

As we conclude, here is a list of questions for you to test your knowledge regarding this chapter's material. You will find the answers in the *Assessments* section of the *Appendix*:

1. Which of the following is the smallest schedulable unit in Kubernetes?

    A. Container

    B. Sidecar

    C. Pod

    D. Deployment

2. Containers running in one pod share which of the following options (pick multiple)?

   A. Name

   B. Storage

   C. Networking

   D. Memory

3. Which of the following types of nodes does Kubernetes have (pick multiple)?

   A. Secondary

   B. Master

   C. Worker

   D. Primary

4. Which of the following are components of control plane nodes (pick multiple)?

   A. Docker, kube-scheduler, cloud-controller-manager

   B. kube-master-server, kubelet, kube-proxy

   C. kube-scheduler, kube-controller-manager

   D. kube-api-server, etcd

5. Which of the following K8s cluster configuration can be recommended?

   A. 1 master node, 5 worker nodes

   B. 2 master nodes, 3 worker nodes

   C. 2 master nodes, 20 worker nodes

   D. 3 master nodes, 10 worker nodes

6. Which of the following components are used to store cluster state in Kubernetes?

   A. kube-api-server

   B. kube-volume

   C. kubelet

   D. etcd

7. Which of the following components is used by Kubernetes to download images and start containers?

    A. Kubelet

    B. Container runtime

    C. etcd

    D. kube-proxy

8. Which of the following components is responsible for Kubernetes controller processes?

    A. kube-api-server

    B. kube-proxy

    C. kube-controller-manager

    D. kube-scheduler

9. What can be used to access the Kubernetes API (pick multiple)?

    A. kubeadmin

    B. kubectl

    C. kubelet

    D. dashboard

10. Kubernetes has a declarative API. What does this mean?

    A. We always need to declare a YAML spec file to use the K8s API

    B. We declare the desired state and K8s will reach it once

    C. We tell Kubernetes exactly what to do with which resource

    D. We declare the desired state and K8s will constantly try to reach it

11. Which of the following Kubernetes API versions are enabled by default (pick multiple)?

    A. Alpha

    B. Beta

    C. Gamma

    D. Stable

12. How can you extend the Kubernetes API with new features (pick multiple)?

    A. Code Resource Definitions

    B. Aggregation layers

    C. Extension layers

    D. Custom Resource Definitions

13. Which of the following projects allows you to extend Kubernetes beyond container orchestration (pick multiple)?

    A. Knative for FaaS

    B. Linkerd for IPAM

    C. Kvirt for VM orchestration

    D. KubeVirt for VM orchestration

14. What helps detect the difference between the current and desired state of Kubernetes resources?

    A. Container runtime

    B. Kubernetes scheduler

    C. Custom Resource Definition

    D. Reconciliation loop

15. What are secondary containers running in pod called?

    A. Flatcars

    B. Sidecars

    C. Podcars

    D. Helpcars

16. Which of the following formats is used to write Kubernetes spec files?

    A. CSV

    B. Protobuf

    C. YAML

    D. Marshal

17. Which of the following Kubernetes components is responsible for allocating new pods to nodes?

   A. kube-api

   B. kube-proxy

   C. kube-scheduler

   D. kube-controller-manager

18. Which of the following K8s CLI commands can be used to list pods in the `development` namespace?

   A. `kubectl list pods -n development`

   B. `kubectl get pods --namespace development`

   C. `kubectl show pods --namespace development`

   D. `kubectl get pods --all-namespaces`

19. Which of the following K8s CLI commands can be used to list all the namespaces in the cluster?

   A. `kubectl list namespaces --all-namespaces`

   B. `kubectl show namespaces`

   C. `kubectl get namespaces`

   D. `kubectl get all`

20. Which of the following pod statuses means its container(s) are currently executing?

   A. Executing

   B. Succeeded

   C. Running

   D. ContainerCreated

21. Which of the following pod statuses means all its containers are running (pick multiple)?

   A. 100%

   B. 1/2

   C. 2/2

   D. 1/1

Further reading

To learn more about the topics that were covered in this chapter, take a look at the following resources:

- Minikube troubleshooting guide: `https://minikube.sigs.k8s.io/docs/handbook/troubleshooting/`

- Commonly used `kubectl` commands: `https://kubernetes.io/docs/reference/kubectl/cheatsheet/`

- K8s pods concept: `https://kubernetes.io/docs/concepts/workloads/pods/`

- K8s namespace concept: `https://kubernetes.io/docs/concepts/overview/working-with-objects/namespaces/`

Further reading

6

Deploying and Scaling Applications with Kubernetes

In this chapter, we'll continue exploring Kubernetes with its rich functionality and ecosystem. We'll see which other Kubernetes resources exist and what their purpose is, how to implement the self-healing and scaling of applications with Kubernetes, how to use Kubernetes service discovery, and how to run stateful workloads with Kubernetes. We will also perform several exercises with the minikube Kubernetes we've installed in the previous chapter (in case you've skipped it – check the last section of *Chapter 5*).

This is going to be one of the densest and most important chapters, so make sure to answer all the questions at the end and complete all practical assignments firsthand before moving further on. If you find it hard to understand some parts, read them twice and refer to the *Further reading* section.

We're about to cover the following exciting topics:

- Deployments, ReplicaSets, and DaemonSets
- Running stateful workloads
- Application configuration and service discovery
- Ensuring applications are alive and healthy

So, let's jump right into it!

Deployments, ReplicaSets, and DaemonSets

As we saw in the previous chapter, there are more resources in Kubernetes than just *Pods* and *namespaces*. Let's learn about *Deployments*, for starters.

> **Deployment**
>
> It is a wrapper for declarative updates for Pods and ReplicaSets. After you describe the desired state in the Deployment resource spec, the Kubernetes Deployment controller changes the current state to the desired state at a configured rate.

It sounds complicated, but essentially Deployment is for controlling Pods and managing the application life cycle of those Pods. Pods are the smallest deployment units that wrap around containers, but they don't provide any advanced Kubernetes features, such as *self-healing, rolling updates,* or *autoscaling.* However, Deployments do.

Because Pods are not resilient, an application container that fails in a pod *takes* the pod *down* with it. That is why in practice you'll often use one of the advanced Kubernetes resources such as Deployment to automatically recreate Pods in case of failure. The deployment controller constantly watches the current state of the Pods it is managing and ensures that the desired number of Pods is running. We will shortly have a demonstration to see how this works.

> **ReplicaSet**
>
> A ReplicaSet is used to maintain the given number of replica Pods running at any given time. ReplicaSets are also used by Deployments to ensure the desired number of Pods (even if only one pod should be running at a time).

Compared to ReplicaSet, Deployment is a higher-level wrapper resource that manages ReplicaSets itself and provides other useful features. ReplicaSet does not allow you to implement custom update orchestration and therefore it is recommended that you use Deployments instead of directly using ReplicaSets.

Let's get back to our minikube Kubernetes setup from the previous chapter for a quick demo. If you've stopped the cluster before, start it first with the `minikube start` command:

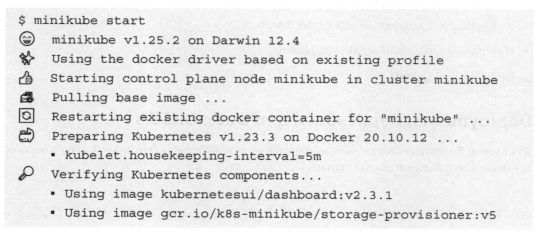

```
$ minikube start
😄   minikube v1.25.2 on Darwin 12.4
✨   Using the docker driver based on existing profile
👍   Starting control plane node minikube in cluster minikube
🚜   Pulling base image ...
🔄   Restarting existing docker container for "minikube" ...
🐳   Preparing Kubernetes v1.23.3 on Docker 20.10.12 ...
    ▪ kubelet.housekeeping-interval=5m
🔎   Verifying Kubernetes components...
    ▪ Using image kubernetesui/dashboard:v2.3.1
    ▪ Using image gcr.io/k8s-minikube/storage-provisioner:v5
```

```
    ▪ Using image kubernetesui/metrics-scraper:v1.0.7
🎇    Enabled addons: storage-provisioner, default-storageclass,
dashboard
🦭    Done! kubectl is now configured to use "minikube" cluster
and "default" namespace by default
```

If you are not sure about the state of your minikube Kubernetes, you can also use the `minikube` `status` command. Make sure that you have `host`, `kubelet`, and `apiserver` in a `Running` state:

```
$ minikube status
minikube
type: Control Plane
host: Running
kubelet: Running
apiserver: Running
kubeconfig: Configured
```

Previously, we created a simple pod running the `Nginx` web server in the `kcna` Kubernetes namespace. Let's create a Deployment of the same nginx web server, but with three replicas (three Pods):

```
$ minikube kubectl -- create -f https://k8s.io/examples/
controllers/nginx-deployment.yaml --namespace kcna
deployment.apps/nginx-deployment created
```

The complete Deployment specification (found in `nginx-deployment.yaml` in the GitHub repository accompanying this book) looks like the following:

```
apiVersion: apps/v1
kind: Deployment
metadata:
  name: nginx-deployment
  labels:
    app: nginx
spec:
  replicas: 3
  selector:
    matchLabels:
      app: nginx
  template:
    metadata:
```

```
        labels:
          app: nginx
      spec:
        containers:
        - name: nginx
          image: nginx:1.14.2
          ports:
          - containerPort: 80
```

It is somewhat similar to the specification of the pod we used previously, but with a number of differences, such as the following:

- `kind: Deployment`
- `apps/v1` indicating the API version
- An additional `app: nginx` label in the metadata
- The number of Pods is defined by `replicas: 3`
- There is a selector for matching Pods by the `app: nginx` label
- It labels templates with an `app: nginx` label

The `selector:` under the `spec:` field defines how this Deployment finds the pods that it manages. In this example, it picks the Pods that have an `app: nginx` label.

The `template` block has the same pod `containers:` specification with the `image:` and `ports:` fields like we used in the previous chapter for the standalone pod scenario. Additionally, it has metadata with an `app: nginx` label that will be added to each pod created by this specification. Once again, the label is needed for the Deployment to be able to find its Pods.

Let's check what happened in the `kcna` namespace after we applied our Deployment specification:

```
$ minikube kubectl -- get pods -n kcna
NAME                                  READY
    STATUS     RESTARTS    AGE
nginx-deployment-9456bbbf9-c195h      1/1
        Running    0           10m
nginx-deployment-9456bbbf9-ghxb2      1/1
        Running    0           10m
nginx-deployment-9456bbbf9-nvl7r      1/1
        Running    0           10m
```

We can see the three `nginx` Pods, each with its own unique name. Those names will look slightly different for you because the second part of the string is randomized. Now let's query ReplicaSets in the `kcna` namespace with the `kubectl get replicasets` command:

```
$ minikube kubectl -- get replicasets -n kcna
NAME                         DESIRED   CURRENT   READY   AGE
nginx-deployment-9456bbbf9   3         3         3       12m
```

OK, we can see one ReplicaSet; however, we did not define it! It was the nginx Deployment that automatically created a ReplicaSet in order to keep the desired number of Pods. So, it is the Deployment that works on top of ReplicaSets; ReplicaSets that works on top of Pods; and Pods are wrappers on top of containers, as shown in *Figure 6.1*. You can also see that ReplicaSet gets a unique ID, and the final Pods inherit this ID in their names.

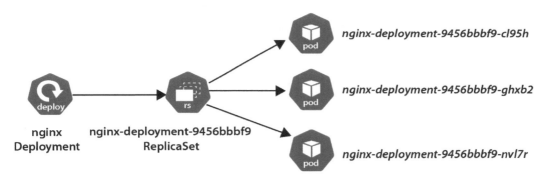

Figure 6.1 – The hierarchy of Deployment, ReplicaSet, and Pod

Let's carry out a quick experiment, let's delete one of the three `nginx` pods created by our Deployment and see what happens (*you'll have to specify the name of one pod that you have as pod names are unique*):

```
$ minikube kubectl -- delete pods nginx-deployment-9456bbbf9-
cl95h -n kcna
pod "nginx-deployment-9456bbbf9-cl95h" deleted
```

Now, even if you are really fast at typing, you probably won't notice how the deleted pod terminated and a new one was created. Next, get the list of Pods in the `kcna` namespace:

```
$ minikube kubectl -- get pods -n kcna
NAME                              READY
    STATUS    RESTARTS    AGE
nginx-deployment-9456bbbf9-9zv5c   1/1
    Running    0           3s
```

```
nginx-deployment-9456bbbf9-ghxb2    1/1
    Running    0         42m
nginx-deployment-9456bbbf9-nvl7r    1/1
    Running    0         42m
```

And there we go – we have a new pod with an AGE of 3 seconds with a status of Running, and the old, deleted pod (nginx-deployment-9456bbbf9-cl95h) is completely gone. Now that's the *Kubernetes self-healing magic* we've talked about so much! In just a couple of seconds, Kubernetes detected that the current state of the Nginx deployment was different because only two replicas (Pods) were running when the desired state is three replicas. The Kubernetes *reconciliation loop* kicked in and spawned a new, third replica of the nginx pod.

Self-healing is great and helps to keep our applications running in situations such as node hardware failure (of course, assuming that you run multiple Kubernetes nodes **as you should do in production**); when an application has a bug and crashes on a certain request type; and in the case of planned or unplanned maintenance when we have to migrate the payloads to another node.

But that's only the beginning. Let's imagine for a second that we are anticipating a high number of requests for an application we run on Kubernetes, so we have to get ready and add additional replicas in our application. With Kubernetes, it is as easy as executing a single kubectl scale deployment command:

```
$ minikube kubectl -- scale deployment nginx-deployment
--replicas 5 -n kcna
deployment.apps/nginx-deployment scaled
```

If you check the state of the respective ReplicaSet fast enough, you might see that new Pods are spawning:

```
$ minikube kubectl -- get replicaset -n kcna
NAME                          DESIRED   CURRENT   READY   AGE
nginx-deployment-9456bbbf9    5         5         4       52m
```

And voilà! Just a moment later, both new Pods are already up and running:

```
$ minikube kubectl -- get pods -n kcna
NAME                                READY
    STATUS      RESTARTS    AGE
nginx-deployment-9456bbbf9-9zv5c    1/1
    Running    0         30m
nginx-deployment-9456bbbf9-ghxb2    1/1
    Running    0         52m
nginx-deployment-9456bbbf9-hgjnq    1/1
    Running    0         23s
```

```
nginx-deployment-9456bbbf9-nvl7r    1/1
    Running    0           52m
nginx-deployment-9456bbbf9-
pzm8q    1/1       Running    0           23s
```

> **Note**
>
> Obviously, adding more application replicas on a single node K8s cluster does not bring a lot of practicality for performance or service availability. In production, you should always run multi-node Kubernetes clusters and spread the replicas of your applications across multiple nodes. We are doing these exercises on a single node Kubernetes instance, only for demonstration and educational purposes.

Next, let's see how we can perform *rolling updates* with Deployments. Rolling updates play an important role because they help to ensure rapid software development cycles with frequent releases and allow us to make updates with *zero downtime* for customers.

> **Zero downtime**
>
> Zero downtime is a deployment method where the updated application is able to serve requests as usual, with no interruptions or errors.

With rolling updates, we can do the following:

- Promote application changes from one environment to another (for example, a new image version, configuration, or labels)
- Rollback to the previous version in case of any issues
- Define how many application replicas can be replaced at a time

Let's see this in action with our Nginx deployment. We will update the nginx container image version tag to 1.20 using kubectl. First, check that our deployment is intact:

```
$ minikube kubectl -- get deployment -n kcna
NAME               READY   UP-TO-DATE   AVAILABLE   AGE
nginx-deployment   5/5     5            5           9h
```

Now, change the image to `nginx:1.20`:

```
$ minikube kubectl -- set image deployment/nginx-deployment
nginx=nginx:1.20 -n kcna
deployment.apps/nginx-deployment image updated
```

Then observe what is happening to the Nginx Pods right after you have changed the image (*you have to be quick to witness the process!*):

```
$ minikube kubectl -- get pods -n kcna
NAME                                       READY
   STATUS                  RESTARTS   AGE
nginx-deployment-7b96fbf5d8-dwskw          0/1
     ContainerCreating       0          2s
nginx-deployment-7b96fbf5d8-grkv6          0/1
     ContainerCreating       0          2s
nginx-deployment-7b96fbf5d8-jcb4p          0/1
     ContainerCreating       0          2s
nginx-deployment-9456bbbf9-9zv5c           1/1
     Running                 0          6h
nginx-deployment-9456bbbf9-ghxb2           1/1
     Running                 0          9h
nginx-deployment-9456bbbf9-hgjnq           1/1
     Running                 0          2h
nginx-deployment-9456bbbf9-nvl7r           1/1
     Running                 0          9h
nginx-deployment-9456bbbf9-pzm8q           1/1
     Terminating             0          2h
```

From five replicas of our Nginx deployment, we see that one has a `Terminating` status, four have a `Running` status, and three new have appeared and are in the `ContainerCreating` status. Just a moment later, we may see that the last few Pods with an old Nginx image are have a `Terminating` status, four new ones are in the `Running` state and one more is in the `ContainerCreating` state:

```
$ minikube kubectl -- get pods -n kcna
NAME                                       READY
   STATUS                  RESTARTS   AGE
nginx-deployment-7b96fbf5d8-6dh9q          0/1
     ContainerCreating       0          2s
nginx-deployment-7b96fbf5d8-dwskw          1/1
     Running                 0          25s
```

```
nginx-deployment-7b96fbf5d8-grkv6    1/1
        Running                 0         25s
nginx-deployment-7b96fbf5d8-jcb4p    1/1
        Running                 0         25s
nginx-deployment-7b96fbf5d8-
zt7bj    1/1      Running            0         4s
nginx-deployment-9456bbbf9-
ghxb2    1/1      Terminating        0         9h
nginx-deployment-9456bbbf9-
nvl7r    1/1      Terminating        0         9h
```

It won't take long before all old Pods are gone and the last new ones enter a `Running` state. We can also verify that the new image is used, by performing `kubectl describe pod` on any new pod (on Windows, use `findstr` instead of `grep` command):

```
$ minikube kubectl -- describe pod nginx-deployment-7b96fbf5d8-
dwskw -n kcna | grep Image
    Image:          nginx:1.20
```

Now, what do we do if a new image of the deployed application is not the right one or if it has a bug that may cause Pods to crash? Just as easy as updating a Kubernetes Deployment, we can roll back to the previous revision of our Deployment. Each change will be tracked by Kubernetes and gets its own revision version that we can see with the `kubectl rollout history` command:

```
$ minikube kubectl -- rollout history deployment -n kcna
deployment.apps/nginx-deployment
REVISION   CHANGE-CAUSE
1          <none>
2          <none>
```

> **Note**
>
> `CHANGE-CAUSE` is an optional description that can be set by adding an annotation to the Deployment. For example, we can do the following: `kubectl -n kcna annotate deployment/nginx-deployment kubernetes.io/change-cause="image updated to 1.20"`.

If we realized that we need to get our deployment back to a previous revision, we can simply call kubectl rollout undo and optionally specify the exact, possibly older deployment revision. Let's try to roll back to the previous, first revision of the nginx deployment (current revision is 2):

```
$ minikube kubectl -- rollout undo deployment/nginx-deployment
-n kcna
deployment.apps/nginx-deployment rolled back
```

A moment later, all Pods are recreated in the same rolling update fashion. And we can verify that the image version tag is back to 1.14.2 using the kubectl get pods command with an extra -o yaml option that will show us complete, detailed information about the pod (*the naming will be different in your case, pick any pod from your output list*):

```
$ minikube kubectl -- get pods -n kcna
NAME                                   READY
    STATUS    RESTARTS    AGE
nginx-deployment-9456bbbf9-6xpq2    1/1
        Running    0          22s
nginx-deployment-9456bbbf9-75m7d    1/1
        Running    0          22s
nginx-deployment-9456bbbf9-hbglw    1/1
        Running    0          22s
nginx-deployment-9456bbbf9-hxdjd    1/1
        Running    0          16s
nginx-deployment-9456bbbf9-mtxzm    1/1
        Running    0          17s
$ minikube kubectl -- get pod nginx-deployment-
9456bbbf9-6xpq2 -n kcna -o yaml
apiVersion: v1
kind: Pod
... LONG OUTPUT OMITTED ...
spec:
  containers:
  - image: nginx:1.14.2
    imagePullPolicy: IfNotPresent
    name: nginx
... LONG OUTPUT OMITTED ...
```

You'll see a long, long output with all the details about this particular pod. You can also use `kubectl get` in combination with `-o yaml` for any other Kubernetes resources (*namespaces*, *Deployments*, and others we're about to learn) to get full information about the object. You don't need to understand each and every line of the output at this stage, but it is very helpful to know about `imagePullPolicy`, which defines the rules for how container images should be pulled from the registry. The policy can be one of the following:

- `IfNotPresent` – this is the default setting. The image will be downloaded only if the requested `name:tag` combination is not already present locally (cached) on the node where the pod was scheduled.

- `Always` – this means that every time a pod with the respective container is started, the image registry will be asked for an image digest (resolved from the image tag). If an image with this *exact digest* is already cached locally on the node, it will be used; otherwise, a Kubernetes kubelet will pull the image with the digest resolved by the registry on the target node.

- `Never` – this means the kubelet won't attempt to fetch the image from the registry. The image should be delivered to the node somehow in advance; otherwise, the container will fail to spawn.

Additionally, we can control the rolling update process with a number of optional settings and timeouts. The two most important ones are as follows:

- `maxUnavailable` – this defines the maximum number of unavailable pods during a rolling update. It can be specified as a percentage (for example, `25%`) or as an absolute number (for example, `3`).

- `maxSurge` – this defines the maximum number of pods that can be created over the desired number of replicas. It can also be specified as a percentage or an absolute number. If set, for example to `25%`, then the total number of *old* and *new* Pods won't exceed `125%` of the desired number of replicas.

Finally, if we don't want to do rolling updates, we can instead choose the `Recreate` strategy, which means all existing Pods are killed at once and new ones are only created after all old Pods have been terminated. Obviously, this strategy doesn't allow you to perform zero-downtime updates, as all Pods of an application will be down for at least a few seconds. The strategy can be configured by defining the `.spec.strategy.type` setting in the YAML spec file of the respective deployment.

Now that we know about deployments, let's move on to **DaemonSets**. As you probably know, **Daemon** in Unix/Linux world is a background process or service that provides additional functionality or supervises the system. A common example is `sshd`, a service that allows us to log in to remote systems over the **Secure Shell** protocol.

> **DaemonSet**
>
> DaemonSet is a wrapper for pods that ensures that all or certain nodes in the Kubernetes cluster each run a single replica of the target pod. If more nodes are added to the cluster, DaemonSet will ensure that a pod is automatically spawned on a new node as soon as it joins the cluster.

Where Deployment is considered a universal resource in Kubernetes for all kinds of user workloads, DaemonSet's typical use cases are as follows:

- To run a log collection service on every Kubernetes node (for example, software such as **Fluent Bit**)

- To run a node-monitoring daemon on every node (for example, a node exporter for **Prometheus**)

- To run a cluster storage daemon on every node

Similar to ReplicaSet, DaemonSet will ensure that the desired state is met, meaning that in the case of a pod failure, it will automatically spawn a new one. By default, DaemonSet will create Pods on all worker nodes in the cluster, but it is also possible to select specific nodes in the cluster or control plane nodes (how to do this will be covered in the next chapter, *Chapter 7*). What cannot be done with DaemonSet is setting the number of replicas per node, because DaemonSet will always run only one pod per node. The spec file of DaemonSet is very similar to that of a Deployment, with a few differences, such as `kind: DaemonSet` or a lack of the `replicas:` setting.

Moving on, we will not create a DaemonSet now, because a proper demonstration requires a multi-node Kubernetes cluster. Feel free to check out the *Further reading* section at the end of the chapter and try it out yourself if you'd like. In the following section, we'll see how to run applications that need to persist information on the disk with Kubernetes.

Running stateful workloads

Everything we've tried so far with Kubernetes has not answered one important question – what do we do if we need to persist the application state between pod restarts? Data written on a container filesystem is not persisted by default. If you just take a deployment spec from the recent examples with Nginx and replace the image with **PostgreSQL**, that won't be enough. Technically, your pod with PostgreSQL will come up, and the database will run, but any data written to that database instance won't survive a pod restart. But, of course, Kubernetes has something to offer for stateful applications too.

As you hopefully remember from *Chapter 4*, *Exploring Container Runtimes, Interfaces, and Service Meshes*, Kubernetes has a **Container Storage Interface** or **CSI** that allows you to integrate various storage solutions into a K8s cluster. In order to augment Pods with external storage, we need *volumes* that can be dynamically provisioned via the Kubernetes API. Let's begin with two new resource definitions:

- **PersistentVolume (PV)**: This is a piece of storage in the cluster that can be provisioned either dynamically (by K8s when requested) or statically (for example, provisioned in some way by the cluster administrator and exposed for use in K8s).

- **PersistentVolumeClaim** (**PVC**): This is a request for storage by the user that consumes *PVs*.

When we want to use persistent storage for our containerized application, we need to define a PVC spec in YAML format that can look like the following:

```yaml
apiVersion: v1
kind: PersistentVolumeClaim
metadata:
  name: kcna-pv-claim
spec:
  storageClassName: standard
  accessModes:
    - ReadWriteOnce
  resources:
    requests:
      storage: 3Gi
```

This PVC can then be referenced in deployments and Pods as a volume. Claim allows you to request a specific size (3Gi in the previous example) and one of the following four accessModes:

- ReadWriteOnce – this allows the volume to be mounted as a read-write by a single node. This mode can allow multiple Pods on this node to access the volume.

- ReadOnlyMany – this allows the volume to be mounted as read-only by one or multiple nodes.

- ReadWriteMany – this allows the volume to be mounted as read-write by many nodes. This should be supported by the storage solution and protocol (for example, **NFS**).

- ReadWriteOncePod – This is the same as ReadWriteOnce, but with a hard limit of only one pod in the whole cluster being able to write to this volume.

Since PVs are the actual storage resources in the Kubernetes cluster, we might have a situation when there is no suitable PV for the PVC request. In that case, Kubernetes can dynamically provision a PV based on the storage class specified in the PVC spec (storageClassName: standard in the previous example).

> **Storage classes**
>
> Storage classes provide a way to classify different storage options available in the cluster. Those might differ by performance, supported access modes and protocols, backup policies, and more.

It is also possible to instruct Kubernetes to only use already provisioned (possibly statically) and available PVs by setting storageClassName: " " (empty string) in the PVC spec. In the case of dynamic PV provisioning, the volume will always be of the exact size requested in the PVC spec. However, where we ask to only use already available PVs, we might get a larger volume than specified in PVC resource requests (for example, 3Gi is requested, but if the closest available PV in the cluster is 5Gi, it will be taken and all 5Gi will be usable by the container that mounts it).

Let's get back to the minikube setup to see this in action. First, create kcna-pv-claim with the previous specification (the file can be downloaded from the book's GitHub repository):

```
$ minikube kubectl -- create -f kcna-pv-claim.yaml -n kcna
persistentvolumeclaim/kcna-pv-claim created
```

Now, get the list of PVs in the cluster (the name will be unique in this case):

```
$ minikube kubectl -- get pv -n kcna
NAME
        CAPACITY    ACCESS MODES    RECLAIM POLICY    STATUS    CLAIM
                    STORAGECLASS    REASON    AGE
pvc-6b56c062-a36b-4bd5-9d92-
f344d02aaf5c    3Gi         RWO
            Delete              Bound
    kcna/kcna-pv-claim    standard                     74s
```

A PV was automatically provisioned by Kubernetes in seconds! At this point, we can start using kcna-pv-claim as a volume in our deployment or pod specifications. Let's delete the old nginx-deployment that we created at the beginning of this chapter:

```
$ minikube kubectl -- get deployment -n kcna
NAME                  READY    UP-TO-DATE    AVAILABLE    AGE
nginx-deployment    5/5      5             5            2d
$ minikube kubectl -- delete deployment nginx-deployment -n
kcna
deployment.apps "nginx-deployment" deleted
```

And create another one, with our new volume attached. For that, we'll need to make a few changes to the old nginx-deployment.yaml spec file (the modified version is available on GitHub):

```
$ cat nginx-deployment-with-volume.yaml
apiVersion: apps/v1
kind: Deployment
metadata:
```

```
    name: nginx-deployment-with-volume
    labels:
      app: nginx
spec:
  replicas: 1
  selector:
    matchLabels:
      app: nginx
  template:
    metadata:
      labels:
        app: nginx
    spec:
      containers:
      - name: nginx
        image: nginx:1.14.2
        ports:
        - containerPort: 80
        volumeMounts:
        - name: kcna-volume
          mountPath: "/usr/share/nginx/html"
      volumes:
      - name: kcna-volume
        persistentVolumeClaim:
          claimName: kcna-pv-claim
```

Besides a new name for the deployment (nginx-deployment-with-volume) and the number of replicas being set to 1, the changes are as follows:

- We have added a volumeMounts: block under the respective nginx container stating which volume (kcna-volume) should be mounted at which path ("/usr/share/nginx/html" – this is a location for static HTML content).

- Additionally, we have defined the volumes: block that maps kcna-volume to our PVC named kcna-pv-claim that we created in the previous step.

> **Note**
>
> The `volumeMounts` is located within the individual container section because different containers in one pod can mount different (or the same) volumes. The `volumes` block is located at the same level as `containers`, and it should list all volumes that will be used within the Pods.

Now, let's create a modified nginx deployment and see what happens:

```
$ minikube kubectl -- create -f nginx-deployment-with-volume.
yaml -n kcna
deployment.apps/nginx-deployment-with-volume created
$ minikube kubectl -- get pod -n kcna
NAME
            READY    STATUS    RESTARTS    AGE
nginx-deployment-with-volume-6775557df5-bjmr6
    1/1      Running   0            39s
```

At this stage, nothing looks different, but we can use the `kubectl exec -it` command to get inside our container by starting a new shell process. You might remember that we did something similar in *Chapter 3*, when we used `docker run -it`. You'll need to specify the name of your unique pod here:

```
$ minikube kubectl -- -n kcna exec -it nginx-deployment-with-
volume-6775557df5-bjmr6 -- bash
root@nginx-deployment-with-volume-6775557df5-bjmr6:/#
```

Let's see whether there is a volume mount at `/usr/share/nginx/html` as we've requested:

```
root@nginx-deployment-with-volume-6775557df5-bjmr6:/# mount |
grep nginx
/dev/vda1 on /usr/share/nginx/html type ext4 (rw,relatime)
```

There it is! Our dynamically provisioned PV was automatically mounted to the node where our pod runs. If the pod dies, the data on the volume is preserved, and if the new pod starts on another node, Kubernetes will take care of unmounting and remounting the volume to the right node reaching the desired state we described in the spec file. To make sure that the data really is persisted, we can do a small exercise inside the container. Let's install the `curl` utility and try to run it against `localhost`:

```
root@nginx-deployment-with-volume-6775557df5-bjmr6:/# apt
update
... LONG OUTPUT OMITTED ...
root@nginx-deployment-with-volume-6775557df5-bjmr6:/# apt -y
```

```
install curl
Reading package lists... Done
Building dependency tree
Reading state information... Done
... LONG OUTPUT OMITTED ...
root@nginx-deployment-with-volume-6775557df5-bjmr6:/ # curl
localhost
<html>
<head><title>403 Forbidden</title></head>
<body bgcolor="white">
<center><h1>403 Forbidden</h1></center>
<hr><center>nginx/1.14.2</center>
</body>
</html>
```

Next, let's create a simple one-liner index.html file in the /usr/share/nginx/html path and try running curl again:

```
root@nginx-deployment-with-volume-6775557df5-bjmr6:/# echo
"Kubernetes Rocks!" > /usr/share/nginx/html/index.html
root@nginx-deployment-with-volume-6775557df5-bjmr6:/# curl
localhost
Kubernetes Rocks!
```

The last part of this exercise is on you. Log out of the container (by either entering the exit command or by pressing *Ctrl + D*) and delete the pod with the kubectl delete pods command and log in to the new pod when it is spawned. Check whether the index.html file that we created is still present at the mount point and has the correct Kubernetes Rocks! string inside.

While it is normal practice to use PVs with Kubernetes deployments, another workload resource was specifically made to manage stateful applications.

StatefulSet

StatefulSet is a resource to manage the deployment and scaling of Pods that guarantees the ordering and uniqueness of these Pods.

What that means is that Pods created by StatefulSets have stable naming (without randomly generated UUIDs) and allow ordered, graceful deployment as well as ordered rolling updates. In addition to that, StatefulSets can provision a PV per pod replica. That means you won't need to define and apply a new PVC every time you want to scale your application by adding a new replica. Let's have a quick look at a StatefulSet example spec:

```yaml
apiVersion: apps/v1
kind: StatefulSet
metadata:
  name: nginx-statefulset
spec:
  selector:
    matchLabels:
      app: nginx
  serviceName: "nginx"
  replicas: 3
  template:
    metadata:
      labels:
        app: nginx
    spec:
      containers:
      - name: nginx
        image: nginx:1.14.2
        ports:
        - containerPort: 80
        volumeMounts:
        - name: nginx-html
          mountPath: /usr/share/nginx/html
  volumeClaimTemplates:
  - metadata:
      name: nginx-html
    spec:
      accessModes: [ "ReadWriteOnce" ]
      storageClassName: "standard"
      resources:
```

```
      requests:
        storage: 1Gi
```

As you can see, the PVC spec is essentially a part of the StatefulSet spec located under the `volumeClaimTemplates` block at the end. Feel free to apply this StatefulSet spec yourself and see what happens. You should get three new PVCs and three new Pods spawned with PVs automatically provisioned and attached.

While this might seem complicated at first, think about how many *manual* steps you'd have to do to achieve the same result *without* Kubernetes. How much time would it take to create multiple volumes, download container images, and configure and start containers? Kubernetes makes many operational tasks trivial, and in the upcoming section, we will learn more about how Kubernetes allows you to configure applications running in containers and how service discovery works.

Application configuration and service discovery

So far, we have explored quite a few of K8s features and resources, but how do we do application configuration? We could add configuration files or environment variables to the container images during the build, but *this is wrong*. If you do so, for even the smallest configuration change, you'll have to rebuild container images. Also, where you need to have different settings for different environments, you'll need to maintain multiple images of the same application. Things get messy, complicated, and error-prone, so don't do this.

Instead, the better approach in Kubernetes is to use **ConfigMaps** and **Secrets**.

> **ConfigMap**
>
> A ConfigMap is a resource to store non-confidential data and configuration settings in key-value pairs that can be consumed inside Pods as environment variables, command-line arguments, or configuration files. ConfigMaps do not provide secrecy or encryption, so they are not suitable for keeping confidential information, such as passwords or access tokens.

> **Secret**
>
> A Secret is a resource to store sensitive data such as passwords, tokens, and access keys. Similar to ConfigMaps, Secrets can be consumed inside Pods as environment variables or configuration files.

Both ConfigMaps and Secrets allow us to decouple configuration from container images, enabling better application portability and reuse of the same container images for different environments.

Let's explore a quick example. Imagine you are developing a web application that requires access to the database. The application is written in a way that it looks for the DATABASE_HOST, DATABASE_ USERNAME, and DATABASE_PASSWORD environment variables. In this case, you can use a ConfigMap to set DATABASE_HOST and a Secret to keep information about the username and the password. This configuration would be consumed in the container with the application and would allow us to use different settings for different environments (for example, different databases and passwords for development, testing, and production).

Besides mapping ConfigMaps and Secrets to environment variables inside containers, we can also mount them inside as if they were regular files. This is done with the *volume* concept that we have just covered in the preceding section when learning about PVs and PVCs.

Let's get back to the keyboard and create a simple Secret using the kubectl create secret command:

```
$ minikube kubectl -- create secret generic kcna-secret --from-
literal="username=kcnauser" --from-literal="password=topsecret"
-n kcna
secret/kcna-secret created
```

> **Note**
>
> Needless to say, it is also possible to create Secrets by defining a YAML spec file with kind: Secret and calling kubectl create -f like we previously did for other resources.

Next, find the nginx-statefulset spec file that we used in the last section and modify it to mount our new kcna-secret as an additional volume at /etc/nginx/kcna.secret. Try to do this on your own, but if you experience any difficulties, the following are the relevant changes to the spec file (a complete modified spec file is also available on GitHub):

```
... BEGINNING OF THE SPEC OMITTED ...
    containers:
    - name: nginx
      image: nginx:1.14.2
      ports:
      - containerPort: 80
      volumeMounts:
      - name: nginx-html
        mountPath: /usr/share/nginx/html
      - name: nginx-kcna-secret
        mountPath: /etc/nginx/kcna/
    volumes:
```

```
        - name: nginx-kcna-secret
          secret:
            secretName: kcna-secret
  volumeClaimTemplates:
  - metadata:
      name: nginx-html
    spec:
      accessModes: [ "ReadWriteOnce" ]
      storageClassName: "standard"
      resources:
        requests:
          storage: 1Gi
```

> **Note**
>
> It is possible to modify resources already created in Kubernetes instead of deleting them and creating them again from the scratch. However, some fields and resources are immutable and cannot be modified *on the fly*.

Now, let's apply the modified spec file using the kubectl apply -f command (the spec filename is statefulset_with_secret.yaml, as follows):

```
$ minikube kubectl -- apply -f statefulset_with_secret.yaml -n
kcna
statefulset.apps/nginx-statefulset configured
```

Because we've added a new volume, Pods will be recreated straight after:

```
$ minikube kubectl -- get pods -n kcna
NAME
            READY    STATUS    RESTARTS    AGE
nginx-statefulset-0
      1/1      Running    0            12s
nginx-statefulset-1
      1/1      Running    0            15s
nginx-statefulset-2
    1/1      Running    0            18s
```

Let's execute into one of the pods to see whether our Secret was correctly mounted inside:

```
$ minikube kubectl -- -n kcna exec -it nginx-statefulset-0 --
bash
root@nginx-statefulset-0:/# cat /etc/nginx/kcna/username
kcnauser
root@nginx-statefulset-0:/# cat /etc/nginx/kcna/password
topsecret
```

There you go, the Secret has been mounted inside our nginx containers. It is worth mentioning that Kubernetes makes it possible to perform all sorts of combinations: Secrets (and individual keys) can be used as environment variables; Secrets can be created from existing files; Secrets can be used to store and mount SSL certificates or SSH keys; individual keys from K8s Secrets can be mounted into different paths and more.

ConfigMaps are very similar in terms of their capabilities, but their purpose is to store generic configuration. For example, we can create a new `ConfigMap` with nginx configuration and mount it over the `/etc/nginx/nginx.conf` in container overriding the default config file.

In terms of the scope of the KCNA exam, you are not expected to know all details, but as you get to work with Kubernetes, you'll encounter the need to do one or another, therefore, feel free to check out the links in the *Further reading* section at the end of the chapter if you have time.

Coming next, we will talk about service discovery in Kubernetes.

> **Service discovery**
>
> Service discovery provides the automatic detection of devices and the services offered by these devices on a network.

As you may remember, in the case of microservice architectures, we have a lot of small services that need to talk to each other over the network. That means service discovery plays a huge role because it helps services to find their counterparts, for example, a backend service that has to discover the database it shall connect to. Luckily, Kubernetes solves that problem, too, with its service discovery mechanism based on **Domain Name System (DNS)**.

Kubernetes implements an internal DNS system that keeps track of applications with their names and respective pod IPs (each pod gets its own unique cluster-wide IP address on start). This allows different applications to easily find the endpoints of each other by resolving application names to pod IPs. Kubernetes **Service** resource comes into play here.

Service

Service is an abstraction layer that enables loose coupling between dependent pods. It is a resource that allows you to publish application names *inside* the cluster and expose applications to be reachable from *outside* the cluster.

Kubernetes Pods can have a relatively short life cycle. If we add a new volume or update the deployment image, or if the node dies, in all cases, Pods are recreated with a new name and a new IP address. That means we cannot rely on pod names, and we should use a Service that will target one or multiple Pods by matching Kubernetes **labels** and **selectors**.

Labels and selectors

Labels are simple key/value metadata pairs that can be attached to any Kubernetes objects during or after creation. Labels can contain the name of the application, version tags, or any other object classification.

Selectors allow the identification of a set of Kubernetes objects. For example, a label selector can be used to find a group of objects that have the same app label, as shown in *Figure 6.2*.

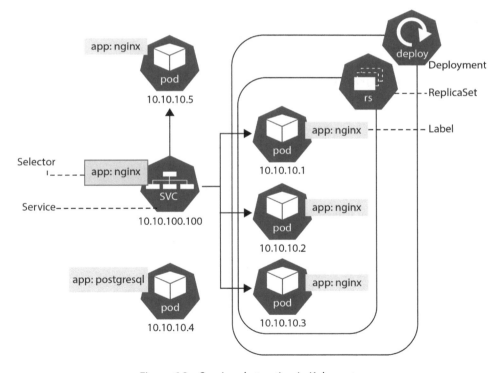

Figure 6.2 – Service abstraction in Kubernetes

Figure 6.2 demonstrates how a Service selects all pods that have an `app: nginx` label assigned. Those can be pods created by a Deployment as well as any other pods that have the selected label assigned. You can list the labels of objects by adding the `--show-labels` parameter to `kubectl get` commands, for example:

```
NAME
READY     STATUS     RESTARTS     AGE     LABELS
nginx-deployment-with-volume-6775557df5-f6ll7     1/1
     Running   0           23h        app=nginx,
pod-template-hash=6775557df5
nginx-statefulset-0
1/1       Running   0           46m        app=nginx,
controller-revision-hash=nginx-statefulset-6fbdf55d78,
statefulset.kubernetes.io/pod-name=nginx-statefulset-0
nginx-statefulset-1
1/1       Running   0           46m        app=nginx,
controller-revision-hash=nginx-statefulset-6fbdf55d78,
statefulset.kubernetes.io/pod-name=nginx-statefulset-1
nginx-statefulset-2                                1/1
     Running   0           46m        app=nginx,controller-
revision-hash=nginx-statefulset-6fbdf55d78,statefulset
.kubernetes.io/pod-name=nginx-statefulset-2
```

See, our nginx deployment pod as well as pods from the `nginx-statefulset` all have the same `app=nginx` label because both the Deployment and StatefulSet have it defined in their spec templates:

```
template:
  metadata:
    labels:
      app: nginx
```

Now, let's create a Service that will target all pods with this label. The following is what a simple spec targeting port `80` of selected pods might look like:

```
apiVersion: v1
kind: Service
metadata:
  name: nginx
spec:
  selector:
    app: nginx
```

```
    ports:
      - protocol: TCP
        port: 80
        targetPort: 80
```

Go on and create the Service:

```
$ minikube kubectl -- create -f nginx-service.yaml -n kcna
service/nginx created
$ minikube kubectl -- get service -n kcna
NAME     TYPE         CLUSTER-IP        EXTERNAL-
IP    PORT(S)     AGE
nginx    ClusterIP    10.105.246.191    <none>          80/
TCP      36s
```

After creation, you should be able to see the endpoints behind the Service that are, in fact, the IPs of running pods with an app=nginx label. Listing endpoints can be done with the kubectl get endpoints command, as follows:

```
$ minikube kubectl -- get endpoints -n kcna
NAME     ENDPOINTS
                         AGE
nginx    172.17.0.2:80,172.17.0.6:80,172.17.
0.7:80 + 1 more...    4m
```

If we're now execute inside to one of the Pods again and run curl nginx (the name of the service we created) we should get a reply. Run it a few times (5-10 times) after installing curl into the container:

```
$ minikube kubectl -- -n kcna exec -it nginx-statefulset-0 --
bash
root@nginx-statefulset-0:/# apt update && apt -y install curl
... LONG OUTPUT OMITTED ...
root@nginx-statefulset-0:/# curl nginx
Kubernetes Rocks!
root@nginx-statefulset-0:/# curl nginx
Kubernetes Rocks!
root@nginx-statefulset-0:/# curl nginx
<html>
<head><title>403 Forbidden</title></head>
<body bgcolor="white">
```

```
<center><h1>403 Forbidden</h1></center>
<hr><center>nginx/1.14.2</center>
</body>
</html>
```

And we get different replies! One of the four pods that we're currently running has a custom `index.html` file that we created earlier in this chapter, while the three others don't.

What happens is the service we created load balances the requests between all available `nginx` pod IPs. The Service will also automatically update the list of endpoints if we scale out the number of replicas or if we do the opposite.

Now, let's see which Service types exist and what they allow you to accomplish:

- **ClusterIP**: This type exposes an application on an internal cluster IP. Only Pods running in the same cluster can reach such a service. This is the default type that gets created unless overridden in the spec.

- **NodePort**: This type exposes the application on the same static port of each node in the cluster. Users will be able to reach the application from outside the cluster by requesting the IP of any node and configured port.

- **LoadBalancer**: This type exposes the application outside of cluster using a cloud provider's load balancer.

- **ExternalName**: This type maps the service to an external DNS name (for example, `mybestservice.app.com`) by returning a **CNAME** record (to map one domain to another) with a configured value. `ExternalName` is not acting as a proxy for application requests like other service types do.

What that means is that in practice you'll use the `LoadBalancer` type in most cases when you need to expose an application running in Kubernetes outside of the cluster (assuming your cloud provider or on-premises infrastructure offers load balancers). And in case of multiple applications that need to communicate with each other within the cluster, you'll use the default `ClusterIP` type. For example, when your backend deployment needs to talk with the database running as a StatefulSet and the database should not be exposed to the internet.

Coming next is the final section of the chapter. As you were doing all of the exercises, you might have wondered how Kubernetes knows that the application is actually running when a pod is running. What happens if an application needs time before it can serve the requests? How do we know that the application is not stuck in a deadlock? Let's figure that out!

Ensuring applications are alive and healthy

By default, Kubernetes ensures that the desired state of applications in a cluster is reached. It will restart and recreate failed containers when a process exits or a node fails. However, that might not be enough to tell if the application running inside the pod is healthy. In order to ensure that the workloads are alive and healthy, Kubernetes implements the concept of **probes**.

> **Probe**
>
> A probe is a diagnostic that is performed by a Kubernetes kubelet on a container. A diagnostic can be an arbitrary command executed inside a container or TCP probe, or an HTTP request.

Kubernetes offers three types of probes, as shown in the following list:

- **Liveness**: Ensures that a process in a container is alive and, if not, restarts the container. For the case when the application catches a deadlock, restarting the container usually helps to make the application more available despite bugs.

- **Readiness**: Ensures that the application is ready to accept traffic. A pod with multiple containers is considered ready when all its containers are ready and all readiness probes succeed.

- **Startup**: Allows you to know when an application in a container has started. If a startup probe is configured, it disables liveness and readiness probes until it succeeds. This might be needed for slow-starting applications to avoid them being killed due to a failed liveness probe before they are up.

All those probes serve the purpose of increasing the availability of containerized applications, but they cover different scenarios. For example, a liveness probe will cause a container to restart if a probe fails. Complex applications running for a long time might eventually transition to a broken state, and this is where the Kubernetes liveness probe helps.

> **Note**
>
> The whole pod is not recreated when the liveness probe of a single container has failed. Only a certain container within the pod is restarted. This is different from the case when the application in the container exits and the pod gets recreated by a controller such as a Deployment, ReplicaSet, or StatefulSet.

A readiness probe is needed when an application in a container is unable to serve the traffic. Some applications might take a long time to start because of the large datasets they are loading into memory or because they need to perform an initial configuration that takes time. An application might also depend on an external service. In all those situations, we don't want to kill and restart the container; rather, we don't want to send any traffic to it.

Readiness probes help to determine which Pods behind a Service are ready to accept connections and serve traffic. If a container fails the readiness probe, its pod IP is automatically taken out from the list of endpoints of the Service. This helps prevent situations when a user request is routed to a *not-yet-working* application replica.

> **Note**
>
> If both liveness and readiness probes are defined, the first does not wait for the second to succeed. It is possible to set initial delays for probes (via the `initialDelaySeconds` setting) or use a `startupProbe` that temporarily disables the liveness and readiness checks.

Each probe can execute a custom command, perform an HTTP request, or a TCP probe. In addition to that, liveness and readiness probes are tunable with several parameters: how often the check should be performed (configurable via `periodSeconds`), how long to wait for a probe to finish (configurable via `timeoutSeconds`) or the thresholds for how many times the probe should be retried before giving up and either restarting the container or stopping the traffic depending on the probe type.

Now, let's examine the following pod with a simple liveness probe defined:

```
apiVersion: v1
kind: Pod
metadata:
  labels:
    test: liveness
  name: liveness-exec
spec:
  containers:
  - name: liveness
    image: k8s.gcr.io/busybox
    args:
    - /bin/sh
    - -c
    - touch /tmp/healthy; sleep 30; rm -f /tmp/healthy; sleep
600
    livenessProbe:
      exec:
        command:
        - cat
        - /tmp/healthy
```

```
        initialDelaySeconds: 5
        periodSeconds: 5
```

When the pod container is started it creates an empty file at the `/tmp/healthy` path, waits for 30 seconds, and deletes that file. After that, the container does nothing for another 600 seconds before exiting. The liveness probe executes the `cat /tmp/healthy` command every 5 seconds after an initial check delay of 5 seconds.

Let's create the spec and see it in action:

```
$ minikube kubectl -- create -f https://k8s.io/examples/pods/
probe/exec-liveness.yaml -n kcna
pod/liveness-exec created
```

At first, the pod runs fine, its liveness probe succeeds, and its restart counter shows 0 restarts:

```
$ minikube kubectl -- get pod -n kcna
NAME
            READY   STATUS     RESTARTS    AGE
liveness-exec
      1/1     Running    0            59s
```

Sometime later, we can see that there was a restart:

```
$ minikube kubectl -- get pod -n kcna
NAME
            READY   STATUS     RESTARTS     AGE
liveness-exec
      1/1     Running    1 (20s ago)  95s
```

If we describe the pod, we can see the timeline of events:

```
$ minikube kubectl -- describe pod liveness-exec -n kcna
... LONG OUTPUT OMITTED ...
Events:
  Type      Reason      Age              From
              Message
  ----      ------      ----             ----
              -------
  Normal    Scheduled   85s
default-scheduler  Successfully assigned kcna/
liveness-exec to minikube
  Normal    Pulled      81s                      kubelet
```

```
                Successfully pulled image "k8s.gcr.io/busybox" in
3.4078911s
  Warning  Unhealthy  41s (x3 over
51s)  kubelet              Liveness probe failed: cat: can't open
'/tmp/healthy': No such file or directory
  Normal   Killing    41s                   kubelet
           Container liveness failed liveness probe,
will be restarted
  Normal   Pulling    11s (x2 over 85s)  kubelet
           Pulling image "k8s.gcr.io/busybox"
  Normal   Created    10s (x2 over 81s)  kubelet
           Created container liveness
  Normal   Pulled     10s                   kubelet
           Successfully pulled image "k8s.gcr.io/busybox" in
1.2501457s
  Normal   Started    9s (x2 over 81s)   kubelet
           Started container liveness
```

We are now approaching the end of this long and intense chapter. By now, you've learned a lot about Kubernetes features and some of its advanced resources. Many of the in-depth details explained here are not required to pass the KCNA exam, but they will be required to start working with Kubernetes and will undoubtedly help you in the future if you decide to become CKA or CKAD certified. If you have not been able to grasp 100% of this chapter's content, that is unlikely to stop you from passing the KCNA exam, but try to get into it as much as you can now. Check out the *Further reading* section resources and do additional research if needed.

Summary

In this chapter, we've seen Kubernetes' self-healing capabilities in action and how K8s reconciliation loops allow it to reach the desired state of resources in a very short time. Since Pods themselves do not have any means to recover from a failure, we commonly use Kubernetes *Deployments* to ensure that the requested number of application replicas are running. *Deployments* also allow us to perform controllable *rolling updates*, *rollbacks,* and *zero-downtime* deployments to enable rapid software development cycles that require the frequent release of versions.

DaemonSet is another resource for the scenario when we need to run one replica of the application on each or a particular set of nodes. *DaemonSets* are often used for running logging or monitoring agents across the cluster.

StatefulSet is a resource for managing stateful workloads with Kubernetes. It allows us to easily integrate volumes to Pods to keep persistent data between container restarts and automate the dynamic provisioning of PVs.

Next, we have explored ways to provide configuration and sensitive information to applications running in Kubernetes. *ConfigMaps* are suitable for generic non-confidential data, and *Secrets* are intended to be used for passwords, tokens, and so on. Both ConfigMaps and Secrets are essentially volumes that can be mounted into specific file paths inside containers.

We have also learned that service discovery plays an important role and allows applications to find and communicate with each other within the Kubernetes cluster. The *Service* resource allows for the exposure of the application with its Pods both inside and outside of the cluster using distinct Service types such as `LoadBalancer`, `NodePort`, or `ClusterIP`.

Last but not least, we've explored the options for ensuring that applications running in Kubernetes are alive and healthy. Kubernetes offers three types of probes (*liveness*, *readiness*, and *startup*) that serve the purpose of verifying the state of the application on startup or periodically at regular intervals. If the application fails the liveness probes, its container is restarted and in case it fails the Readiness probes, it just won't receive any traffic, and the pod IP will be excluded from the list of Service endpoints. The startup probes are intended for slow-starting applications that need extra time before they can handle other probes or real traffic.

> **Note**
> Feel free to delete any Kubernetes resources created in this chapter unless you're planning to come back to them later.

In the upcoming chapter, we will continue exploring Kubernetes and its features. We will learn about placement controls, resource requests, and ways to debug applications running on Kubernetes. Make sure to answer all recap questions and check out the *Further reading* section if you'd like to learn more about the topics in this chapter.

Questions

As we conclude, here is a list of questions for you to test your knowledge regarding this chapter's material. You will find the answers in the *Assessments* section of the *Appendix*:

1. Which of the following Kubernetes resources allows you to recover an application if the node it was running on has failed (select multiple)?

    A. Pod

    B. Service

    C. StatefulSet

    D. Deployment

2. Which of the following Kubernetes resources ensures that the defined number of replicas are always running (select multiple)?

   A. Pod

   B. ReplicaSet

   C. Deployment

   D. DaemonSet

3. Which of the following Kubernetes resources allows us to perform rolling updates and zero-downtime deployments?

   A. Service

   B. Deployment

   C. ReplicaSet

   D. DeploySet

4. Which statement best describes the relationship between Pods and various Kubernetes controllers (resources)?

   A. Pods are managing the resources

   B. Pods are managed by the container runtime

   C. Pods are always managed by one of the Kubernetes controllers

   D. Pods can be managed by one of the Kubernetes controllers

5. What is the purpose of label selectors?

   A. They help to determine the purpose of each pod in the cluster

   B. They help to distinguish more important Pods from less important ones

   C. They are simply auxiliary metadata

   D. They allow us to group and select resources by labels

6. Which of the following image pull policies will cause a download from the registry only when the image is not already cached on the node?

   A. `IfNotCached`

   B. `IfNotPresent`

   C. `IfNotAvailable`

   D. `Always`

7. How does a Service determine the Pods that are ready to accept traffic?

    A. Pods that are ready will have the `ready: true` label on them

    B. Only Pods managed by Deployment can accept traffic from a Service

    C. A pod's readiness probe has to succeed

    D. A pod's startup probe has to succeed

8. Which type of probe delays the execution of other probes?

    A. Delayed

    B. Liveness

    C. Startup

    D. Readiness

9. Which spec setting controls the number of Pods managed by a Deployment?

    A. podnum

    B. Replicas

    C. Containers

    D. Instances

10. Which Kubernetes controller is best suited for applications that need to save data to disk?

    A. `Deployment`

    B. `DaemonSet`

    C. `ReplicaSet`

    D. `StatefulSet`

11. Which of the following allows Kubernetes controllers to detect drift from the desired state?

    A. Replica controller

    B. Kubelet

    C. Reconciliation loop

    D. Liveness probes

12. Which type of service allows the exposure of applications inside the cluster?

     A. LoadBalancer

     B. ClusterIP

     C. InternalIP

     D. NodePort

13. Which technology is used behind service discovery in Kubernetes?

     A. Avahi

     B. Iptables

     C. NTP

     D. DNS

14. Which of the following service types are suitable for exposing applications outside of the Kubernetes cluster (select multiple)?

     A. ClusterIP

     B. NodePort

     C. LoadBalancer

     D. ExternalIP

15. Which of the following resources is suitable for storing and injecting generic configuration into containers?

     A. ConfigMap

     B. Secret

     C. SettingMap

     D. PV

16. Which object in Kubernetes represents an actual storage volume?

     A. StatefulSet

     B. PVC

     C. PV

     D. SV

17. Which resource is suitable for representing sensitive information to applications in containers?

    A. ConfigMap

    B. Secret

    C. Volume

    D. PVC

18. Which probe will restart the container if failed?

    A. Aliveness

    B. Readiness

    C. Startup

    D. Liveness

Further reading

To learn more about the topics that were covered in this chapter, take a look at the following resources:

- Dynamic Volume provisioning: `https://kubernetes.io/docs/concepts/storage/dynamic-provisioning/`

- Managing Kubernetes Secrets: `https://kubernetes.io/docs/tasks/configmap-secret/`

- Creating and using ConfigMaps: `https://kubernetes.io/docs/tasks/configure-pod-container/configure-pod-configmap/`

- Kubernetes probes configuration: `https://kubernetes.io/docs/tasks/configure-pod-container/configure-liveness-readiness-startup-probes/`

7

Application Placement and Debugging with Kubernetes

In this chapter, we'll see how we can control the placement of workloads on Kubernetes, how its scheduler works, and how we can debug applications running on K8s when something goes wrong. This chapter covers aspects from the *Kubernetes Fundamentals* as well as *Cloud Native Observability* domains of the **Kubernetes and Cloud Native Associate** (**KCNA**) exam at the same time.

As before, we will perform a few exercises with our minikube Kubernetes, so keep your setup handy. We're going to cover the following topics:

- Scheduling in Kubernetes

- Resource requests and limits

- Debugging applications in Kubernetes

Let's continue our Kubernetes journey!

Scheduling in Kubernetes

We've already touched the surface of what Kubernetes scheduler (`kube-scheduler`) does in *Chapter 5*. The scheduler is the component of the K8s control plane that decides on which node a pod will run.

> **Scheduling**
> Scheduling is the process of assigning Pods to Kubernetes nodes for the kubelet to run them. The scheduler watches for newly created Pods that have no *node* assigned in an infinite loop, and for every Pod it discovers, it will be responsible for finding the optimal node to run it on.

The default `kube-scheduler` scheduler selects a node for a pod in two stages:

1. **Filtering**: The first stage is where the scheduler determines the set of nodes where it is feasible to run the pod. This includes checks for nodes to have sufficient capacity and other requirements for a particular pod. This list might be empty if there are no suitable nodes in the cluster, and in such a case, the pod will hang in an unscheduled state until either the requirements or cluster state is changed.

2. **Scoring**: The second stage is where the scheduler ranks the nodes filtered in the first stage to choose the most suitable pod placement. Each node in the list will be ranked and gets a score, and at the end, the node with the highest score is picked.

Let's have a real-world example. Imagine we have an application that requires nodes with certain hardware. For example, you run **machine learning** (**ML**) workloads that can utilize GPUs for faster processing, or an application requires a particular CPU generation that is not available on every node in the cluster. In all such cases, we need to instruct Kubernetes to restrict the list of suitable nodes for our pods. There are multiple ways to do that:

- Specifying a `nodeSelector` field in the pod spec and labeling nodes

- Specifying an exact `nodeName` field in the pod spec

- Using **affinity** and **anti-affinity** rules

- Using pod **topology spread constraints**

Now let's get back to our minikube setup and extend the cluster by adding one more node with the `minikube node add` command (*this operation might take some time*):

```
$ minikube node add
😄   Adding node m02 to cluster minikube
❗   Cluster was created without any CNI, adding a node to it
might cause broken networking.
👍   Starting worker node minikube-m02 in cluster minikube
🚜   Pulling base image ...
🔥   Creating docker container (CPUs=2, Memory=2200MB) ...
📦   Preparing Kubernetes v1.23.3 on Docker 20.10.12 ...
🔎   Verifying Kubernetes components...
🐎   Successfully added m02 to minikube!
```

We should have a two-node minikube cluster at this point! Let's check the list of nodes:

```
$ minikube kubectl get nodes
NAME            STATUS    ROLES                   AGE    VERSION
minikube        Ready     control-plane,master    22d    v1.23.3
minikube-m02    Ready     <none>                  84s    v1.23.3
```

> **Note**
>
> If your system does not have sufficient resources to run another Kubernetes node, you can also continue as before with just one node. In such cases, however, you will need to adjust the example commands you encounter in this chapter to label the first node.

We will now create a modified version of the nginx deployment from before, which will require the node to have `purpose: web-server` appended to it. The respective `Deployment` spec could look like this:

```
$ cat nginx-deployment-with-node-selector.yaml
apiVersion: apps/v1
kind: Deployment
metadata:
  name: nginx-deployment-with-node-selector
  labels:
    app: nginx
spec:
  replicas: 1
  selector:
    matchLabels:
      app: nginx
  template:
    metadata:
      labels:
        app: nginx
    spec:
      containers:
      - name: nginx
        image: nginx:1.14.2
```

```
        ports:
        - containerPort: 80
    nodeSelector:
        purpose: web-server
```

> **Note**
>
> If you have not yet deleted the resources from the previous chapter's exercises, do so now by executing `kubectl delete deployment`, `kubectl delete sts`, or `kubectl delete service` in the kcna namespace respectively.

Go ahead and create the aforementioned nginx deployment spec:

```
$ minikube kubectl -- create -f nginx-deployment-with-node-
selector.yaml -n kcna
deployment.apps/nginx-deployment-with-node-selector created
```

Let's check what happened; for example, query pods in the kcna namespace:

```
$ minikube kubectl -- get pods -n kcna
NAME
                    READY    STATUS
RESTARTS    AGE
nginx-deployment-with-node-selector-7668d66698
-48q6b    0/1    Pending    0            1m
```

There it goes – the created Nginx pod is stuck in a Pending state. Let's check more details with the `kubectl describe` command (*your pod naming will differ*):

```
$ minikube kubectl -- describe pods nginx-deployment-with-node-
selector-7668d66698-48q6b -n kcna
... LONG OUTPUT OMITTED ...
Events:
  Type      Reason           Age
        From               Message
  ----      ------           ----
        ----               -------
  Warning  FailedScheduling  1m
     default-scheduler  0/2 nodes are available: 2 node(s)
didn't match Pod's node affinity/selector.
```

The message is clear – we have requested a node with a certain label for our nginx deployment pod and there are no nodes with such a label available.

We can check which labels our nodes have by adding the --show-labels parameter:

```
$ minikube kubectl -- get nodes --show-labels
NAME             STATUS    ROLES
  AGE     VERSION    LABELS
minikube          Ready        control-plane,master
   22d     v1.23.3    beta.kubernetes.io/arch=amd64,
beta.kubernetes.io/os=linux,kubernetes.io/
arch=amd64,kubernetes.io/hostname=minikube,kubernetes.
io/os=linux,minikube.k8s.io/
commit=362d5fdc0a3dbee389b3d3f1034e8023e72bd3a7,minikube.
k8s.io/name=minikube,minikube.k8s.io/primary=true,minikube.
k8s.io/updated_at=2022_06_19T17_20_23_0700,minikube.k8s.io/
version=v1.25.2,node-role.kubernetes.io/control-plane=,node-
role.kubernetes.io/master=,node.kubernetes.io/exclude-from-
external-load-balancers=
minikube-m02    Ready    <none>                 19m
v1.23.3    beta.kubernetes.io/arch=amd64,beta.kubernetes.io
/os=linux,kubernetes.io/arch=amd64,kubernetes.io/
hostname=minikube-m02,kubernetes.io/os=linux
```

Default labels include some useful information about the roles of the nodes, CPU architecture, OS, and more. Let's now label the newly added node with the same label our nginx deployment is looking for (*the node name might be similar in your case, so adjust accordingly*):

```
$ minikube kubectl -- label node minikube-m02  "purpose=web-
server"
node/minikube-m02 labeled
```

And just a moment later, we can see the nginx pod is being created:

```
$ minikube kubectl -- get pods -n kcna
NAME
                    READY    STATUS
    RESTARTS    AGE
nginx-deployment-with-node-selector-7668d66698
-48q6b    0/1      ContainerCreating    0            22m
```

By adding the -o wide option, we can see which node the pod was assigned to:

```
$ minikube kubectl -- get pods -n kcna -o wide
```

```
NAME
          READY    STATUS     RESTARTS    AGE    IP
          NODE               NOMINATED NODE    READINESS GATES
nginx-deployment-with-node-selector-7668d66698-48q6b
   1/1     Running    0            23m    172.17.0.2
minikube-m02    <none>                   <none>
```

That was a demonstration of perhaps the most common way to provide placement instructions to a Kubernetes scheduler with `nodeSelector`.

Let's move on to discuss the other scheduling controls Kubernetes offers. `nodeName` should be obvious – it allows us to specify exactly which node we want the workload to be scheduled to. Affinity and anti-affinity rules are more interesting. Conceptually, affinity is similar to `nodeSelector` but has more customization options.

---

nodeAffinity and podAffinity

These allow you to schedule Pods either on certain nodes (`nodeAffinity`) in a cluster or to nodes that are already running specified Pods (`podAffinity`).

---

nodeAntiAffinity and podAntiAffinity

The opposite of affinity. These allow you to either schedule Pods to different nodes than the ones specified (`nodeAntiAffinity`) or to schedule to different nodes where the specified Pods run (`podAntiAffinity`).

In other words, affinity rules are used to attract Pods to certain nodes or other Pods, and anti-affinity for the opposite – to push back from certain nodes or other Pods. Affinity can also be of two types – *hard* and *soft*:

- `requiredDuringSchedulingIgnoredDuringExecution` – Hard requirement, meaning the pod won't be scheduled unless the rule is met
- `preferredDuringSchedulingIgnoredDuringExecution` – Soft requirement, meaning the scheduler will try to find the node that satisfies the requirement, but if not available, the pod will still be scheduled on any other node

---

Note

`IgnoredDuringExecution` means that if the node labels change after Kubernetes already scheduled the pod, the pod continues to run on the same node.

Last on our list is pod **topology spread constraints**.

Topology spread constraints

These allow us to control how Pods are spread across the cluster among failure domains such as regions, **availability zones (AZs)**, nodes, or other user-defined topologies.

Essentially, these allow us to control where Pods run, taking into account the physical topology of the cluster. In today's cloud environments, we typically have multiple AZs in each region where the cloud provider operates.

AZ

This is one or multiple discrete data centers with redundant power, networking, and internet connectivity.

It is a good practice to run both the control plane and worker nodes of Kubernetes across multiple AZs. For example, in the `eu-central-1` region, **Amazon Web Services (AWS)** currently has three AZs, so we can run one control plane node in each AZ and multiple worker nodes per AZ. In this case, to achieve **high availability (HA)** as well as efficient resource utilization, we can apply topology spread constraints to our workloads to control the spread of Pods by nodes and zones, as shown in *Figure 7.1*:

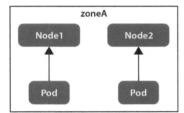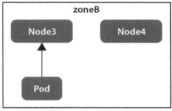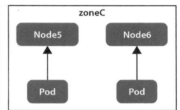

Figure 7.1 – Example of Pods spread across a cluster

This way, we can protect our workloads against individual node outages as well as wider cloud provider outages that might affect a whole AZ. Besides, it is possible to combine different methods and rules for more precise and granular control of where the Pods will be placed – for example, we can have topology spread constraints together with `nodeAffinity` and `podAntiAffinity` rules in one deployment.

> **Note**
>
> It is possible to combine multiple rules per pod - for example, `nodeSelector` together with hard `nodeAffinity` rules (`requiredDuringSchedulingIgnoredDuringExecution`). Both rules must be satisfied for the pod to be scheduled. In cases where at least one rule is not satisfied, the pod will be in a `Pending` state.

Altogether, scheduling in Kubernetes might seem to be a bit complicated at first, but as you start getting more experience, you'll see that its extensive features are great and let us handle complex scenarios as well as very large and diverse K8s installations. For the scope of the KCNA exam, you are not required to know in-depth details, but if you have some time, you are encouraged to check the *Further reading* section at the end of this chapter.

Resource requests and limits

As we were exploring the features of the K8s scheduler previously, have you wondered how Kubernetes knows *what is the best node in the cluster for a particular pod*? If we create a Deployment with no affinity settings, topology constraints, or node selectors, how can Kubernetes decide what is the best location in the cluster for the application we want to run?

By default, K8s is not aware of how many resources (CPU, memory, and other) each container in a scheduled pod requires to run. Therefore, for Kubernetes to make the best scheduling decisions, we need to make K8s aware of what each container requires for normal operation.

> **Resource requests**
>
> A resource request is an optional specification of how many resources each container in a pod needs. Containers can use more resources than requested if the node where the Pod runs has available resources. The specified request amounts will be reserved on the node where the pod is scheduled.

Kubernetes also allows us to impose hard limits on resources that the container can consume.

> **Resource limits**
>
> A resource limit is an optional specification of the maximum resources a running container can consume that are enforced by the kubelet and container runtime.

For example, we can set that the nginx container requires 250 MiB. If the pod with this container gets scheduled on a node with 8 GiB total memory with few other running Pods, our nginx container could possibly use 1 GiB or even more. However, if we additionally set a limit of 1 GiB, the runtime will prevent nginx from going beyond that limit. If a process tries to allocate more memory, the node kernel will forcefully terminate that process with an **Out Of Memory** (**OOM**) error, and the container gets restarted.

In the case of the CPU, limits and requests are measured by absolute units, where 1 CPU unit is an equivalent of 1 **virtual CPU** (**vCPU**) core or an actual 1 physical CPU core, depending on whether the worker node is a **virtual machine** (**VM**) or a physical server. A CPU unit of 0.5 CPU is the same as 500m units, where m stands for *milliCPU*, and—as you probably guessed—it allows us to specify a fraction of CPU this way. Unlike with memory, if a process tries to consume more CPU time than allowed by the limit, it won't be killed; instead, it simply gets throttled.

> **Note**
>
> When a resource limit is specified but not the request, and no default request is set (for example, the default might be inherited from the namespace settings), Kubernetes will copy the specified limit and use it as the request too. For example, a 500 MiB limit will cause the request to be 500 MiB as well.

Time to see these in action! Let's get back to our minikube setup and try creating the following example pod with a single container in the kcna namespace:

```
apiVersion: v1
kind: Pod
metadata:
  name: memory-demo
spec:
  containers:
  - name: memory-demo-ctr
    image: polinux/stress
    resources:
      requests:
        memory: "100Mi"
      limits:
        memory: "200Mi"
    command: ["stress"]
    args: ["--vm", "1", "--vm-bytes", "150M", "--vm-hang", "1"]
```

Execute the following command:

```
$ minikube kubectl -- create -f memory-request-limit.yaml -n
kcna
pod/memory-demo created
```

The application inside is a simple stress test tool that generates configurable load and memory consumption. With the arguments specified in the preceding spec, it consumes exactly 150 Mi of memory. Because 150 Mi is less than the limit set (200 Mi), everything is working fine.

Now, let's modify the stress arguments in the spec to use 250M instead of 150M. The respective changes are highlighted in the following code snippet:

```
        memory: "200Mi"
    command: ["stress"]
    args: ["--vm", "1", "--vm-bytes", "250M", "--vm-hang", "1"]
```

Delete the old pod and apply the updated spec, assuming that the file is now called memory-request-over-limit.yaml:

```
$ minikube kubectl -- delete pods memory-demo -n kcna
pod "memory-demo" deleted
$ minikube kubectl -- apply -f memory-request-over-limit.yaml
-n kcna
pod/memory-demo created
$ minikube kubectl -- get pods -n kcna
NAME
                    READY    STATUS
        RESTARTS    AGE
memory-demo
        0/1      ContainerCreating   0             3s
```

If you're typing quickly enough, you should be able to see the OOMKilled status and, eventually, CrashLoopBackOff:

```
$ minikube kubectl -- get pods -n kcna
NAME
                READY   STATUS      RESTARTS   AGE
memory-demo
    0/1     OOMKilled   0           5s
$ minikube kubectl -- get pods -n kcna
NAME
```

```
                READY      STATUS                 RESTARTS         AGE
memory-demo
        0/1        CrashLoopBackOff    2 (31s ago)    54s
```

Also, you can invoke `minikube kubectl -- describe po memory-demo -n kcna` to see more details:

```
... LONG OUTPUT OMITTED ...
      State:           Waiting
      Reason:          CrashLoopBackOff
   Last State:         Terminated
      Reason:          OOMKilled
      Exit Code:       1
```

Because the process allocates `250 MiB` with a limit of `150 MiB` set on the container, it gets killed. Remember that if you run multiple containers in a pod, the whole pod will stop accepting requests if at least one container of that pod is not running.

To sum all this up, requests and limits are very important, and **the best practice is to configure both for all workloads running in Kubernetes** because Kubernetes does not know how many resources your applications need, and you might end up with overloaded or underutilized worker nodes in your cluster, impacting stability when resource requests are undefined. Resource limits, on the other hand, help protect from rogue pods and applications with bugs that might be leaking memory or trying to use all available CPU time, affecting the neighbor workloads.

After you're done, feel free to delete the pod and other resources in the `kcna` namespace, if any. Next, we will continue exploring Kubernetes and learn about the ways to debug applications running on Kubernetes.

Debugging applications in Kubernetes

As you start using Kubernetes to run various applications, you'll eventually face the need to debug at least some of them. Sometimes, an application might have a bug that causes it to crash – maybe it was misconfigured or misbehaving under certain scenarios. Kubernetes provides multiple mechanisms that help us figure out what is wrong with the containerized payload and individual pod containers, including the following:

- Fetching logs from all containers in a pod, and also logs from the previous pod run
- Querying events that happened in a cluster recently
- Port forwarding from a pod to a local environment
- Running arbitrary commands inside containers of a pod

Logs play a crucial role and are very helpful to understand what is not working as intended. Applications often support multiple log levels categorized by the severity and verbosity of information that gets recorded, such as received requests and their payload; interrupted connections; failures to connect to a database or other services; and so on.

Common log levels are INFO, WARNING, ERROR, DEBUG, and CRITICAL, where the ERROR and CRITICAL settings will only record events that are considered errors and major problems as such. INFO and WARNING levels might provide generic information about what is happening or what might indicate an application problem, and DEBUG usually gives the most details by recording everything that happened with the application. As the name suggests, it might be wise to enable maximum verbosity by enabling the DEBUG log level to help debug problems. While this level of categorization is pretty standard across the industry, some software might have its own ways and definitions of log verbosity, so refer to the respective documentation and configuration samples. A standard log representation format today is JSON, and it is widely supported by development libraries in any language and all sorts of applications.

When it comes to logging architecture, the best way is to use a separate backend to store, analyze, and query logs that will persist the log records independent from the lifecycle of Kubernetes nodes, Pods, and containers. This approach is known as **cluster-level logging**. Kubernetes does not provide a native log storage solution and only keeps the most recent logs on each node. However, there are plenty of logging solutions that offer seamless integration with Kubernetes, such as **Grafana Loki** or **Elastic Stack (ELK)**, to name a few. The opposite of cluster-level logging is when logging is configured individually for each pod (application) running in the cluster. This is not a recommended way to go with Kubernetes.

In order to collect logs from each Kubernetes node for aggregation and longer storage, it is common to use **node logging agents**. Those are small, containerized agents that run on every node and push all collected logs to a logging backend server. Because they need to run on each node in the cluster, it is common to define them as a **DaemonSet**. A schematic of such a setup is shown in *Figure 7.2*:

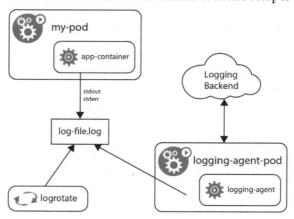

Figure 7.2 – Using a node logging agent for log collection and aggregation

For a moment, let's get back to our minikube setup and see in action how to fetch application logs. Let's start with a basic pod that simply writes the current date and time into the **standard output (stdout)**:

```
$ minikube kubectl -- apply -f
https://k8s.io/examples/debug/counter-pod.yaml -n kcna
pod/counter created
$ minikube kubectl -- get pods -n kcna
NAME
                   READY    STATUS    RESTARTS    AGE
counter
          1/1      Running   0            22s
```

Execute kubectl logs to get the container logs. If a pod has multiple containers, you'll have to additionally specify which particular container you want to get the logs from with the --container argument:

```
$ minikube kubectl -- logs counter -n kcna
0:  Sun Aug   7 13:31:21 UTC 2022
1:  Sun Aug   7 13:31:22 UTC 2022
2:  Sun Aug   7 13:31:23 UTC 2022
3:  Sun Aug   7 13:31:24 UTC 2022
4:  Sun Aug   7 13:31:25 UTC 2022
5:  Sun Aug   7 13:31:26 UTC 2022
6:  Sun Aug   7 13:31:27 UTC 2022
7:  Sun Aug   7 13:31:28 UTC 2022
8:  Sun Aug   7 13:31:29 UTC 2022
9:  Sun Aug   7 13:31:30 UTC 2022
10: Sun Aug   7 13:31:31 UTC 2022
11: Sun Aug   7 13:31:32 UTC 2022
12: Sun Aug   7 13:31:33 UTC 2022
```

> **Note**
> It is also possible to fetch logs from the previous container execution (before it was restarted) by adding the --previous argument to the kubectl logs command.

What we can see here is actually what the application inside the container writes to stdout and stderr (**standard error**) Linux output streams. If the logs are written to any file in the local container filesystem, those won't be visible with kubectl logs.

However, if an application does not have a configuration to log to `stdout` and `stderr`, it is possible to add a logging sidecar – a separate container running in the same pod that captures the logs from the main container and forwards those to either a logging server or its own `stdout` and `stderr` output streams. Such a setup is depicted in *Figure 7.3*:

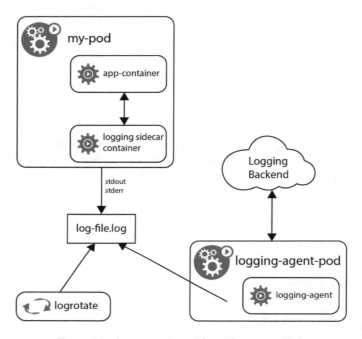

Figure 7.3 – Log steaming with a sidecar container

Next on our list are events that can provide valuable insights into what is happening in your Kubernetes cluster.

> **Kubernetes event**
>
> This is a record documenting a change in the state of Kubernetes resources—for example, changes to nodes, pods, and any other resources when a node becomes `NotReady` or when a **PersistentVolume (PV)** fails to be mounted.

Events are namespaced, and the `kubectl get events` command can be used to query recent events. For example, if we recently scaled an nginx deployment, we could see something similar to this:

```
$ minikube kubectl -- get events -n kcna
LAST SEEN    TYPE      REASON           OBJECT
                                                 MESSAGE
```

```
5s              Normal    Scheduled           pod/nginx-deployment-
with-node-selector-7668d66698-bx7kl     Successfully assigned
kcna/nginx-deployment-with-node-selector-7668d66698-bx7kl to
minikube-m02
3s              Normal    Pulled              pod/nginx-deployment-
with-node-selector-7668d66698-bx7kl     Container image
"nginx:1.14.2" already present on machine
3s              Normal    Created             pod/nginx-deployment-
with-node-selector-7668d66698-bx7kl     Created container nginx
3s              Normal    Started             pod/nginx-deployment-
with-node-selector-7668d66698-bx7kl     Started container nginx
5s              Normal    SuccessfulCreate    replicaset/nginx-
deployment-with-node-selector-7668d66698    Created pod: nginx-
deployment-with-node-selector-7668d66698-bx7kl
5s              Normal    ScalingReplicaSet   deployment/nginx-
deployment-with-node-selector              Scaled up replica
set nginx-deployment-with-node-selector-7668d66698 to 2
```

> **Note**
> By default, only events that happened in the last hour are kept. The duration can be increased in the kube-apiserver configuration.

Coming next is another useful feature that can help during debugging or development with Kubernetes—**port forwarding**. Using a simple kubectl command, you can configure to forward connections made on the local port on your system to the specified remote port of any pod running in your K8s cluster. The syntax of the command is shown here:

```
kubectl port-forward POD_NAME LOCAL_PORT:REMOTE_POD_PORT
```

This is very helpful if you need to access a Kubernetes payload as though it is running locally on your workstation. For example, you have a web application listening on port 80 in the pod, and you forward your local port 8080 toward remote port 80 of the respective pod. While port forwarding is running, you can reach the application locally under localhost:8080.

Port forwarding is not a part of the KCNA exam; however, if you have time, feel free to check the *Further reading* section at the end of the chapter for examples of how to use it.

The last point on our list is about starting processes inside already running containers of a pod. We've already done that previously, in *Chapter 6, Deploying and Scaling Applications with Kubernetes*.

The respective `kubectl exec` command allows us to start transient, arbitrary processes in containers, and most of the time, you'd probably use it to start a shell (`bash` or `sh`) in interactive mode. This *feels* much like logging inside a container with a **Secure Shell** (**SSH**) protocol. Here's an example:

```
kubectl exec -it POD_NAME -c CONTAINER_NAME bash
```

Kubernetes also allows us to copy files between your local system and remote containers. The respective command is `kubectl cp`, which works very similarly to the Linux `scp` tool, but in the Kubernetes context.

Both `exec` and `cp` are very practical for understanding what is going on inside the container with an application we're debugging. It allows us to quickly verify configuration settings, perform an HTTP request, or fetch logs that are not written to `stdout` or `stderr`.

Summary

All in all, in this chapter, we've learned a few important aspects of running and operating workloads with K8s. We've seen how pod scheduling works with Kubernetes, its stages (**filtering** and **scoring**), and how we can control placement decisions with `nodeSelector`, `nodeName`, and **affinity** and **anti-affinity** settings, as well as **topology spread constraints**. Extensive features of the Kubernetes scheduler allow us to cover all imaginable scenarios of controlling how a certain workload will be placed within the nodes of a cluster. With those controls, we can spread Pods of one application between nodes in multiple AZs for HA; schedule Pods that require specialized hardware (for example, a GPU) only to nodes that have it available; magnet multiple applications together to run on the same nodes with affinity; and much more.

Next, we've seen that **resource requests** help Kubernetes make better scheduling decisions, and **resource limits** are there to protect the cluster and other Pods from misbehaving apps or simply restrict resource utilization. With the container reaching the specified memory limit, its process gets killed (and the container restarted), and when reaching allocated CPU units, the process gets throttled.

After, we explored ways to debug applications on K8s. Logs are one of the basic and most important tools in any problem analysis. Kubernetes follows a **cluster-level** approach to logging and does not provide long-term log storage. In case of Kubernetes node failure, the logs of the node's Pods are all gone. Therefore, it is important to set up a logging solution for aggregation and log storage. To collect and ship logs from all nodes, we use **node logging agents**, which can be deployed with a help of **DaemonSet**. If an application running in K8s cannot send its log output to `stdout` and `stderr`, the solution is to run a **logging sidecar container** in the same pod as the application that will stream the logs.

Other practical ways to debug applications and get insights about what is happening in a cluster include Kubernetes events, port forwarding, and execution of arbitrary processes such as a **shell** inside containers with the `kubectl exec` command.

Coming next is the final chapter from the Kubernetes part, where we will learn some of the best practices and explore other operational aspects of K8s. If you would like to go deeper into the content described in this section, check out the *Further reading* section.

Questions

As we conclude, here is a list of questions for you to test your knowledge regarding this chapter's material. You will find the answers in the *Assessments* section of the *Appendix*:

1. Which of the following stages are part of scheduling in Kubernetes (pick multiple)?

    A. Spreading

    B. Launching

    C. Filtering

    D. Scoring

2. What happens if the Kubernetes scheduler cannot assign a pod to a node?

    A. It will be stuck in a `CrashLoopBackOff` state

    B. It will be stuck in a `Pending` state

    C. It will be stuck in a `NotScheduled` state

    D. It will be forcefully run on one of the control plane nodes

3. Which of the following scheduler instructions will not prevent a pod from being scheduled if a condition cannot be satisfied (soft affinity or soft anti-affinity)?

    A. `requiredDuringSchedulingIgnoredDuringExecution`

    B. `preferredDuringSchedulingIgnoredDuringExecution`

    C. `neededDuringSchedulingIgnoredDuringExecution`

    D. `softAffinity`

4. Which Kubernetes scheduler feature should be used to control how Pods are spread across different failure domains (such as AZs, nodes, and so on)?

    A. Pod failure domain constraints

    B. Pod topology spread constraints

    C. `podAntiAffinity`

    D. `nodeName`

5.   What is the purpose of `podAffinity` in Kubernetes?

   A.   To schedule Pods to certain nodes in the cluster

   B.   To group two or more Pods together for better performance

   C.   To schedule Pods to nodes where other Pods already running

   D.   To schedule Pods to different nodes where other Pods already running

6.   What is the purpose of resource requests in Kubernetes?

   A.   They help to plan ahead the cluster extension

   B.   They define more important workloads in the cluster

   C.   They are needed to pick the right hardware in the cluster for the workload

   D.   They are needed for optimal pod placement in the cluster

7.   What happens if a container has a memory limit of `500Mi` set but tries to allocate `550Mi`?

   A.   `550Mi` is within a 10% margin, so the container will allocate memory normally

   B.   Pods have higher limits than containers, so memory allocation will work

   C.   The container process will be killed with an OOM error

   D.   The container process will be stuck when it gets over `500Mi`

8.   What will be the value of the container CPU request if the limit is set to `1.5` and there are no defaults for that namespace?

   A.   `0.0`

   B.   `0.75`

   C.   `1.5`

   D.   `1.0`

9.   What happens with a pod if its containers request a total of `10.0` CPU units, but the largest node in the cluster only has `8.0` CPUs?

   A.   Requests are not hard requirements; the pod gets scheduled

   B.   Requests are hard requirements; the pod will be stuck in a `Pending` state

   C.   Because of the `preferredDuringScheduling` option, the pod gets scheduled anyway

   D.   The pod will be in a `CrashLoopBackOff` state due to a lack of resources in the cluster

10. Which logging level typically provides maximum verbosity for debugging purposes?

    A. `INFO`

    B. `ERROR`

    C. `MAXIMUM`

    D. `DEBUG`

11. What does cluster-level logging mean for log storage in Kubernetes?

    A. K8s aggregates all cluster logs on control plane nodes

    B. K8s needs separate log collection and aggregation systems

    C. K8s provides a complete log storage and aggregation solution

    D. K8s provides storage only for the most important cluster health logs

12. What do node logging agents in Kubernetes do (pick multiple)?

    A. Collect logs only from worker nodes

    B. Collect logs from all nodes

    C. Send logs from worker nodes to control plane nodes

    D. Send logs for aggregation and storage to a logging backend

13. What is the purpose of logging sidecar agents in Kubernetes?

    A. To collect and stream logs from applications that cannot log to `stdout` and `stderr`

    B. To provide a backup copy of logs in case of a node failure

    C. To allow logging on verbosity levels such as ERROR and DEBUG

    D. To enable the `kubectl logs` command to work

14. Which of the following `kubectl` commands allows us to run an arbitrary process in a container?

    A. `kubectl run`

    B. `kubectl start`

    C. `kubectl exec`

    D. `kubectl proc`

15. Which of the following commands will return logs from a pod container that has failed and restarted?

    A. `kubectl logs POD_NAME --previous`

    B. `kubectl logs POD_NAME`

    C. `kubectl previous logs POD_NAME`

    D. `kubectl logs`

16. Which Kubernetes scheduler feature provides a simple way to constrain Pods to nodes with specific labels?

    A. `kubectl local`

    B. `nodeConstrain`

    C. `nodeSelector`

    D. `nodeName`

Further reading

To learn more about the topics that were covered in this chapter, take a look at the following resources:

- Scheduling and assigning Pods to nodes: `https://kubernetes.io/docs/concepts/scheduling-eviction/assign-pod-node/`

- Pod topology spread constraints: `https://kubernetes.io/docs/concepts/scheduling-eviction/topology-spread-constraints/`

- Resource management in Kubernetes: `https://kubernetes.io/docs/concepts/configuration/manage-resources-containers/`

- Using port forwarding to access applications in a K8s cluster: `https://kubernetes.io/docs/tasks/access-application-cluster/port-forward-access-application-cluster/`

- Getting a shell to a running container: `https://kubernetes.io/docs/tasks/debug/debug-application/get-shell-running-container/`

8

Following Kubernetes Best Practices

We have finally reached the last chapter of the Kubernetes part! Congrats on making it here—you're now more than halfway through becoming **Kubernetes and Cloud Native Associate (KCNA)** certified!

In this chapter, we are going to discuss some of the best practices for operating Kubernetes and some of the security gaps and ways to address those.

We'll learn about Kubernetes networking and **network policies** for traffic control; restricting access with **role-based access control (RBAC)**; using **Helm** as a K8s package manager, and more. As before, we'll need the minikube setup from the previous chapters to perform a few hands-on exercises.

The topics of this chapter include the following:

- Kubernetes networking essentials
- RBAC
- Helm—the package manager for K8s
- Kubernetes best practices

Let's get started!

Kubernetes networking essentials

Without exaggeration, K8s networking is probably the hardest part to understand, and even for very experienced engineers and operators, it might be tough. As you hopefully remember from *Chapter 4*, Kubernetes implements the **Container Networking Interface (CNI)**, which allows us to use different overlay network plugins for container networking. Yet there are so many CNI providers out there (**Flannel, Calico, Cilium, Weave**, and **Canal**, to name a few) that it is easy to get confused. Those providers rely on different technologies such as **Border Gateway Protocol (BGP)** or **Virtual Extensible LAN (VXLAN)** to deliver different levels of overlay network performance and offer different features.

But don't worry – for the scope of KCNA, you are not required to know many details. For now, we will cover Kubernetes networking essentials.

Have a look at the following diagram:

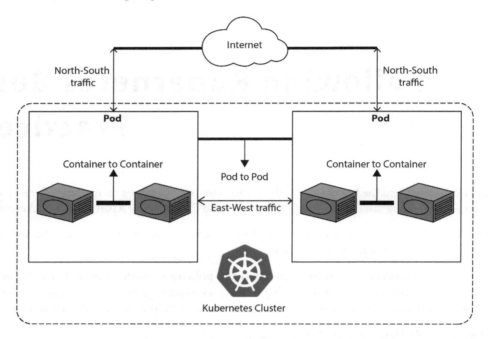

Figure 8.1 – Kubernetes networking model

As *Figure 8.1* suggests, there are three types of communication happening in a Kubernetes cluster:

- **Container to container**—Within a pod, all containers can easily communicate with each other via `localhost` because they are collocated together as one unit.

- **Pod to pod**—Communication on the level of the overlay network (sometimes called the **pod network**) spanning all nodes in the cluster. The overlay network makes it possible for a pod on one node to talk with other pods on any nodes in a cluster. This kind of communication is often called **East-West** traffic.

- **The outside world** (for example, the internet or other networks)—Communication that requires a Service resource of either a `NodePort` or a `LoadBalancer` type to expose a pod or a group of pods with the same application outside of the cluster. Communication with the outside world is also known as **North-South** traffic.

In practice, when a pod needs to communicate with other pods, this will also involve Kubernetes' service discovery mechanism. Since every new pod started in Kubernetes automatically gets an IP address in the flat overlay network, it is almost impossible to refer to IP addresses in any configuration as addresses change all the time. Instead, we will use the ClusterIP Service, which automatically tracks all changes to the list of endpoints when a new pod comes up or an old pod is terminated (refer to *Chapter 6* for a detailed explanation). Kubernetes also allows the use of **IP Address Management** (**IPAM**) plugins to control how pod IP addresses are allocated. By default, a single IP pool is used for all pods in a cluster. Using IPAM plugins, it is possible to subdivide the overlay network IP pool into smaller blocks and allocate pod IP addresses based on annotations or the worker node where a pod is started.

Moving on, it is important to understand that all pods in the cluster pod network can talk to each other *without any restriction by default.*

> **Note**
> Kubernetes namespaces do not provide network isolation. Pods in namespace A can reach pods in namespace B by their IP address in the pod network and the other way around unless restricted by a NetworkPolicy resource.

NetworkPolicy is a resource allowing us to control network traffic flow in Kubernetes in an application-centric way. NetworkPolicy allows us to define how a pod can communicate with other pods (selected via label selectors), pods in other namespaces (selected via namespace selector), or IP block ranges.

Network policies are essentially a pod-level firewall in Kubernetes that allows us to specify which traffic is allowed to and from pods that match selectors. A simple example might be when you have one application per Kubernetes namespace consisting of many microservices. You might want to disallow communication of pods between the namespaces in such a scenario for better isolation. Another example scenario: you might want to restrict access to a database running in Kubernetes to only pods that need to access it because allowing every pod in the cluster to reach the database imposes a security risk.

But why, exactly, do we need to apply network policies in Kubernetes?

As applications shifted from monolithic to microservice architectures, this added a lot of network-based communication. Monolithic applications have most communication happening *within themselves*, as being one big executable program, while microservices rely on message buses and web protocols to exchange data, which causes an increased amount of **East-West** network traffic that should also be secured.

Under the hood, network policies are implemented by the CNI provider, and to use network policies, the provider should support those. For example, **Kindnet**—the CNI used by default with minikube-provisioned Kubernetes—does not support network policies. Therefore, if we create any `NetworkPolicy` definition in our minikube Kubernetes, it will not have any effect on the traffic in the cluster. Nevertheless, feel free to check the *Further reading* section if you'd like to learn more about K8s networking and network policies.

Coming up next, we will explore RBAC and see how it helps in securing a Kubernetes cluster.

RBAC

You've probably noticed that in our minikube cluster, we have unlimited access and control over all resources and namespaces. While this is fine for learning purposes, when it comes to running and operating production systems, you'll most likely need to restrict the access. This is where Kubernetes RBAC becomes very helpful.

> **Kubernetes RBAC**
>
> This is the main security mechanism in Kubernetes to ensure that users only have access to resources according to their assigned roles.

A few examples of what can be done with K8s RBAC:

- Restricting access to a specific namespace (for example, production namespace or namespace for a certain application) for a limited group of people (such as with an administrator role)
- Restricting access to be read-only for certain resources
- Restricting access to a certain group of resources (such as **Pod**, **Service**, **Deployment**, **Secret**, or anything else)
- Restricting access to an application that interacts with the Kubernetes API

Kubernetes RBAC is a very powerful mechanism, and it allows us to implement the **least privilege** principle, which is considered the best practice for access management.

> **Least privilege principle**
>
> This is when each user or account receives only the minimum privileges required to fulfill their job or process.

As for the scope of the KCNA exam, this is pretty much all you need to know about restricting access in Kubernetes. The intention of this book, however, is to take you one step further and closer to the real-world scenarios of operating a Kubernetes cluster, so we'll dig a little deeper.

Let's see what happens when you execute `kubectl apply` or `kubectl create` with some resource specification:

1. `kubectl` will read the Kubernetes configuration from the file at the `KUBECONFIG` environment variable.

2. `kubectl` will discover available Kubernetes APIs.

3. `kubectl` will validate the specification provided (for example, for malformed YAML).

4. Send the request to `kube-apiserver` with the spec in the payload.

5. `kube-apiserver` receives the request and verifies the authenticity of the request (for example, *who* made the request).

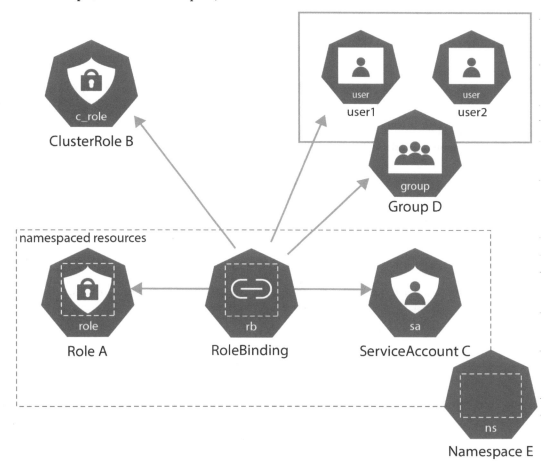

Figure 8.2 – Application of Role and ClusterRole rules via RoleBinding

While Kubernetes RBAC might seem complex at first, the moment you start applying it in practice, it gets much easier and clear. You'll see that RBAC mechanisms are very flexible and granular and allow us to cover all possible scenarios, including a case when an application inside the pod needs to access a Kubernetes API.

Let's check the following simple `pod-reader` Role definition:

```
apiVersion: rbac.authorization.k8s.io/v1
kind: Role
metadata:
  namespace: kcna
  name: pod-reader
rules:
- apiGroups: [""] # "" indicates the core API group
  resources: ["pods"]
  verbs: ["get", "watch", "list"] # the actions allowed on
resources
```

It can be used to grant read-only access to pod resources in the kcna namespace using RoleBinding, such as in the following code snippet:

```
apiVersion: rbac.authorization.k8s.io/v1
kind: RoleBinding
metadata:
  name: read-pods
  namespace: kcna
subjects:
# subjects can be multiple users, groups or service accounts
- kind: User
  name: jack # name is case sensitive
  apiGroup: rbac.authorization.k8s.io # the standard API group
for all RBAC resources
roleRef:
  # roleRef specifies the binding to a Role or ClusterRole
  kind: Role # either a Role or ClusterRole
  name: pod-reader # name of the Role or ClusterRole to bind to
  apiGroup: rbac.authorization.k8s.io
```

Go ahead and create first a `Role` and then a `RoleBinding` resource in our minikube playground:

```
$ minikube kubectl -- create -f role.yaml -n kcna
role.rbac.authorization.k8s.io/pod-reader created
$ minikube kubectl -- create -f rolebinding.yaml -n kcna
rolebinding.rbac.authorization.k8s.io/read-pods created
```

The `RoleBinding` was referencing user `jack` as the only subject, but a single `RoleBinding` can also be used to reference any number of users, groups, and service accounts.

Now, when it comes to testing permissions, Kubernetes has a very neat feature that allows us to check permissions without the actual user credentials (which can be an x509 client certificate). The respective `kubectl auth can-I` command allows us to verify what is allowed and what is not for a certain user, group, or service account. Try the following:

```
$ minikube kubectl -- auth can-i get pods --as=jack
no
```

But hey, didn't we allow it to `get` in our preceding `pod-reader` role definition for a user named `jack`? We did, but only in the `kcna` namespace! Let's try again by specifying the namespace:

```
$ minikube kubectl -- auth can-i get pods -n kcna --as=jack
yes
```

Looks much better now. How about the creation or deletion of pods? Let's try the following:

```
$ minikube kubectl -- auth can-i create pods -n kcna --as=jack
no
$ minikube kubectl -- auth can-i delete pods -n kcna --as=jack
no
```

As expected, this is not allowed, just as nothing else is allowed to be done with other resources than pods in the `kcna` namespace according to the role and binding we've created. You've probably noticed that the *verbs* in the role definition are very precise—we've specified `get`, `watch`, and `list`, and they are not the same:

- `watch` is a verb that allows us to see updates to resources in real time

- `list` allows us to only list resources, but not to get further details about a particular object

- `get` allows us to retrieve information about a resource, but you need to know the name of the resource (to find this out, you'll need the `list` verb)

And of course, there are write permission verbs such as `create`, `update`, `patch`, and `delete`, which can be a part of a role definition spec.

If you'd like to learn more about RBAC, feel free to explore on your own and check the materials in the *Further reading* section at the end of the chapter. Moving forward, we're going to learn about the Kubernetes package manager in the next section.

Helm – the package manager for K8s

A package manager for Kubernetes—that might sound confusing at first. We are building images with system packages and pushing those to the image registry with Docker or another tool. Why do we need a package manager?

> **Note**
>
> This section is not a prerequisite for passing the KCNA exam; however, it is strongly recommended reading as it might help you to avoid mistakes when using Kubernetes in real-world, practical setups.

Imagine the following scenario—you are operating a few Kubernetes clusters for a small enterprise. Those Kubernetes clusters are similar in size and configuration and run exactly the same applications, but for different environments such as *development*, *testing*, and *production*. The dev team was pushing for microservices architecture, and now there are about 50 microservices that run on Kubernetes working together as a part of bigger applications.

The naive way to manage the Kubernetes specifications for all those would be the creation of individual spec files for each microservice and each environment. The number of YAML files to maintain might easily grow to over 100, and they will likely include a bunch of duplicated code and settings that are even harder to manage in the long run. There must be a better way, and using a package manager such as Helm is one possible solution.

Let's clarify that in more detail. Helm is not for building container images and packaging application executables inside. Helm is used for the standardized management of Kubernetes specifications that represent the payload we want to run in Kubernetes clusters.

> **Helm**
>
> This is a tool for automating the creation, packaging, deployment, and configuration of Kubernetes applications. It helps to define, install, and update applications on Kubernetes.

Coming back to the previous example with 50 microservices and 3 environments, instead of writing duplicated spec files, with Helm you can create reusable templates once and simply apply configuration values that are different based on the environment where the application should be deployed.

Next, you realize that 20 out of those 50 microservices you run rely on individual **Redis** instances, and instead of duplicating the same Redis deployment specification with different names 20 times, you create a single one that is templated, reusable, and can be simply added as a requirement for other applications that need it.

In order to understand Helm a little better, let's talk about its three main concepts:

- **Helm chart**—This is a package that contains all K8s resource definitions (specs) required to run an application in Kubernetes. Think of it as the Kubernetes equivalent of a Linux **DEB** package, an **RPM** package, or a **Homebrew** formula.

- **Helm repository**—This is a place where *charts* are collected and shared; it could be thought of as a Kubernetes equivalent to the **Python Package Index** (**PyPI**) or the **Comprehensive Perl Archive Network** (**CPAN**) for Perl. Charts can be downloaded from and uploaded to the *repository*.

- **Helm release**—This is an instance of a *chart* running in a Kubernetes cluster. One *chart* can be installed many times into the same cluster, and on each installation, a new release is created. For the previous example with Redis, we can have 1 Redis *chart* that we can install 20 times on the same cluster where each installation will have its own *release* and *release name*.

In a nutshell, Helm installs charts onto Kubernetes, creating a new release on each installation. Using Helm repositories, it is very easy to find and reuse ready charts for common software to be run on Kubernetes. It is also easy to install multiple charts together that need to work as one application by specifying dependencies between the charts.

Helm comes with a CLI tool that is also called `helm`. Using the `helm` CLI tool, we can search chart repositories, package charts, install, update, and delete releases, and do pretty much anything else that Helm allows. Helm uses the same Kubernetes config file that `kubectl` is using and interacts directly with the Kubernetes API, as shown in *Figure 8.3*:

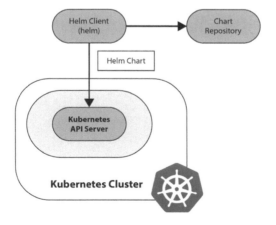

Figure 8.3 – Helm v3 architecture

Helm also makes updates and rollbacks of applications easier. If something goes wrong with the changes introduced by the release, one simple command—`helm rollback` —can help to go back to the previous release version in a matter of seconds or minutes. Rollbacks with Helm are similar to the Kubernetes Deployment rollbacks that we have tried before in *Chapter 6*, but the difference is that Helm can roll back any chart spec changes. For example, you have modified a Secret spec file that is a part of a Helm chart and triggered `helm upgrade` to roll out the changes. A few moments later, you realize that the change broke the chart application, and you need to get back to the previous version quickly. You execute `helm rollback` with an optional release revision and release name and get back to the working revision.

At this time, we are not going to dive deeper into Helm and do any hands-on assignments because, again, Helm is not a part of the KCNA exam. The goal of this section is to give you a quick introduction to Helm—a tool that significantly simplifies the management of applications on Kubernetes. Helm is a graduated **Cloud Native Computing Foundation** (CNCF) project and comes with a powerful templating engine that allows the definition of custom functions and flexible control actions (`if/else/with/range`, and so on).

You can also consider other tools such as **Kustomize** and **YTT** that serve the same purpose yet follow a different approach. Neither is a part of KCNA, but as usual, the *Further reading* section will include resources about those if you'd like to go the extra mile.

Kubernetes best practices

While KCNA is not a security-focused certification, you are expected to know a few basics and best practices about Kubernetes and Cloud Native, and now is the time to talk about those.

Kubernetes' documentation suggests the **4Cs of Cloud Native security**: *Cloud*, *Clusters*, *Containers*, and *Code*—an approach with four layers for in-depth defense:

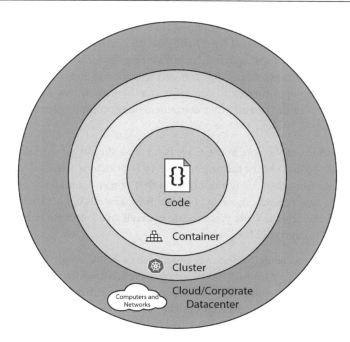

Figure 8.4 – 4Cs of Cloud Native security

In this approach, the inner circle security builds upon the next outermost layers. This way, the *Code* layer is protected by the bases of the *Container*, *Cluster*, and *Cloud* layers, and you cannot safeguard against poor security standards and practices in the base layers by addressing the security on the level of *Code*, just as you cannot disregard the need to secure the innermost circle even when you have very strong security in the outer layers. Let's see why in more detail and what each layer of the 4Cs means.

Starting with the base, the cloud or other infrastructure (such as a corporate database or co-located servers) acts as a trusted base for the Kubernetes cluster. If the *Cloud* layer is vulnerable or misconfigured, there is no guarantee that the components built on top are secure.

At the beginning of the book, we discussed what the *shared responsibility model* means in the cloud, where both the cloud provider and the users must take action in order to keep workloads safe and secure. Therefore, always refer to and follow the security documentation from your cloud provider.

When it comes to the *Cluster* layer, there are multiple best practices for Kubernetes— specifically, things such as *etcd* encryption, RBAC configuration, limiting access to nodes, restricting API server access, keeping the Kubernetes version up to date, and more. But don't worry—you are not required to memorize any of those to pass the KCNA exam.

Next is the *Container* layer. As you might remember from *Chapter 4*, there are *Namespaced*, *Sandboxed*, and *Virtualized* containers, and they all have their pros and cons, *Virtualized* being the most secure yet *heavy*, and *Namespaced* the most lightweight, but sharing the same host kernel and thus providing lower levels of security. Which one to run depends on the workload and other requirements you might have. Also, avoid running applications in containers as the `root` user. Doing so means there is a high chance of the whole node with all other containers being compromised if that `root` container is compromised.

And reaching the middle, at the core is the *Code* layer. You should not run sources that you don't trust—for example, if you don't know the origin of the code or exactly what it does. We also discussed that aspect in detail in *Chapter 4*. Container images that you've found somewhere might package malicious code inside, and running those in your environment can open a backdoor for an attacker. At a minimum, build and test the code you execute yourself and automate vulnerability scanning as a part of the container image build process.

Should you be running Kubernetes clusters over unsecured or public networks, consider implementing a service mesh to encrypt all pod traffic. Otherwise, by default, Kubernetes' overlay network transports all data unencrypted, although a few CNI providers support **Transport Layer Security** (**TLS**) too. Consider using network policies to isolate and further protect your workloads. The right way to do it is to *deny* all communication between pods by default and put tailored *allow* rules for each application and microservice in place. And yes, you can have both a service mesh and network policies in one cluster, and their usage is not exclusive.

Finally, a few basic good practices when dealing with Kubernetes. Some might be a repetition of what we have learned, but better repeat twice than learn the *hard way later on*:

- **Use controllers to create**

  Simple pod specification does not provide fault tolerance and any additional functions such as rolling updates. Use `Deployment`, `StatefulSet`, `DaemonSet`, or `Job` controllers to create pods.

- **Use namespaces to organize workloads**

  Deploying everything into one, default namespace will quickly make it a mess. Create multiple namespaces for better workload organization and ease of operation. Namespaces are also great for RBAC configuration and restricting traffic with network policies.

- **Use resource requests and limits**

  These are required for Kubernetes to make the best scheduling decisions and protect clusters against misbehaving applications utilizing all resources and causing nodes to crash.

- **Use readiness and liveness probes**

  These ensure that requests reach pods only when they *are ready* to process those. If we don't define `readinessProbe` and the application takes too long to start, then all requests forwarded to that pod will fail or time out first. `livenessProbe` is just as important because it will make the container restart in case its process is caught in a deadlock or stuck.

- **Use small container images when possible**

  Avoid installing optional packages into container images you're building and try to get rid of all unnecessary packages. Large images take longer to download (and thus more time for the pod to start first) and consume more disk space. Specialized, minimal images such as **Alpine** can only be 5-10 MB in size.

- **Use labels and annotations**

  Add metadata to Kubernetes resources to organize your cluster workloads. This is helpful for operations and for tracking how different applications interact with each other. The K8s documentation recommends including `name`, `instance`, `version`, `component`, `part-of`, and other labels. Where labels are used to identify resources, annotations are used to store additional information about K8s resources (`last-updated`, `managed-by`, and so on).

- **Use multiple nodes and topology awareness**

  Use an uneven number of control plane nodes (such as 3 or 5) to avoid *split-brain* situations and use multiple worker nodes spread across multiple failure domains (such as **availability zones** or **AZs**) where possible. Apply pod topology spread constraints or anti-affinity rules to ensure that all replicas of microservices are not running on the same node.

The list can be extended with many further points, but this should be enough to let you continue in the right direction with Kubernetes. Monitoring and observability topics will be discussed additionally in the upcoming chapters.

Summary

With that, we've reached the end of the Kubernetes part – well done!

Remember – the more hands-on you get, the faster you'll learn and understand Kubernetes and its concepts. If some points still feel a bit blurry, that is fine. You can always go back and read some parts again and check the *Further reading* sections at the end of each chapter. Refer to the official Kubernetes documentation at `https://kubernetes.io/docs/home/` if you have any questions.

This chapter discussed which three types of network communication happen in a Kubernetes cluster and that by default, there is nothing restricting communication between two pods in the cluster. Therefore, it is a good idea to use network policies in order to only allow required communication and deny the rest for security reasons. Not all CNI providers support network policies, therefore make sure to check that when planning a Kubernetes installation.

Every new pod in the cluster automatically gets an IP address in the overlay network, and Kubernetes also takes care of cleaning it up when a pod is terminated. However, using pod IP addresses in any configuration is not practical, and we should use Kubernetes Services for both **East-West** and **North-South** communication.

Next, we learned about the RBAC features of Kubernetes and how they allow restricting access to the API. It is strongly recommended to implement RBAC rules for any cluster that is accessed by more than one person or if an application running in Kubernetes talks with the K8s API.

Managing a large number of microservices and environments might be challenging, and a package manager tool can become very handy. Helm is a powerful tool for packaging, configuring, and deploying Kubernetes applications. We've seen that Helm introduces additional concepts of charts, repositories, and releases.

When it comes to security, Kubernetes suggests a 4Cs layered approach: *Cloud*, *Clusters*, *Containers*, and *Code*. Each layer requires its own practices and actions to be taken, and only together do they make infrastructure and workloads secure. Depending on the security requirements and the K8s cluster setup, it might be necessary to use virtualized containers instead of namespaced containers and have a service mesh integrated to encrypt pod traffic.

Finally, we collected seven basic Kubernetes practices based on materials from this and previous chapters that should help to get you moving in the right direction. In the upcoming chapter, we will continue exploring the world of Cloud Native and learn about Cloud Native architectures.

Questions

As we conclude, here is a list of questions for you to test your knowledge regarding this chapter's material. You will find the answers in the *Assessments* section of the *Appendix*:

1. Which of the following is another name for pod-to-pod network traffic?

    A. East-South

    B. North-East

    C. East-West

    D. North-South

2. What can be applied to restrict pod-to-pod traffic?

    A. `PodPolicy`

    B. `PodSecurityPolicy`

    C. `TrafficPolicy`

    D. `NetworkPolicy`

3. Which layers are part of the 4Cs of Cloud Native security?

    A. Cloud, Collocations, Clusters, Code

    B. Cloud, Clusters, Containers, Code

    C. Cloud, Collocations, Containers, Code

    D. Code, Controllers, Clusters, Cloud

4. Pod A is running in Namespace A and pod B is running in Namespace B. Can they communicate via their IP addresses?

    A. No, because different namespaces are isolated with a firewall

    B. Yes, but only if they are running on the same worker node

    C. Yes, if not restricted with `NetworkPolicy`

    D. No, because different namespaces have different IP **Classless Inter-Domain Routing (CIDR)** blocks

5. How do two containers in the same pod communicate?

    A. Via a network policy

    B. Via `localhost`

    C. Via the `NodeIP` Service

    D. Via the `ClusterIP` Service

6. Which of the following service types is typically used for internal pod-to-pod communication?

    A. `InternalIP`

    B. `LoadBalancer`

    C. `ClusterIP`

    D. `NodePort`

7. What can be used to encrypt pod-to-pod communication in a cluster?

    A. `NetworkPolicy`

    B. Service mesh

    C. `EncryptionPolicy`

    D. Security Service

8. Which of the following container types provides maximum isolation?

    A. Virtualized

    B. Namespaced

    C. Isolated

    D. Sandboxed

9. What can be used to restrict access to the Kubernetes API?

    A. Service mesh

    B. Helm

    C. Network policies

    D. RBAC

10. Why is it important to build your own container images?

    A. Newly built images are often smaller in size

    B. Due to copyrights and license restrictions

    C. Newly built images always include the newest packages

    D. Images found on the internet might include malware

11. Which of the following can be used to provide fault tolerance for pods (pick multiple)?

    A. Service

    B. Deployment

    C. Ingress

    D. StatefulSet

12. Why it is better to have three and not four control plane nodes?

    A. Because four nodes consume too many resources; three is enough

    B. An uneven number of nodes helps prevent split-brain situations

    C. More nodes make the overlay pod network slower

    D. More nodes introduce more operational burden for version upgrades

13. Why is it not recommended to use pod IP addresses in `ConfigMap` configurations?

    A. Because pods are ephemeral

    B. Because the pod IP is not reachable from the internet

    C.   Because pods are using an old IPv4 protocol

    D.   Because it is hard to remember IP addresses

14. What could be the reasons why a request forwarded to a running pod ends up in a timeout error (pick multiple)?

    A.   The Kubernetes API overloaded, affecting all pods

    B.   Network policy rules add additional network latency

    C.   A process in a pod is stuck and no `livenessProbe` is set

    D.   A process in a pod is still starting and no `readinessProbe` is set

15. Which RBAC entity is used to give an identity to an application?

    A.   `Role`

    B.   `ServiceAccount`

    C.   `RoleBinding`

    D.   `ServiceIdentity`

Further reading

To learn more about the topics that were covered in this chapter, take a look at the following resources:

- Network policies: `https://kubernetes.io/docs/concepts/services-networking/network-policies/`

- Network policies with miniKube Kubernetes: `https://minikube.sigs.k8s.io/docs/handbook/network_policy/`

- RBAC: `https://kubernetes.io/docs/reference/access-authn-authz/rbac/`

- Helm quickstart guide: `https://helm.sh/docs/intro/quickstart/`

- Kustomize: `https://kustomize.io/`

- YTT: `https://carvel.dev/ytt/`

- 4Cs of Cloud Native security: `https://kubernetes.io/docs/concepts/security/overview/`

- Recommended Kubernetes labels: `https://kubernetes.io/docs/concepts/overview/working-with-objects/common-labels/`

- Kubernetes in a production environment: `https://kubernetes.io/docs/setup/production-environment/`

Part 4:
Exploring Cloud Native

This part will explain in more detail what is behind cloud native, what makes an application cloud native, and which concepts should apply to cloud native applications, as well as how to deliver and operate such applications in modern environments.

This part contains the following chapters:

- *Chapter 9, Understanding Cloud Native Architectures*
- *Chapter 10, Implementing Telemetry and Observability in the Cloud*
- *Chapter 11, Automating Cloud Native Application Delivery*

9

Understanding Cloud Native Architectures

With this chapter, we are moving on to explore further aspects of Cloud Native in more detail. We will see which concepts are a part of Cloud Native and what is the architecture of Cloud Native, talk about **resiliency** and **autoscaling**, and get to know some of the best practices. This chapter covers further requirements of the *Cloud Native Architecture* domain of the **Kubernetes and Cloud Native Associate (KCNA)** exam, which makes up a total of 16% of questions.

This chapter has no practical part, so we won't perform any hands-on exercises, but it is still very important to understand it in order to pass the KCNA exam and advance in the field. We will focus on the following topics:

- Cloud Native architectures
- Resiliency and autoscaling
- Serverless
- Cloud Native best practices

If you've skipped the first two chapters of the book and you find some terms discussed here unclear, please go back and read *Chapters 1* and *2* to cover the gaps first.

Cloud Native architectures

In the first two chapters, we've already covered the definition of Cloud Native. Let's check it one more time for a quick recap.

> **Cloud Native**
>
> This is an approach to building and running applications on modern, dynamic infrastructures such as clouds. It emphasizes application workloads with high resiliency, scalability, a high degree of automation, ease of management, and observability.

Yet, despite the presence of the word *cloud*, a Cloud Native application is not strictly required to run in the cloud. It's an approach that can be followed when building and running applications also on-premises. And yes—you can also build resilient, scalable, highly automated applications on-premises that are Cloud Native, albeit not running in the cloud.

It is important to understand that simply picking a well-known public cloud provider and building on top of its service offerings (whether IaaS, PaaS, SaaS, or FaaS) does not mean your application automatically becomes Cloud Native. For example, if your application requires manual intervention to start then it cannot scale automatically, and it won't be possible to restart it automatically in case of failure, so it's not Cloud Native.

Another example: you have a web application consisting of a few microservices, but it is deployed and configured manually without any automation and thus cannot be easily updated. This is not a Cloud Native approach. If you forgot about microservices in the meantime, here is a definition one more time .

> **Microservices**
>
> These are small applications that work together as a part of a larger application or service. Each microservice could be responsible for a single feature of a big application and communicate with other microservices over the network. This is the opposite of monolithic applications, which bundle all functionality and logic in one big deployable piece (tightly coupled).

In practice, to implement a Cloud Native application, you'll most likely turn to microservices. Microservices are loosely coupled, which makes it possible to scale, develop, and update them independently from each other. Microservices solve many problems but they also add operational overhead as their number grows, and that is why many of the Cloud Native technologies such as Kubernetes and Helm aim to make microservices easy to deploy, manage, and scale.

Again, strictly speaking, you are not required to run microservices managed by Kubernetes to have Cloud Native architecture. But this combination of containerized, small, loosely coupled applications orchestrated by Kubernetes works very well and paves the way toward Cloud Native. It is much, much easier to implement resiliency, autoscaling, controllable rolling updates, and observability with Kubernetes and containers than doing so with many **virtual machines** (**VMs**) and homegrown shell scripts. Kubernetes is also infrastructure-agnostic, which makes it very attractive for many environments and use cases. It can run on bare-metal servers, on VMs, in public and private clouds, and could be consumed as a managed service or run in a hybrid environment consisting of cloud resources and on-premises data centers.

Now, before diving deeper into some of the aspects, let's see at a high level the benefits Cloud Native provides:

- **Reduced time to market (TTM)** – A high degree of automation and easy updates make it possible to deliver new Cloud Native application features rapidly, which offers a competitive advantage for many businesses.

- **Cost efficiency** – Cloud Native applications scale based on demand, which means paying only for resources required and eliminating waste.

- **Higher reliability** – Cloud Native applications can self-heal and automatically recover from failures. This means reduced system downtime, resulting in a better user experience.

- **Scalability and flexibility** – Microservices can be scaled, developed, and updated individually allowing us to handle various scenarios and provide more flexibility for development teams.

- **No vendor lock-in** – With the right approach and use of open source technologies, a Cloud Native application could be shifted between different infrastructures or cloud providers with minimum effort.

The list can be continued, but it should be enough to give you an idea of why most modern applications follow Cloud Native approaches and practices. Moving on, we will focus on some of the most important aspects of Cloud Native, such as resiliency and autoscaling.

Resiliency and autoscaling

As funny as it may sound, in order to design and build resilient systems, we need to expect things to fail and break apart. In other words, in order to engineer resilient systems, we need to engineer for failure and provide ways for applications and infrastructure to recover from failures automatically.

Resiliency

This characterizes an application and infrastructure that can automatically recover from failures. The ability to recover without manual intervention is often called *self-healing*.

We've already seen self-healing in action in *Chapter 6* when Kubernetes detected that the *desired state* and the *current state* were different and quickly spawned additional application replicas. This is possible thanks to the Kubernetes *reconciliation loop*.

There are, of course, ways to build resilient applications and infrastructure without Kubernetes. For example, the **Amazon Web Services (AWS)** public cloud offers **Autoscaling Groups**, which allow you to run a desired number of VMs in a group or increase and decrease the number automatically based on the load. In case of VM failure, it will be detected and reacted upon with the creation of a new VM. In case CPU utilization in the group reaches a certain, pre-defined threshold, new VMs can be provisioned to share the load. And this brings us to another important concept: autoscaling.

Autoscaling

This is an ability to add or reduce computing resources automatically to meet the current demand.

Needless to say, different cloud providers offer many options for configuring autoscaling today. It can be based on various metrics and conditions, where CPU or RAM utilization are just common examples.

Previously, in the times of traditional IT, applications and infrastructure were designed to account for peak system usage, and this resulted in highly underutilized hardware and high running costs. Autoscaling has been a huge improvement, and it became one of the most important features of Cloud Native.

When we talk about autoscaling, it applies to *both the application and the infrastructure it runs on*, because scaling one without another won't be sufficient. Let's consider the following example to explain—you manage multiple microservice applications running in a Kubernetes cluster that under typical load require 10 worker nodes to operate. If additional worker nodes are created and joined into the K8s cluster, there won't be any pods running on those new nodes until one of the following happens:

- The number of replicas of applications is increased so that new pods are created
- Some of the existing pods exit and get recreated by a controller (such as Deployment, StatefulSet, and so on)

That is because Kubernetes won't reschedule already running pods when a new node joins the cluster. So, it would be required to increase the number of microservice replicas besides adding new nodes. *Why won't simply adding more replicas be enough?* Doing so will eventually max out the CPU/RAM utilization and make Kubernetes nodes unresponsive as the payloads will be *fighting* for resources.

Scaling in general can also be distinguished into two types, as shown in *Figure 9.1*:

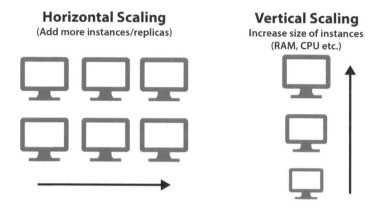

Figure 9.1 – Comparison of horizontal and vertical scaling

Let's look at this in more detail:

- **Horizontal**—When we add or reduce the number of instances (VMs or nodes), as in the preceding example. Horizontal scaling is also known as **scaling out** (adding new VMs) and **scaling in** (terminating VMs).

- **Vertical**—When we keep the number of instances the same but change their configuration (such as the number of vCPUs, GB of RAM, size of the disks, and so on). Vertical scaling is also known as **scaling up** (adding CPU/RAM capacity) and **scaling down** (reducing CPU/RAM capacity).

To keep it simple, you can memorize horizontal autoscaling as an automatic increase (or decrease) in numbers and vertical autoscaling as an increase (or decrease) in size. Cloud Native microservice architectures commonly apply horizontal autoscaling, whereas old monolithic applications were scaled vertically most of the time. Vertical autoscaling is also more restricting because even the largest flavors of VMs and bare-metal servers available today cannot go beyond certain technological limits. Therefore, scaling horizontally is the preferred way.

From the previous chapters, we already know that we can change the number of Deployment replicas with Kubernetes in just one simple command; however, that is not automatic, but a manual scaling. Apart from that, there are three mechanisms in Kubernetes that allow us to implement automatic scaling:

- **Horizontal Pod Autoscaler (HPA)**—This updates the workload resource (such as Deployment, StatefulSet) to add more pods when the load goes up and removes pods when the load goes down to match demand. HPA requires configuration of lower and upper bounds of replicas (for example, 3 replicas minimum and 10 maximum).

- **Vertical Pod Autoscaler (VPA)**—This updates the workload resource requests and limits for containers (CPU, memory, huge page size). It can reduce requests and limits of containers *over-requesting* resources and scale up requests and limits for *under-requesting* workloads based on historical usage over time. VPA does not change the number of replicas like HPA does, as shown in *Figure 9.2*. VPA also optionally allows us to define minimum and maximum request boundaries.

- **Cluster Autoscaler**—This adjusts the size of the Kubernetes cluster by adding or removing worker nodes when either there are pods that fail to run due to insufficient resources or there are underutilized nodes for an extended period of time and their pods can be placed on other nodes in the cluster. It is recommendable to limit the maximum number of nodes in the cluster to protect against making the cluster too large. Cluster Autoscaler also requires integration with your cloud provider to operate:

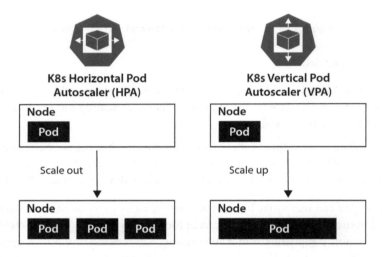

Figure 9.2 – Comparison of Kubernetes HPA and VPA

Those mechanisms are especially powerful as they get combined. As you remember, we need to scale both application and the infrastructure where it runs, so using only HPA or only using Cluster Autoscaler won't be sufficient. In fact, all three mechanisms can be used together, but this is a complex topic that you should not approach without getting enough K8s experience first. For the scope of KCNA, you only need to know what autoscaling is and which autoscaling mechanisms Kubernetes has to offer.

At the end of the day, autoscaling is a crucial part of Cloud Native that is required to strike a balance between workload performance and infrastructure size and costs.

Moving on, we are going to learn more about Serverless—an evolution of computing that gained adoption over the last years.

Serverless

In the very first chapter, we briefly touched on a definition of Serverless—a newer cloud delivery model that appeared around 2010 and is known as *Function as a Service* or *FaaS*.

> **Serverless**
>
> This is a computing model where code is written as small functions that are built and run without the need to manage any servers. Those functions are triggered by events (for example, the user clicked a button on the web page, uploaded a file, and so on).

Despite the name, the truth is that Serverless computing still relies on real hardware servers underneath. However, servers running the functions **are completely abstracted away** from the application development. In this model, the provider handles all operations that are required to run the code: provisioning, scaling, maintenance, security patching, and so on. Since you don't need to take care of servers ever, the model is called Serverless.

Serverless brings in several advantages besides a lack of routine server operations. The development team can simply upload code to the Serverless platform, and once deployed, the application and infrastructure it runs on will be scaled automatically as needed based on demand.

When a Serverless function idles, most cloud providers won't charge anything as with no events, there are no executions of the functions and thus no costs are incurred. If there are 10,000 events that trigger 10,000 function executions, then in most cases, their *exact execution times* will be billed by the provider. This is different from a typical *pay-as-you-go* VM in the cloud where you pay for all time the VM is running, regardless of the actual CPU/RAM utilization. A sample Serverless architecture is shown in *Figure 9.3*:

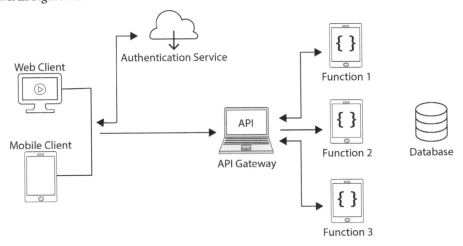

Figure 9.3 – Serverless architecture example

> **Note**
>
> An API Gateway is a part of Serverless that allows us to define endpoints for the REST API of an application and connect those endpoints with corresponding functions implementing the actual logic. API Gateway typically handles user authentication and access control and often provides additional features for observability.

It's worth mentioning that many popular programming languages (Java, Golang, Python, and Ruby, to name a few) are supported by the cloud providers offering Serverless today, yet not all providers allow the use of our own container images. In fact, most public cloud providers offering Serverless today rely on their own proprietary technology. So, if you develop a Serverless application for **AWS Lambda** (the Serverless offering of AWS) then migrating it to **Google Cloud Functions** (the Serverless offering of Google Cloud) will require considerable effort.

Besides fully managed cloud Serverless platforms, there are a few open source alternatives available today that reduce the risk of vendor lock-in. For example, the following Serverless frameworks can be installed on top of Kubernetes with functions code packaged and run as containers:

- **OpenFaaS**
- **CloudEvents**
- **Knative**
- **Fn**

Knative and CloudEvents are currently curated **Cloud Native Computing Foundation** (**CNCF**) projects.

To wrap it up, FaaS can be seen as an evolution of cloud computing models (IaaS, PaaS, and SaaS) that fits well for Cloud Native architectures. While the Serverless market share is still growing, it has become apparent that it will not replace common VMs and managed platform offerings due to limitations that we briefly cover here:

- To persist data, Serverless applications must interact with other stateful components. So, unless you never need to keep the state, you'll have to involve databases and other storage options.

- In most cases, there is little to no control over runtime configuration. For instance, you won't be able to change OS or **Java Virtual Machine** (**JVM**) parameters when using FaaS offered by a cloud provider.

- **Cold start**—Initialization of container or infrastructure where the function code will execute takes some time (typically in the range of tens of seconds). If a particular function has not been invoked for a while, the next invocation will suffer from a cold-start delay. The way to go around it is to call the functions periodically to keep them *pre-warmed*.

- Monitoring, logging, and debugging Serverless applications is often harder. While you don't need to take care of servers and metrics such as CPU or disk utilization, the ways to debug functions at runtime are limited. You won't be able to run code line by line as you would do locally in an IDE.

- Risk of vendor lock-in. As already mentioned, FaaS offerings are not standardized, and thus migrating from one provider to another would require significant work.

The list is not exhaustive, but hopefully, it gives you an idea of why you should not necessarily rush your development team to move completely to Serverless. Both cloud provider and open source FaaS offerings have improved a lot in the recent years, so there is a chance that many of the limitations will be resolved in the near future.

Again, we are diving deeper here than required to pass KCNA. You'll not be questioned about the limitations of Serverless, but you need to understand the concept of the billing model and be able to name a few projects that let you operate your own FaaS on top of Kubernetes.

In the last section of the chapter, we're going to summarize some key points we've learned about Cloud Native.

Cloud Native best practices

As the world is changing fast, users get more and more demanding, and the IT landscape has to change in order to meet expectations. Today, not many people tolerate waiting for a web page to open if it takes 30 seconds and people complain if online banking is not working for a whole hour long.

Cloud Native has signified major improvements in the field by bringing a new approach to building and running applications. Cloud Native applications are designed to expect failures and automatically recover from most of them. A lot of focus is put on making **both the application and the infrastructure resilient**. This can be achieved in many ways with or without Kubernetes. If using Kubernetes, make sure to run multiple control plane and worker nodes spread across different failure domains such as your cloud provider **availability zones (AZs)**. Always run at least two replicas (pods) of an application using a controller such as Deployment and make sure to spread them across the topology of your cluster. In the case of pod failure, the K8s reconciliation loop will kick in and self-heal the application.

Some companies have taken further steps to improve resiliency by introducing random failures across the infrastructure, allowing them to detect weak spots that need improvement or system redesign. For example, Netflix has become known for its **Chaos Monkey** tool that randomly terminates VMs and containers in order to incentivize engineers to build highly resilient services.

Next on the list is autoscaling—a crucial element for both performance and cost efficiency. Again, autoscaling must be implemented for **both the application and the infrastructure**. If running Kubernetes, make sure to set up at least HPA and Cluster Autoscaler. And don't forget to configure resource requests and limits for all workloads, as it helps K8s to schedule pods in an optimal way.

When it comes to application architecture, apply the principle of *loose coupling*—develop microservices performing small tasks working together as a part of a larger application. Consider event-driven Serverless architecture if that fits your scenarios. In many cases, Serverless might be more cost-efficient and require almost zero operations.

When it comes to roles, we've already learned in *Chapter 2* that organizations need to hire the right people for the job. This is not only about hiring DevOps and site reliability engineers to handle infrastructure, but it is also about team collaboration and corporate culture supporting constant change and experimentation. Learnings that come along provide valuable insights and lead to improvements in architecture and system design.

Furthermore, we briefly mentioned before that Cloud Native applications should feature a high degree of automation and ease of management. In *Chapter 11*, we'll see in detail how automation helps shipping software faster and more reliably. And in the upcoming *Chapter 10*, we'll discuss telemetry and observability.

Summary

In this chapter, we've learned about Cloud Native architectures, applications, and their features. Not every application that runs in the cloud automatically becomes Cloud Native. In fact, Cloud Native principles can be successfully applied also on-premises and not just in the cloud. We've briefly discussed the benefits of Cloud Native and in-depth about two core features—**resiliency** and **autoscaling**. While Cloud Native applications do not strictly require Kubernetes to run them, K8s makes things much easier with its *self-healing* capabilities and multiple autoscaling mechanisms: **HPA**, **VPA**, and **Cluster Autoscaler**.

Next, we covered Serverless or FaaS—a newer, event-driven computing model that comes with autoscaling and requires almost no operations at all. With Serverless, we are not responsible for any OS, security patching, or server life cycle. Serverless is also billed based on the actual usage calculated by the number of actual function invocations and the time they run. Serverless technologies can be leveraged to implement Cloud Native applications; however, be aware of their limitations.

Finally, we summarized the points about Cloud Native that we've learned in this chapter and previously, in *Chapter 2*. In the upcoming chapter, we will focus on monitoring Cloud Native applications and see how telemetry and observability can be implemented.

Questions

As we conclude, here is a list of questions for you to test your knowledge regarding this chapter's material. You will find the answers in the *Assessments* section of the *Appendix*:

1. Which of the following helps to get better resiliency with Kubernetes?

    A. Resource requests

    B. Multi-container pods

    C. Reconciliation loop

    D. Ingress controller

2. Which of the following Kubernetes autoscalers allows us to automatically increase and decrease the number of pods based on the load?

    A. VPA

    B. HPA

    C. RPA

    D. Cluster Autoscaler

3. Which of the following Kubernetes autoscalers adjusts container resource requests and limits based on statistical data?

    A. VPA

    B. HPA

    C. RPA

    D. Cluster Autoscaler

4. Why is it important to downscale the application and infrastructure?

    A. To reduce the possible attack surface

    B. To avoid hitting cloud provider limits

    C. To reduce network traffic

    D. To reduce costs when computation resources are idling

5. What best describes horizontal scaling?

    A. Adding more CPU to the same service instance

    B. Adding more replicas/instances of the same service

    C. Adding more RAM to the same service instance

    D. To schedule pods to different nodes where other pods already running

6. Which scaling approach is preferred for Cloud Native applications?

    A. Cluster scaling

    B. Cloud scaling

    C. Vertical scaling

    D. Horizontal scaling

7. Which of the following projects allow us to operate our own Serverless platform on Kubernetes (pick multiple)?

    A. KubeVirt

    B. KEDA

    C. Knative

    D. OpenFaaS

8. What characterizes Serverless computing (pick multiple)?

    A. Servers are not needed anymore

    B. It supports all programming languages

    C. It is event-based

    D. The provider takes care of server management

9. What is correct about scaling microservices?

    A. Individual microservices can be scaled in and out

    B. Only all microservices can be scaled in and out at once

    C. Microservices do not need to be scaled—only the infrastructure needs to be

    D. Microservices are best scaled up

10. Which application design principle works best with Cloud Native?

   A. Self-healing
   B. Tight coupling
   C. Decoupling
   D. Loose coupling

11. What describes a highly resilient application and infrastructure?

   A. Ability to automatically shut down in case of issues
   B. Ability to automatically recover from most failures
   C. Ability to preserve the state in case of failure
   D. Ability to perform rolling updates

12. What represents the smallest part of a Serverless application?

   A. Gateway
   B. Method
   C. Container
   D. Function

13. Which of the following is a correct statement about Serverless?

   A. It is only billed for the actual usage
   B. It is free as no servers are involved
   C. It is billed at a constant hourly price
   D. It is billed the same as IaaS services

14. Which of the following features do Cloud Native applications have (pick multiple)?

   A. High scalability
   B. High efficiency
   C. High resiliency
   D. High portability

15. What should normally be scaled in order to accommodate the load?

    A. The application and the infrastructure it runs on

    B. The load balancer and ingress

    C. The number of application pods

    D. The number of Kubernetes worker nodes

16. Which resiliency testing tool can be used to randomly introduce failures in the infrastructure?

    A. Chaos Monster

    B. Chaos Kube

    C. Chaos Donkey

    D. Chaos Monkey

Further reading

To learn more about the topics that were covered in this chapter, take a look at the following resources:

- Autoscaling: `https://glossary.cncf.io/auto-scaling/`
- Kubernetes HPA walkthrough: `https://kubernetes.io/docs/tasks/run-application/horizontal-pod-autoscale-walkthrough/`
- Kubernetes Cluster Autoscaler: `https://github.com/kubernetes/autoscaler`
- Chaos Monkey: `https://github.com/Netflix/chaosmonkey`
- OpenFaaS: `https://www.openfaas.com/`
- Knative: `https://knative.dev/docs/`

10

Implementing Telemetry and Observability in the Cloud

As we already know, Cloud Native applications typically consist of multiple small services that communicate over the network. Cloud Native apps are frequently updated and replaced with newer versions and in this chapter, we emphasize the need to monitor and optimize them based on observations for best performance with cost in mind.

This chapter covers further requirements from *Cloud Native Observability* domain of KCNA exam that makes up 8% of the total exam questions. The following are the topics we're going to focus on:

- Telemetry and observability
- Prometheus for monitoring and alerting
- FinOps and cost management

Let's get started!

Telemetry and observability

With the evolution of traditional monolithic architectures towards distributed loosely coupled microservice architectures, the need for detailed high-quality telemetry quickly became apparent. Before elaborating any further, let's first define what **Telemetry** is in the context of IT infrastructure.

> Telemetry
>
> Refers to monitoring and collection of data about system performance for analysis that helps identify issues. Telemetry is a broad term for **logs**, **metrics**, and **traces** that are also known as telemetry types or signals.

With Cloud Native applications being distributed by design, the ability to track and trace all communication between the parts plays a major role for troubleshooting, finding bottlenecks and providing insights on how application performs.

All three telemetry signals (**logs**, **metrics** and **traces**) help us to better understand the state of the application and infrastructure at any given point of time and take a corrective action if needed.

> **Observability**
>
> Is the capability to continuously generate insights based on telemetry signals from the observed system. In other words, an observable system is the one, the state of which is clear with the *right data* provided at the *right time* to make the *right decision*.

Let's explain what this *right data* at the *right time* to make the *right decision* means with an example. Consider you are operating microservices on Kubernetes with most of the services persisting data in a database layer backed by **Persistent Volumes** (**PV**).

Obviously, you need to make sure that all databases are operational and that there is enough disk space available on the storage appliance serving the PVs. If you only collect and analyze the *logs* of the services, that will not be enough to make decision when the storage capacity should be extended. For instance, services using databases can crash suddenly because they cannot write to their databases anymore. Logs of the databases will point to the fact that the storage space has run out and more capacity is urgently required.

In this case, the logs are helpful to find the culprit, but they are not exactly the right data provided at the right time. The *right data* would be continuous disk utilization metrics collected from the storage appliance. The *right time* would be predefined threshold (let's say appliance is 70% full) that gives operator enough time to make the *right decision* of extending or freeing the capacity. Informing operator that the database storage is 100% full and services are down at 2AM is clearly not the best way to go.

That is why relying on only one telemetry signal is almost never enough and we should have all three in place to ensure observability. Observability is one of the keys behind faster incident responses, increased productivity and optimal performance. However, having more information does not necessary translate into a more observable system. Sometimes, having too much information can have an opposite effect and make it harder to distinguish the valuable insights from the noise (e.g., excessive log records produced by the maximum debug level of an application).

Let's now see each of the telemetry signals in more details starting with logs.

> **Logs**
>
> Are events described as text which are recorded by an application, an operating system or an appliance (for example, firewall, load balancer, etc.).

The events that log records represent could be pretty much anything ranging from a service restart and user login to an API request with payload received or an execution of a certain method in code. Logs often include timestamp, text message and further information such as status codes, severity levels (DEBUG, INFO, WARNING, ERROR, CRITICAL), user ids and so on.

> **Note**
>
> The log severity levels as well as instructions on how to access container logs in Kubernetes have been discussed in detail in *Chapter 7* in section *Debugging applications in Kubernetes*. Make sure to go back, if you've skipped it before for any reason.

Below you'll find a sample log message recorded by Nginx webserver when processing an HTTP v1.1 GET request received from client with IP 66.211.65.62 on the 4th of October 2022:

```
66.211.65.62 - - [04/Oct/2022:19:12:14 +0600] "GET /?q=%E
0%A6%A6%E0%A7%8B%E0%A7%9F%E0%A6%BE HTTP/1.1" 200 4556 "-"
"Mozilla/5.0 (compatible; Googlebot/2.1; +http://www.google.
com/bot.html)"
```

Additional information can be derived from the message, such as:

- response status code 200 (HTTP OK)

- the number of bytes sent to the client 4556

- the URL and query string /?q=%E0%A6%A6%E0%A7%8B%E0%A7%9F%E0%A6%

- as well as user agent Mozilla/5.0 (compatible; Googlebot/2.1; +http://www.google.com/bot.html) that in fact tells us that the request is done by Google's web crawler.

Depending on the application, the log format can be adjusted to only include the information you'd like and skip any unnecessary details.

Next on the signals list are metrics. Let's figure out what they are.

> **Metrics**
>
> Are regular measurements that describe the performance of an application or a system over the course of time in a time-series format.

Common examples include metrics like CPU, RAM utilization, number of open connections or response time. If you think about it, single, irregular measurements do not provide much value or insight about the state of the system. There might be a short spike in utilization that is over in less than a minute, or the other way around: utilization dropping for some time.

With single measurements, it is not possible to make any prediction or analyze how the application or the system behaves. With time-series, we can analyze how one or another metric has changed, determine trends and patters, and envision upcoming changes. That is why metrics should be collected at a regular, short intervals typically in a range between 30 seconds to a few minutes. Time-series can also be plotted as a graph for visual representation as shown on *Figure 10.1* below:

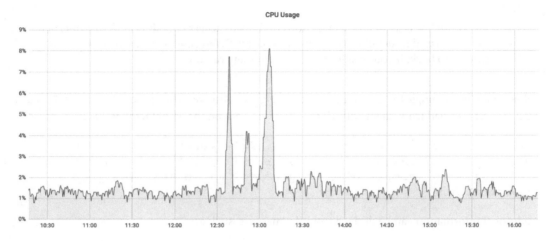

Figure 10.1 – CPU usage metric visualization (X = time, Y = utilization).

While it looks like there been a huge increase in CPU usage between 12:30 to 13:15 according to the graph, the maximum utilization over the period shown was always under 10% suggesting that the system is heavily underutilized. Basic metrics like CPU, memory, or disk usage should always be collected, but often they are not enough to make the *right decisions*.

Therefore, it is recommended to collect multiple application-specific metrics which could include number of API requests per minute, number of messages waiting in a queue, request response times, number of open connections, and so on. Some of those metrics can be well suited to making right autoscaling decisions and some to provide valuable insights on application performance.

That's it about metrics for now. Let's continue with request tracing as next.

> **Tracing**
> Is a complete tracking of the requests passing through the components of a distributed system. It allows to see which components are involved in the processing of a particular request, how long the processing takes, and any additional events that happen along. *Traces* are the results of tracing requests.

Now imagine the following situation. You are investigating longer response times of a distributed, microservice based application you operate, yet the number of requests or load has not changed much. Since most of the application requests traverses' multiple services, you'll need to verify each and every service to find the one (or several ones) that are not performing well. However, if you integrate a tracing utility such as **Jaeger** or **Zipkin**, it would allow you to trace requests and store and analyze the results. Traces would show which service is having longer response times and might be slowing the whole application down. The traces collected can then be viewed in a dashboard such as the one shown on *Figure 10.2* below:

Figure 10.2 – example trace view in Jaeger dashboard.

All-in-all, tracing contributes a lot to observability. It helps to understand the flow of traffic and detect the bottlenecks or issues quickly. Along with logs and metrics, the three telemetry types are a must for monitoring of modern applications and infrastructure. Without those, operators are *blind* and cannot be sure that all systems are operational and perform as expected. It might take some effort and time to implement the telemetry and observability right, but it always pays off as eventually it will save you a lot of time when it comes to troubleshooting problems.

Speaking about implementation – there is a CNCF project called **OpenTelemetry** or **OTel** for short. It provides a set of standardized vendor-agnostic APIs, SDKs and tools to ingest, transform and send data to an observability backend. Support for a large number of open-source and commercial protocols and programming languages (*C++*, *Java*, *Go*, *Python*, *PHP*, *Ruby*, *Rust* and more) makes it easy to incorporate telemetry into practically any application. It is not strictly required for the scope of KCNA, but if you'd like to know more about it – there will be links in the *Further Reading* section below.

Moving on, in the next section we'll learn about **Prometheus** – number one tool for Cloud Native observability.

Prometheus for monitoring and alerting

After its initial appearance in 2012, Prometheus quickly gained popularity with its rich functionality and **Time Series Database** (**TSDB**) that allowed to persisting metrics for querying, analysis, and predictions. Interestingly, Prometheus was inspired by Google's **Borgmon** – tool used for monitoring Google's **Borg** – the predecessor of Kubernetes.

In 2016, Prometheus was accepted as the second CNCF project (after K8s) that has reached *Graduated* status by the year 2018. Today, Prometheus is considered an industry standard for monitoring and alerting and widely used with Kubernetes and other CNCF projects.

But enough history, let's get to the point. First, what is a TSDB?

> **TSDB**
>
> Is a database optimized for storage of data with timestamps. The data could be measurements or events that are tracked and aggregated over time. In case of Prometheus, the data are metrics collected regularly from applications and parts of the infrastructure. The metrics are kept in Prometheus TSDB and can be queried with its own, powerful *PromQL* query language.

How are the metrics being collected? In general, there are two approaches on collecting monitoring metrics:

- **Pull** – when a (micro-)service exposes an HTTP endpoint with metrics data, that is periodically *scraped (collected)* by the monitoring software. Commonly, it is a /metrics URL that is called with a simple HTTP GET request. This is the dominant way how Prometheus works. The service should make the metrics available and keep them up-to-date and Prometheus should make GET requests against /metrics to fetch the data regularly.

- **Push** – opposite of pull, the service or an application should send the metrics data to the monitoring software. Also supported by Prometheus with Pushgateway and done with HTTP PUT requests. Helpful for the cases when service metrics cannot be *scrapped (pulled)* due to network restrictions (service behind a firewall or NAT gateway) or simply when the source of the metric has very short lifespan (e.g., quick batch job).

When we say *metrics data*, it means not just the metric name and value but also a timestamp and often additional labels. Labels indicate certain attributes of a metric and can hold the hostname of a server where the metric was scraped, the name of an application or pretty much anything else. Labels are very helpful for grouping and querying the metrics data with Prometheus' PromQL language. Let's see the following metric for an example:

```
nginx_ingress_controller_requests{
cluster="production",
container="controller",
controller_class="k8s.io/ingress-nginx",
```

```
endpoint="metrics",
exported_namespace="kcna",
exported_service="kcnamicroservice",
host="kcnamicroservice.prd.kcna.com",
ingress="kcnamicroservice",
instance="100.90.111.22:10254",
job="kube-system-ingress-nginx-controller-metrics",
method="GET",
namespace="kube-system",
path="/",
pod="kube-system-ingress-nginx-controller-7bc4747dcf-4d246",
prometheus="kube-monitoring/collector-kubernetes",
status="200"} 273175
```

Here, `nginx_ingress_controller_requests` is the name of the metric, `273175` is the value of the metric (representing number of requests) and everything else between { } are the labels. As you can see, labels are crucial to narrow down the metric scope, which service it applies to, or what exactly it represents. In this example, it shows the count of HTTP `GET` requests that were responded with HTTP `200 OK` for the service called `kcnamicroservice` located in `kcna` namespace.

One other great feature of Prometheus is the dashboard that lets us visualize the data from TSDB directly in the Prometheus UI. While it is very easy to plot graphs with it, its functionality is somewhat limited and that is why many people use **Grafana** for visualization and metrics analytics.

Now let's think for a moment how we could collect metrics with Prometheus from applications that we cannot modify? We are talking about services that weren't developed within your company and the ones that don't expose the metrics on a `/metrics` endpoint. This also applies to software that does not come with a webserver such as databases and message buses or even for basic OS stats (CPU, RAM, disk utilization). The solution for such cases is called Prometheus **Exporter**.

Prometheus Exporter

Is a small tool that bridges the gap between the Prometheus server and applications that don't natively export metrics. Exporters aggregate custom metrics from a process or a service in the format supported by Prometheus and expose them over `/metrics` endpoint for collection.

Essentially, an exporter is a minimalistic webserver that knows how to capture metrics from an application that must be monitored and transforms those into Prometheus format for collection. Let's take PostgreSQL database as an example. Natively it does not expose any metrics, but we can run an exporter along with it that would query the DB and provide observability data that will be pulled into Prometheus TSDB. If run on Kubernetes, the typical way to place an exporter is to put it in the same Pod with the service monitored as a *Sidecar* container (in case you missed it, *Sidecar* containers are explained in *Chapter 5*).

Today, you'll find a ton of ready-to-use exporters for popular software such as *MySQL*, *Redis*, *Nginx*, *HaProxy*, *Kafka* and more. However, if there is no exporter available – it is not a big deal to write one own using any popular programming language with Prometheus client libraries.

Speaking about Kubernetes and Prometheus, there is a seamless integration between the two. Prometheus has *out-of-the-box* capabilities to monitor Kubernetes and automatically discover the service endpoints of the workloads you run in your K8s cluster. Besides Kubernetes, there is also support for various PaaS and IaaS offerings including those from Google Cloud, Microsoft Azure, Amazon Web Services and many other.

With that, we've covered the part about monitoring with Prometheus and before moving on to the alerting, let's have a look at *Figure 10.3* first:

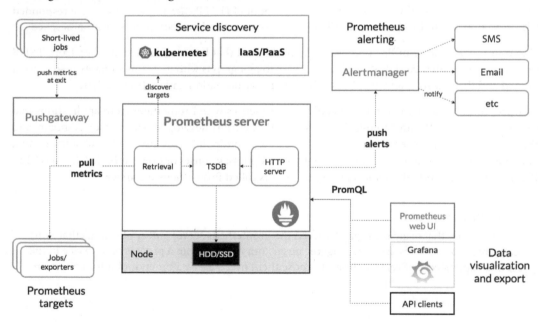

Figure 10.3 – Prometheus architecture.

As you can see, Prometheus server will pull metrics from its *targets* that can be statically configured or discovered dynamically with service discovery. Short-lived jobs or services behind NAT can also push their metrics via `Pushgateway`. The metrics can be queried, displayed, and visualized with `PromQL` in *Prometheus web UI* or third-party tools.

Moving on, we are going to learn about Prometheus **Alertmanager** and its notification capabilities.

> **Alerts**
>
> Are reactive elements of a monitoring system triggered by a metric change or a crossing of a certain threshold.

Alerts are used to notify team or an engineer on duty about the change of state in an application or an infrastructure. The notification can take a form of an e-mail, SMS or a chat message as an example. Alertmanager, as you already guessed, is the component of Prometheus responsible for the alerts and notifications.

An alert is normally triggered when a certain metric (or a combination of multiple metrics) has crossed a predefined threshold and stayed above or beyond it for some minutes. Alert definitions are based on Prometheus expression language and accept mathematical operations which allows flexible definition of conditions. In fact, a quite unique feature of Prometheus is the ability to predict when a metric will reach a certain threshold and raise an alert early, before it actually happens. This way, you can define an alert that will notify you five days in advance before a host runs of disk space, as an example. This is possible thanks to Prometheus TSDB that keeps time-series and allows analyzing the data and its rate of change.

Overall, Prometheus is an ultimate solution for monitoring in the Cloud Native era. It is often used to monitor both Kubernetes itself and workloads that run on top of Kubernetes. Today you'll find plenty of software that supports Prometheus natively by exposing metrics data via `/metrics` endpoint in the Prometheus format. Client libraries available in many languages make it possible to integrate Prometheus support directly in your own applications. This process is sometimes called **direct instrumentation** as it introduces native support of Prometheus. For applications and software that does not offer native support, you are likely to find exporters that extract the data and offer it in Prometheus metric format for collection.

Now, some of you probably cannot wait to make hands dirty with Prometheus, but in fact we've already covered it in more details than it is required to pass KCNA exam. Nevertheless, you are encouraged to check *Further Reading* section and try deploying Prometheus onto our miniKube K8s cluster yourself. And for now, we're moving on to the topic of cost management.

FinOps and cost management

With rapid transition from traditional data centers and collocation towards cloud, it has quickly became apparent that cloud services might be pretty expensive. In fact, if you'd see a bill of a public cloud provider, you'll often find that *everything* is metered and *everything* costs money: cross availability zone traffic and Internet traffic, number of objects or usage of space, number of API requests, Internet IPs, different VM flavors, tiered storage and additional IOPS, storage of VMs that are shut down and the list goes on and on. Sometimes, prices also vary from region to region making it hard to estimate the costs in advance. This has led to the appearance of FinOps in the recent years.

> FinOps
> Is a cloud financial management discipline and cultural practice. It helps organizations to get the maximum business value based on collaboration of engineering, finance, technology and business teams to make data-driven spending decisions.

Where DevOps puts a lot of focus on collaboration between *Development* and *Operations*, FinOps adds *Finance* to the mix. It helps the teams to manage their cloud spending and stresses the need of collaboration between engineering and business teams as a part of continuous improvement and optimization process. While you don't need to know the details for the scope of KCNA exam, you're still encouraged to check about FinOps in the *Further Reading* section.

When we talk about cloud, by default we assume that we can provision and terminate resources such as virtual machines at any time we want. And we only pay for the time the VM was running. This is known as **on-demand** capacity or on-demand pricing model, and this is the most popular way to consume cloud services today. You use it – you pay for it, if you're running nothing – then nothing is charged.

However, there are two more options commonly offered by public cloud providers:

- **Reserved instances** – These are VMs or bare-metal servers that you reserve for a longer period of time (typically one or more years) and pay the costs up front. Reserved instances come with a very good discount (30-70%) from the regular, on-demand pricing, but you don't get the same flexibility. Meaning that you'll keep paying for reserved resources even if you don't need them.

- **Spot instances** (sometimes called **preemptible instances**) – are the instances that can be terminated (deleted) by the cloud provider at any point. Spot instances are leftover and spare capacities that providers offer with huge discounts (60-90%) from on-demand capacity. In some cases, you'll need to bid (as on auction) for Spot instances and as long as you're bidding more than the others your instance continues to run.

So, which instance type should you use?

There is no easy answer to this question as there are many variables that come into play and the answer varies from case to case. The rule of a thumb is to buy Reserved instances only for constant workloads or the minimal capacity that is always needed to run your applications. Spot instances can be used for non-critical workloads, batch processing and various non-real-time analytics. Workloads that can be restarted and completed later are a great fit for Spot. And on-demand can be used for everything else including temporarily scaling to accommodate higher loads. As you remember from the previous chapter, *Autoscaling* is one of the main features of Cloud Native architectures and this is where you'd normally use on-demand instances.

Yet effective cost management in cloud needs more than just right capacity type (on-demand/reserved/spot). The instances should also be of the right size (flavor). This is known as **Righsizing**.

> **Rightsizing**
> Is the continuous process of matching instance size to workload performance and capacity requirements with cost in mind.

We already know that autoscaling is crucial for cost efficiency, and autoscaling can be seen as a part of Rightsizing strategy. You don't want to run too many underutilized instances when the load is low and the opposite – not having enough instances to handle high load. Autoscaling should target the sweet spot between the capacity/performance and the associated infrastructure costs. But besides the number of instances, their size (number of CPUs, GBs of memory, network throughput, etc.) is also important.

For example, running 40 Kubernetes worker nodes as VMs with only 4 CPUs and 8 GB of RAM might cost you more than running 20 worker nodes with 8 CPUs and 16 GB RAM each despite the same total number of CPUs and RAM. Additionally, many providers offer instances based on different CPU generations and flavors optimized for specific workloads. Some instances might be optimized for high network throughput and some for low-latency disk operations and thus be better suited for your applications. All of that should be taken into consideration as a part of rightsizing strategy and cost management in the cloud.

Summary

In this chapter we've learned a lot about Telemetry and Observability. The three telemetry types or signals are *logs*, *metrics* and *traces* which provide valuable insights into the system observed from slightly different perspectives. An observable system is the one that is constantly monitored where we know the state based on the telemetry data that serves as evidence.

We've also learned about projects such as *OpenTelemetry* that can help with instrumentation and simplify the work needed to implement telemetry. Had a quick introduction to projects such as *Zipkin* and *Jaeger* for tracing and had a closer look at Prometheus – a fully featured monitoring platform.

Prometheus supports both *Push* and *Pull* operating models for metric collection, but dominantly uses *Pull* model to periodically scrape the metric data at (/metrics endpoint) and save it in TSDB in time-series format. Having metrics in TSDB allows us visualizing the data in software such as *Grafana* and define alerts that would notify us over the preferred channel when one or another metric is crossing the threshold defined.

Another great point about Prometheus is the Kubernetes integration. Prometheus supports automatic discovery of targets that are running in Kubernetes which makes operator's life easier. For software that doesn't natively provide metrics in Prometheus format it is possible to run exporters – small tools that aggregate the metrics from the service or an application and expose them in Prometheus format via /metrics endpoint for collection. If you are in control of the source code of applications you run – it is also possible to add support for Prometheus with a help of client libraries available in many programming languages. This is known as *direct instrumentation*.

Finally, we've got to know about FinOps and cost management in cloud. Most commonly, the so called *on-demand* capacities are consumed in the cloud. That means resources can be provisioned when needed and deleted when no longer required and only the time when they were running is billed. This is different from *Reserved* capacity when instances are paid in advance for longer periods of time. Reserved capacities come with very good discounts but will still cost money if unused. And *Spot* or *Preemptible* instances are spare capacity that cloud provider might just terminate at any time. They are the cheapest among three options, however, might not be the right choice for critical workloads that require maximum uptime.

Last, but not least, we've covered *Rightsizing*. It's a process of finding the best instance size and number of instances for current workload as a balance between performance requirements and cost.

Next chapter is about automation and delivery of Cloud Native applications. We will learn about best practices and see how we can ship better software faster and more reliably.

Questions

Correct answers can be found at __TBD__

1. Which of the following are valid telemetry signals (pick multiple)?

    A. Tracks

    B. Pings

    C. Logs

    D. Metrics

2. Which is the dominant operation model of Prometheus for metrics collection?

    A. Push

    B. Pull

    C. Commit

    D. Merge

3. Which of the following allows to collect metrics with Prometheus when native application support is missing?

    A. Running application in Kubernetes

    B. Installing Pushgateway

    C. Installing Alertmanager

    D. Installing application exporter

4. Which of the following signals does Prometheus collect?

    A. Logs

    B. Metrics

    C. Traces

    D. Audits

5. Which component can be used to allow applications to push metrics into Prometheus?

    A. Zipkin

    B. Grafana

    C. Alertmanager

    D. Pushgateway

6. Which telemetry signal fits best to see how request traverses a microservice-base application?

    A. Logs

    B. Traces

    C. Metrics

    D. Pings

7. Which software allows visualizing metrics stored in Prometheus TSDB?

    A. Zipkin

    B. Kibana

    C. Grafana

    D. Jaeger

8. Which software can be used for end-to-end tracing of distributed applications (pick multiple)?

    A. Prometheus

    B. Grafana

    C. Jaeger

    D. Zipkin

9. What makes it possible to query Prometheus metrics from the past?

    A. Alertmanager

    B. TSDB

    C. PVC

    D. Graphite

10. Which endpoint Prometheus collects metrics from by default?

    A. `/collect`

    B. `/prometheus`

    C. `/metric`

    D. `/metrics`

11. What is the format of Prometheus metrics?

    A. Timeseries

    B. Traces

    C. Spans

    D. Plots

12. Which of the following allows direct instrumentation for applications to provide metrics in Prometheus format?

    A. K8s service discovery

    B. Pushgateway

    C. Exporters

    D. Client libraries

13. A periodic job takes only 30 seconds to complete, but Prometheus scrape interval is 60 seconds. What is the best way to collect the metrics from such job?

    A. push the metrics to Pushgateway

    B. reduce scrape interval to 30 seconds

    C. reduce scrape interval to 29 seconds

    D. replace job with Kubernetes CronJob

14. Which of the following is a crucial part of Rightsizing?

    A. FinOps

    B. Reserved instances

    C. Autoscaling

    D. Automation

15. Which of the following should be taken into consideration when implementing Autoscaling?

    A. CPU utilization metric

    B. RAM utilization metric

    C. CPU + RAM utilization metrics

    D. CPU, RAM, and application specific metrics

16. Which of the following instance types are offered by many public cloud providers (pick multiple)?

    A. On-demand

    B. Serverless

    C. Spot

    D. Reserved

17. Which of the following instance types fits for constant workloads with no spikes in load that should run for few years straight?

    A. On-demand

    B. Serverless

    C. Spot

    D. Reserved

18. Which of the following instance types fits for batch processing and periodic jobs that can be interrupted if lowest price is the main priority?

    A. On-demand

    B. Serverless

    C. Spot

    D. Reserved

Further reading

- OpenTelemetry: https://opentelemetry.io/docs/

- Jaeger: https://www.jaegertracing.io/

- Grafana: https://grafana.com/grafana/

- Prometheus query language: https://prometheus.io/docs/prometheus/latest/querying/basics/

- Prometheus exporters: https://prometheus.io/docs/instrumenting/exporters/

- Kubernetes metrics for Prometheus: https://kubernetes.io/docs/concepts/cluster-administration/system-metrics/

- Introduction to FinOps: https://www.finops.org/

11

Automating Cloud Native Application Delivery

In this chapter we will focus on Cloud Native application lifecycle. We'll learn about best practices for development and delivery of Cloud Native apps and see how automation helps to *develop better* and *ship faster*.

This chapter covers everything you need to know about *Cloud Native Application Delivery* domain of KCNA exam that makes up 8% of the total exam questions. The following topics we're about to cover:

- Delivery of Cloud Native applications
- CI/CD and GitOps
- Infrastructure as a Code (IaC)

This is the last technically packed chapter of the book. You're almost ready to take the exam and become Kubernetes and Cloud Native associate. Carry on!

Delivery of Cloud Native applications

Modern applications are often developed at a high velocity which requires efficient and robust delivery processes. That is why Cloud Native applications delivery is a rather complex, but highly automated process consisting of multiple stages.

First, developers write code and commit it to a **Version Control System (VCS)** such as **Git**, **Mercurial** or **Subversion** with Git being de-facto standard today. The code is then *built*, *tested* and *released*. Automating those stages makes it possible to speed up the whole process of software delivery and make small, frequent, and well-tested software releases.

> **Release**
>
> Is a version of software including the changes (new features, enhancements, bugfixes, etc.) to be delivered to the users. Each release has **semantic versioning** where v1.0.0 commonly stands for the *first stable* release (More about semantic versioning can be found in *Further Reading* section).
>
> *To release* (as a verb) is also commonly used for describing the process of deploying to a production environment, e.g., making new software version available to the end users.

Strictly speaking, the application delivered doesn't have to be Cloud Native. However, with Cloud Native architectures that are often based on microservices, it is pretty much impossible to do all the *build-test-release* stages manually. Imagine for a moment you'd have to do it 30 times for 30 different microservices – slow, error prone, and tedious work. That is why automation became an essential part of modern application lifecycle and brought us many benefits including the following:

- Faster delivery times and more frequent updates
- More stable releases with automated processes
- More productivity as manual work minimized
- Fewer bugs with automated test runs
- Repeatable results

Obviously, there is more to it than just *build-test-release* as every service should also be deployed, operated and monitored as suggested on *Figure 11.1* below:

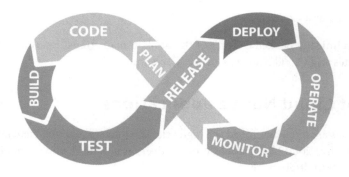

Figure 11.1 – modern application lifecycle.

This loop is infinite, and automation of the stages makes it possible to release the changes and updates even multiple times per day. In fact, it also saves a lot of developer's time so that they could focus on developing new features and fixing bugs. It should also be possible to roll back the changes easily and fast in case of any issues (one example of how to do it with Kubernetes and Helm was discussed previously in *Chapter 8*).

Now that we know about the basics of Cloud Native application delivery, let's dive into CI/CD and GitOps.

CI/CD and GitOps

You might have heard it before, **CI** stands for **Continuous Integration** and **CD** for **Continuous Delivery** or sometimes **Continuous Deployment**.

> **Continuous Integration**
>
> Is a practice and process automation targeting developers. With CI, code changes are regularly *built*, *tested* and *integrated* into a shared repository (branch/trunk/etc.)

CI is viewed as a solution to the problem of having too many changes in development at once that might conflict with each other and being hard *to merge*. The ultimate goal is to ensure that the software is always in the working state and in case automated tests fail, the team has to fix the problem first, before continuing with development.

> **Continuous Delivery**
>
> Usually refers to an automation in the pipeline where the tested code changes mark a *release* that is uploaded to a package repository or container image. From there on, the image or a package can be *deployed* after approval.

Continuous Delivery can be seen as a way to align development and business teams and its purpose is to ensure that it would take minimum time and effort to deploy new code. In Continuous Delivery, there is normally an approval that should be done by a human before the release can be deployed to a production environment.

> **Continuous Deployment**
>
> Is a further automation for deploying changes from the source repository to a development, testing or production environments. It is essentially Continuous Delivery except deployment happens automatically when all the tests and checks have passed.

Schematically, this can be seen as follows in *Figure 11.2*:

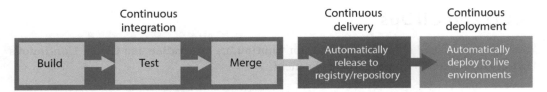

Figure 11.2 – the CI/CD/CD pipelines.

Needless to say, there are many ways how to implement CI or CD automation in any organization, and there is no *single right way* of doing it. We can use different tools, introduce custom checks or deployment schedules, involve various stakeholders for approval, etc. However, one thing that will always be present is a **Pipeline**.

Ci/CD Pipeline

Is a top-level component which implements automation processes. Pipeline typically consists of multiple jobs and stages where output of one job or stage can be used as an input for the next job/stage. Pipeline might invoke multiple tools to compile the code, run unit tests, perform code analysis, create binaries, package code into container and so on.

Why we often refer to pipelines when talking about CI/CD is because many processes in software delivery have sequential steps that are executed one after another. You can think of it as a pipe where the source code comes in on one side and built and tested package come out on another side. Or, possibly, the package is being deployed on the other end. And this process repeats all over again as previously shown on *Figure 11.1*.

Speaking about the packages and change sets, it is considered best to release and deploy small changes often, rather than infrequently do big changes, especially when implementing *Continuous Deployment*. When the change set is small, there is much lower risk of things going wrong, so it is recommended to release and deploy small, tested changes regularly instead of deploying many changes together as *big bang* once in a while.

Now that we've covered the concept, let's mention few tools that can help us to implement CI/CD automation. There are many tools available today and despite different feature sets, they all can be used to build and run CI/CD pipelines. Some might be a better fit for your tech stack with better support for one or another VCS, some provide Kubernetes and various IaaS/PaaS integrations, and some are only available *as a service*. CI/CD system offered as a service means provider will take care of its maintenance, updates, scaling and so on for a monthly fee. Make sure to conduct some research before picking one for your team.

Listed here are a few popular CI/CD systems that you might want to check out:

- **ArgoCD**
- **Jenkins**
- **Gitlab CI**
- **Tekton**
- **GitHub Actions**
- **Spinnaker**
- **FluxCD**
- **GoCD**
- **CircleCI**
- **TravisCI**

> **Note**
> The presence of *CI* or *CD* in the names does not mean you can only implement *CI* or *CD* with that tool. Some of the tools could be used for implementing both *CI* and *CD* and some not.

GitOps

Previously, we've learned about *DevOps, DevSecOps, FinOps,* and now there is one more *Ops* to go – **GitOps**. Introduced in 2017, it is a further evolution of industry best practices and CI/CD applied for modern infrastructure and Cloud Native application delivery.

> **GitOps**
> Is an operational framework combining DevOps practices such as Git version control, collaboration, compliance, declarative configuration, and CI/CD.

Figure 11.3 – overview of GitOps.

GitOps based upon three core elements:

Merge Requests (MR) + Infrastructure as a Code (IaC) + CI/CD

1. **Merge Requests** are the change mechanism offered by Git version control system. MR is where the team collaborates and does code reviews and leaves comments. When a MR is approved, the changes are typically merged into the *main* (`master`) branch and commit messages along with comments serve as an audit log.

2. **IaC** is the topic of the upcoming section, but at a high-level, it is a practice of describing desired infrastructure configuration and setup as a code that is kept in Git repository. IaC is an example of *declarative configuration* that serves as the *source of truth* for your infrastructure.

3. **CI/CD** is an essential part of GitOps and its purpose is not just to automate the delivery stages described in the previous section, but also to avoid manual changes and eliminate **infrastructure drift**. Manual changes are not tolerated with GitOps.

Infrastructure (configuration) drift

Is when the real-time state of the infrastructure does not match what has been defined in your *IaC* configuration. Drift can be caused by manual human actions, applications making unintended changes, software bugs and other reasons.

Drift can cause uncertainty, application failures, and even introduce security holes. That is why eliminating infrastructure drift is very important and GitOps does this job well if implemented right. If someone did manual changes, then latest on the next MR being accepted and merged into the *source of truth* Git repository those manual changes will be overwritten and drift will be eliminated.

Furthermore, some advanced GitOps tools such as *ArgoCD*, *FluxCD* and *Jenkins X* have the capability to constantly watch the changes in Git repository and propagate those to a connected live environment. The system will resync and bring environment to the desired state automatically – any manual change on the live environment will be overwritten in a matter of seconds. New changes coming from code merged in Git will be deployed automatically and fast.

One thing to keep in mind is that *ArgoCD*, *FluxCD* and *Jenkins X* require Kubernetes cluster to run on. That does not mean it is impossible to implement GitOps without Kubernetes, but implementing it with Kubernetes is much easier due to developed ecosystem and its ultimate *reconciliation loop* functionality that brings cluster resources to the desired state (see *Chapter 5* in case you've forgotten).

Let's consider the following example to see how GitOps and K8s can complement each other. Imagine your team operates microservices on Kubernetes and specification definitions are stored in Git repository which acts as the source of truth. You use ArgoCD for GitOps that deploys K8s manifests to the target Kubernetes clusters. A new colleague has recently started in your team and got the task to decommission a microservice that is no longer needed.

Unfortunately, the new colleague was not fully onboarded with the processes and started deleting Kubernetes resources manually with kubectl which is a GitOps anti-pattern. By mistake, he/she has deleted wrong K8 Deployment which belonged to another microservice in production environment. Kubernetes controller loop kicked in and started terminating Pods managed by that Deployment, bringing wrong microservice down. Luckily, ArgoCD had auto-sync turned on and detected that the state of both affected microservices has drifted away from the definition located in Git repository. ArgoCD kicked in and quickly created missing Deployment and other manually deleted resources. The service quickly came back online. A colleague has opened a MR to change the desired state in Git correctly which got approved by the teammates and merged. In an event of wrong changes been merged into Git, it is just as easy to roll them back by simply reverting the respective commit.

Figure 11.4 demonstrates an example GitOps process:

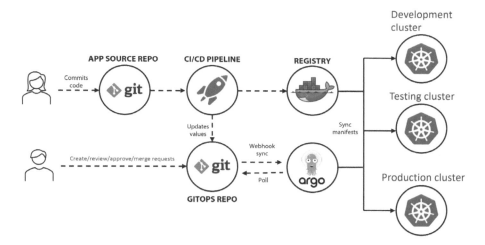

Figure 11.4 – CI/CD and GitOps example with ArgoCD and Kubernetes.

If you decide to implement similar process in your team or organization, consider the fact that ArgoCD is suitable for GitOps and CD, but for implementing CI, you'll need an additional tool. That could be, for example, Argo Workflows or Gitlab CI or similar.

To wrap it up, GitOps is a very powerful framework that primarily focuses on CD and CI. It allows to deliver software at a very fast pace, maximize stability, increase productivity and free up productive time for the team as manual operations are automated. All configurations are transparent, auditable and reviewable. For best results and maximum efficiency, you also need to implement CI to automate testing and building of the applications.

Finally, let's talk about IaC in more detail.

Infrastructure as a Code (IaC)

IaC is the practice of managing and provisioning infrastructure in a declarative way via definition files. You describe the desired state in definition files and let a tool apply the configuration to your environment.

Don't worry, despite the presence of the word *Code* that does not mean you'll need to learn how to code in **C++** or **Java** or other advanced programming language. Most IaC tools allow configuration to be defined in *YAML* or a similar human-readable markup language.

IaC automates and replaces manual operations for infrastructure configuration and provisioning. Essentially, all actions that can be done using your cloud provider UI or CLI manually can be done with an IaC tool. Instead of clicking through the dashboard to configure and provision VM every time you need one, you could describe the desired number and type of VMs you need in IaC and keep that configuration in Git or other version control. Invoking an IaC tool with desired configuration will establish communication with cloud provider API and create described resources. If resources were there before and configured correctly, IaC tool won't do any further changes. Resources that IaC can provision include VMs, load balancers, network attached storage, firewall rules, object storage buckets and much-much more.

Today, **Terraform** is one of the most popular IaC tools on the market. It supports major public and private cloud providers and most of their IaaS/PaaS/SaaS/FaaS offerings.

Terraform accepts JSON as well as own .tf definition file format and here is a small example to give you an idea what it looks like:

```
terraform {
  required_providers {
    aws = {
      source  = "hashicorp/aws"
      version = "~> 4.16"
    }
  }
  required_version = ">= 1.2.0"
}
provider "aws" {
  region  = "eu-central-1"
}

resource "aws_instance" "kcna_demo_vm" {
  ami           = "ami-051835d754b74795c"
  instance_type = „t3.medium"
```

```
    tags = {
      Name = "KCNAExampleInstance"
    }
}
```

If applied, this definition file will provision a t3.medium type VM tagged KCNAExampleInstance in AWS public cloud in eu-central-1 region. This VM can also be referenced again in other definition files, for example, if you'd like to attach a storage block device to it.

For the scope of KCNA, you don't need to memorize the format or .tf specifics, but you need to remember the advantages of IaC which were already mentioned in the previous section since IaC is an essential part of GitOps:

- Faster setup and reproducible results.

- Human-readable and reviewable configuration that can be stored in VCS.

- Elimination of infrastructure drift with desired state definition.

Worth mentioning that some cloud providers have their own, vendor specific IaC tools that might offer better support for their cloud services, but obviously won't be compatible with any other providers. **CloudFormation** – an IaC made by AWS only for AWS would be such an example.

If you remember the exercises we did in *Chapters 5* and *6*, we basically used IaC with Kubernetes. Kubernetes uses declarative resource definitions to describe workloads but can also be used to provision load balancers (with LoadBalancer Service type) and persistent storage (as *PV* and *PVC*). When you run it in a public cloud environment and apply the specification, Kubernetes cloud controller manager will interact with provider APIs and ensure that resources are provisioned and in the desired state.

Summary

In this chapter we've learned about the delivery of Cloud Native applications. Modern applications require CI/CD to automate all stages of software delivery.

Where CI focuses on the first *build-test-release* stages, *Continuous Delivery* focuses on packaging software in container images or installable software packages and uploading them into container registry or package repositories respectively.

Another CD – *Continuous Deployment* focuses on automatic deployment of the tested and packaged *releases* into various live environments.

Next, we've seen how *GitOps* evolved on top of *CI/CD* by adding reviewable merge (or pull) requests together with IaC. This has led to an ultimate, highly automated, and powerful process that works especially well with Kubernetes. Some of the popular tools that help implementing GitOps are *ArgoCD*, *FluxCD* and *Jenkins X*.

IaC is the practice of managing and provisioning infrastructure in a declarative way with definition files. Using IaC allows to eliminate *Infrastructure Drift* and have reviewable and reproducible infrastructure configuration. *Terraform* is one of the most popular IaC tools today.

Going with IaC and GitOps means no manual changes, no manual deployments or live reconfiguration is allowed. The whole team should be aware and follow the process. Git repositories act as a source of truth and CI/CD systems ensure that this desired state is reached and maintained.

And with that we've finished the last technical chapter! Congratulations and well done! In the next two chapters you'll find a mock exam to evaluate your readiness as well as tips on how to pass the exam and what to do after.

Questions

Correct answers can be found at __TBD__

1. What does CI mean?

    A. Continuous Interaction

    B. Continuous Improvement

    C. Continuous Integration

    D. Continuous Inspection

2. Which of the following stages are the focus of CI automation (pick multiple)?

    A. Release

    B. Build, Test

    C. Deploy

    D. Package

3. Which of the following definitions are correct for CD (pick multiple)?

    A. Continuous Debugging

    B. Continuous Delivery

    C. Continuous Destruction

    D. Continuous Deployment

4. Which of the following is considered a CI/CD practice?

    A. Frequent, large releases done by the whole team together

    B. Frequent, small, and fully automated releases

    C. Frequent, small, well tested, and automated releases

    D. Infrequent, large, and automated releases

5. Which of the following tools are suitable for GitOps (pick multiple)?

    A. Jenkins X

    B. FluxCD

    C. TravisCI

    D. ArgoCD

6. Which of the following elements are a part of GitOps (pick multiple)?

    A. Kubernetes

    B. CI/CD

    C. IaC

    D. Merge (or pull) Requests

7. Which VCS is used with GitOps?

    A. Bitbucket

    B. Subversion

    C. Git

    D. Mercurial

8. What is infrastructure drift?

    A. When the infrastructure is fully automated and can drift on autopilot

    B. When the number of VMs in cloud has increased due to autoscaling events

    C. When the performance of VMs varies during the day depending on demand

    D. When the real infrastructure state is different from what is desired and defined by IaC

9.   What should NOT be done with established GitOps process in team?

   A.   Monitoring the system state

   B.   Opening (pull) merge requests

   C.   Manual changes in the live environment

   D.   Reviewing teammate's code as tests are automated

10. What is normally defined with IaC (pick multiple)?

   A.   System architecture

   B.   VMs and load balancers

   C.   Database migrations

   D.   Firewall rules

11. What are the benefits of GitOps (pick multiple)?

   A.   Faster and more stable software delivery

   B.   No need to monitor live environments anymore

   C.   More free time for the team due to high degree of automation

   D.   All Kubernetes operations are handled by CI/CD

12. What are the benefits of CI (pick multiple)?

   A.   Automatic deployment of tested code

   B.   Automatic packaging of tested code

   C.   No developer time spent for running builds or tests

   D.   Issue detection with automated tests

13. What is a correct definition of a *release*?

   A.   A version of software to be delivered to the users

   B.   A current state of application in K8s cluster

   C.   A decision to stop further development

   D.   A complete CI/CD pipeline run

14. Which of the following is a CI/CD tool?

    A. CloudFormation

    B. Terraform

    C. GitlabCI

    D. Subversion

15. What normally triggers a deployment in GitOps?

    A. Push into any Git branch

    B. An event of infrastructure drift

    C. Approved and merged MR (PR)

    D. Manual rebase in Git

16. Which of the following is true about GitOps (pick multiple)?

    A. Overwrite of manual changes

    B. It is only possible with Kubernetes

    C. Uses declarative configuration

    D. Can only be used with a few popular programming languages

17. Which of the following stages are NOT a part of CI/CD (pick multiple)?

    A. Monitor

    B. Build

    C. Plan

    D. Code

Further reading

- Semantic versioning: `https://semver.org/`
- What is GitOps: `https://www.weave.works/blog/what-is-gitops-really`
- ArgoCD: `https://argo-cd.readthedocs.io/`
- ArgoCD examples: `https://github.com/argoproj/argocd-example-apps`
- FluxCD: `https://fluxcd.io/`
- GitLab for CI/CD: `https://docs.gitlab.com/ee/ci/`
- Terraform: `https://www.terraform.io/`

Part 5:
KCNA Exam and Next Steps

In this closing part, you'll find tips for preparing for and passing the exam, along with two mock exams to verify your knowledge. Finally, we'll discuss what your next steps could be after getting certified to start or advance your cloud native career.

This part contains the following chapters:

- *Chapter 12, Practicing for the KCNA Exam with Mock Papers*
- *Chapter 13, The Road Ahead*

12
Practicing for the KCNA Exam with Mock Papers

In this chapter, you'll find several tips on how to make final preparations and tackle the **Kubernetes and Cloud Native Associate (KCNA)** exam. Those are followed by two mock exams that allow you to test your knowledge and make sure you're ready to take the real exam.

About the KCNA exam

As you might remember from *Chapter 2*, KCNA is an entry-level exam offered by the **Cloud Native Computing Foundation (CNCF)**, followed by much harder **Certified Kubernetes Administrator/ Certified Kubernetes Administrator Developer (CKA/CKAD)** and **Certified Kubernetes Security Specialist (CKS)** certifications. Despite being a theoretical, multi-choice exam, KCNA assumes basic knowledge of kubectl commands, Kubernetes resources, architecture, and features. Almost half (46%) of the exam is about Kubernetes, and it is not recommended to attempt the exam if you have not done any hands-on exercises from this book or if you have zero prior K8s experience.

Unlike CKA, CKAD, and CKS, KCNA is broader and tests other domains and competencies, including Cloud Native and microservice architectures, **continuous integration/continuous deployment (CI/ CD)**, observability, and more. However, even without any practical experience with Prometheus, Jaeger, Argo CD, or Helm, you'll be able to pass it based on the theory presented in the previous chapters.

The exam itself is online, remotely proctored, and can be taken from anywhere in the world with a reliable internet connection. Remotely proctored means you'll need a web camera and a microphone, and for the whole examination time, you and your desktop will be recorded. It is not allowed to use multiple screens, so prepare to use only one.

If your internet connection breaks up, you'll be able to rejoin the session, but you'll lose time as the timer keeps going. You are not allowed to take the exam in public spaces such as cafés or if other people are present in the room, and you're not allowed to eat during the exam. Drinking water from a transparent container is allowed.

> **Note**
> Don't cheat or leave any notes and hints around as this will result in the termination of your exam! Your surroundings will be checked via the web camera!

For pricing and the latest information, refer to the official sources:

- `https://www.cncf.io/certification/kcna/`
- `https://training.linuxfoundation.org/certification/kubernetes-cloud-native-associate/`

There, you'll find a candidate handbook, exam scheduling instructions, and answers to common organizational questions.

> **Note**
> Make sure to satisfy the *system requirements* after scheduling the exam, and complete the checklist in order to take the exam. **Do so in advance as being late to the exam will be considered a no-show!**

Make sure to have a valid, government-issued ID with a phone on the day of the exam—this will be verified at the beginning of the session.

Tips on getting ready

If you read all chapters and answered all the questions at the end of the chapters, the recommended way is to try the mock exams here while measuring the time it takes. You'll have 90 minutes to answer all 60 questions, which leaves you with 1.5 minutes per question.

After, calculate your score:

- If the mock exam score is 80% or better, you should be good to go for the real KCNA exam. Go ahead and schedule one right after.
- If the score is close to 75%, go back and check the chapters or at least summaries on the topics where you've made a mistake. Answer questions at the end of the chapters and make another mock exam attempt after a day or two.

The KCNA passing score is 75%, and if you scored significantly less during the mock exam, that means you need more preparation.

Just before the exam, make sure that you get a good night's sleep and do some other activities besides preparing for KCNA. Don't study all night as this might negatively impact your performance on the exam day. And if you feel stressed and worried, try to shift your perspective. You have one completely free retake in case something goes wrong! What's the point in stressing yourself out if a second exam attempt is already included in the price? But if you followed this book carefully, you likely won't need a second attempt anyway.

A few words on how to approach the exam questions. In recent years, I have taken more than 10 professional certification exams and passed all of them on the first attempt, except one. Here is how I normally do it:

1. Read each question completely and carefully.
2. If you don't know the answer or are not sure, mark the question and move on to the next one.
3. Never spend several minutes on a single question as you might not have enough time to attempt all questions.
4. Come back to the marked questions only after attempting all questions.

Now, it's time to take the mock exam. Get paper and a pen, set a 90-minute timer, and nail it!

> **Note**
>
> The mock exam questions here are testing the same domains and competencies as the real exam, yet these are not the questions from the real KCNA exam! Posting online or publishing real exam questions is a violation of the confidentiality agreement that you sign before the exam. Never do that!

Mock exam A

Correct answers can be found in the *Assessment* section of the *Appendix*.

> **Note**
>
> Unless specified otherwise, there is only one correct answer.

1. You're planning a deployment of a Kubernetes cluster in your organization. There is a requirement to make the control plane highly available. How many control plane nodes should be deployed?

   A. 1

   B. 2

   C. 3

   D. 4

2. You're operating a Kubernetes cluster in a production environment where nodes are running in multiple failure domains (also called **Availability Zones**, or **AZs**). You need to ensure that Pods are started across predefined failure domains. Which K8s feature can be used?

    A. PVC

    B. Pod topology spread constraints

    C. Pod network policies

    D. Pod security policies

3. You've been asked to deploy a new application onto a Kubernetes cluster. Which check do you need to implement to constantly ensure that the application is healthy and running?

    A. Prometheus probe

    B. Container runtime check

    C. Reconciliation check

    D. Liveness and readiness probes

4. Which of the following `kubectl` commands can be used to get detailed information about a deployment named `microservice-a`?

    A. `kubectl get pod microservice-a`

    B. `kubectl describe pod microservice-a`

    C. `kubectl explain deployment microservice-a`

    D. `kubectl describe deployment microservice-a`

5. You are operating a Kubernetes cluster and have received a request to run a new application in containers that will reside in its own **virtual machines** (**VMs**), isolated from other workloads. Which technology would allow you to do that?

    A. Namespaced container runtime

    B. Virtualized container runtime

    C. Sandboxed container runtime

    D. Isolated container runtime

6. You're deploying a new stateless microservice application into your Kubernetes cluster. The application must automatically recover from cluster node failures and should be updated regularly in a rolling fashion. Which K8s resource fits best for such a case?

   A. StatelessSet

   B. StatefulSet

   C. ReplicaSet

   D. Deployment

7. Which of the following is the smallest schedulable workload unit in Kubernetes?

   A. Deployment

   B. Container

   C. Pod

   D. Service

8. You're deploying a new stateful application into your Kubernetes cluster that must persist data on the disk. Which Kubernetes controller will fit such a case?

   A. ReplicaSet

   B. Deployment

   C. StatelessSet

   D. StatefulSet

9. You're operating several Kubernetes clusters, and in order to implement GitOps, you've started the evaluation of several tools. Which of the following is well suited for GitOps?

   A. Argo CD

   B. GitLab CI

   C. Prometheus

   D. Travis CI

10. You're managing a Kubernetes cluster running in a big public cloud. The demand fluctuates often, and you need to automate the change of cluster size to add more worker nodes when demand is high and reduce the number when the load is low. Which technology would you use?

    A. Self-healing

    B. **Horizontal Pod Autoscaler (HPA)**

    C. **Vertical Pod Autoscaler (VPA)**

    D. **Cluster Autoscaler (CA)**

11. You're debugging an application running in Kubernetes and you need to get the logs from a Pod called `microservice-b` that was just terminated. Which `kubectl` command allows you to do that?

    A. `kubectl get logs microservice-b`

    B. `kubectl logs microservice-b --previous`

    C. `kubectl logs microservice-b`

    D. `kubectl get logs microservice-b --previous`

12. You're debugging an application in Kubernetes and need to check the logs from a container named app of the `microservice-c` Pod. How can you do that with `kubectl`?

    A. `kubectl logs microservice-c`

    B. `kubectl get logs microservice-c app`

    C. `kubectl get logs microservice-c`

    D. `kubectl logs microservice-c -c app`

13. You're managing a Kubernetes cluster and need to run a logging agent on each node to ship the log to a centralized logging system. Which Kubernetes resource controller can be used for this logging agent?

    A. DaemonSet

    B. Deployment

    C. StatefulSet

    D. ReplicaSet

14. Which of the following is the main operational concept behind Kubernetes controllers?

    A. Readiness probe

    B. Serverless

    C. Reconciliation loop

    D. Rolling update

15. Which of the following projects can be used to implement your own Serverless platform? Pick two.

    A. Knative

    B. Prometheus

    C. OpenFaaS

    D. Jaeger

16. Which of the following technologies can be used to operate a virtualized container runtime with Kubernetes?

    A. containerd

    B. gVisor

    C. Kata

    D. Docker

17. You've been asked to deploy an application to Kubernetes that requires a small helper service running collocated with the main application. The helper service should share data on the disk with the main application. Which of the following resources can be used?

    A. Two Pods with a network policy

    B. Two Pods with an affinity policy

    C. Pod with a single container

    D. Pod with multiple containers

18. You've been asked to help with an application that is been migrated to Kubernetes. The application cannot output its logs to **standard out (stdout)** or **standard error (stderr)**. What can be done in order to ship its logs to the central log aggregation system?

    A. Nothing—the vendor should be asked to implement the feature first

    B. The application should run inside the Pod with a PV attached for the logs

    C. A logging agent should be run on all nodes as a DaemonSet

    D. A logging sidecar container should be used in the Pod with the application

19. Which of the following formats is commonly used today for application logs?

    A. CSV

    B. JSON

    C. YAML

    D. SQL

20. As a part of the process improvement initiative in your organization, you are required to automate, test, and build procedures for several development teams. Which tools and processes would help if there is no need to automatically deploy the changes to various environments?

    A. Tracing

    B. GitOps

    C. CD

    D. CI/CD

21. Which of the following projects can be used to implement a service mesh? Pick two:

    A. Linkerd

    B. containerd

    C. Istio

    D. dockerd

22. You've just deployed a dedicated Kubernetes cluster for a new project, and you already have access to several other clusters. What needs to be done in order to access additional Kubernetes APIs from your workstation?

    A. Add new credentials to the `kubecon` file

    B. Add new credentials to the `ssh-config` file

    C. Add new credentials to the `kube-proxy` file

    D. Add new credentials to the `kubeconfig` file

23. You have been tasked to allow several development teams to use the same Kubernetes cluster. What can be done to logically separate their workloads from each other?

    A. Let each team assign its own labels to each started Pod

    B. Create a namespace for each team

    C. Use affinity rules to schedule each team's Pods to certain nodes

    D. Use a virtualized container runtime such as Kata

24. Your development team is adding telemetry instrumentation to a new microservice that it's working on. It is asking at which endpoint the Prometheus-compatible metrics should be exposed for collection. Which of the following is the correct choice?

    A. `/metrics`

    B. `/metric`

C. /prometheus

D. /collect

25. What are the four Cs of Cloud Native security?

A. Code, Commit, Comply, Cloud

B. Code, Container, Cluster, Cloud

C. Code, Commit, Cluster, Cloud

D. Code, Container, Commit, Collocation

26. You have been assigned to design a Kubernetes setup where all Pod-to-Pod traffic will be encrypted. Which of the following solutions would be suitable?

A. Use cluster network policies

B. Deploy a service mesh into the cluster

C. Use RBAC

D. Ask developers to add TLS to each application in the cluster

27. What is a component of a service mesh that must be part of all workloads in Kubernetes?

A. Service of type LoadBalancer in front of each Pod

B. Secret injected to all Pods

C. ConfigMap injected to all Pods

D. Sidecar container injected to all Pods

28. Which of the following are part of the **Open Container Initiative** (**OCI**) specifications? Select all that apply:

A. Image specification

B. Runtime specification

C. Distribution specification

D. Pod specification

29. Which of the following are the correct maturity levels for projects curated by CNCF?

A. Sandbox, Incubating, Passed

B. Sandbox, Incubating, Graduated

C. Sandboxed, Namespaced, Virtualized

D. Alpha, Beta, Release

30. You've been asked to deploy a tracing tool to analyze a complex microservice-based application. Which of the following could be an option?

    A. Prometheus

    B. Traefik

    C. Knative

    D. Jaeger

31. Which of the following are the attributes of highly resilient systems? Select all correct answers.

    A. Traffic encryption

    B. Latest kernel version

    C. Desired state

    D. Self-healing

32. Which technology is behind the default service discovery mechanism of Kubernetes?

    A. Iptables

    B. DNS

    C. SSL

    D. DHCP

33. You've been asked to implement automatic scaling (depending on the load) for an application running in Kubernetes. Which of the following tools will be helpful?

    A. CA

    B. **Deployment Autoscaler (DA)**

    C. **Horizontal Node Autoscaler (HNA)**

    D. HPA

34. A company is looking to hire a professional who understands the entire application lifecycle and makes security an essential part of it. Which of the following job roles should the company be looking for?

    A. System Administrator

    B. DevSecOps Engineer

    C. Cloud Solution Architect

    D. Data Scientist

35. Which of the following are valid container runtimes? Select all correct answers:

    A. Xen

    B. Kubernetes

    C. gVisor (`runsc`)

    D. containerd

36. Which ways exist to extend Kubernetes API with new features? Pick two:

    A. Code resource definitions

    B. Custom resource definitions

    C. Extension layers

    D. Aggregation layers

37. You have prepared a declarative Kubernetes spec file for a new application. The file is named `microservice-d.yaml`. How would you deploy it to the cluster using `kubectl`?

    A. `kubectl deploy -f microservice-d.yaml`

    B. `kubectl apply -f microservice-d.yaml`

    C. `kubectl run -f microservice-d.yaml`

    D. `kubectl exec -f microservice-d.yaml`

38. Your team is evaluating Kubernetes for container orchestration and would like to know which of the following features are available out of the box. Pick two:

    A. Request tracing

    B. IP Address Management (IPAM)

    C. Service discovery

    D. Full traffic encryption

39. Which of the following is considered a good CI/CD practice?

    A. Frequent, large releases done by the whole team together

    B. Frequent, small, and fully automated releases

    C. Infrequent, large, and automated releases

    D. Frequent, small, well-tested, and automated releases

40. What are the advantages of using Kubernetes controllers such as Deployment or StatefulSet compared to static definitions of simple Pods?

   A. Controlled Pods start and run faster

   B. They allow self-healing and rolling updates

   C. They allow affinity settings to be defined

   D. They allow Pods to be exposed via a Service

41. Which of the following is a valid statement about Serverless?

   A. It is only available in the public cloud

   B. It only works with Kubernetes

   C. It does not use any server hardware

   D. It abstracts away all server management operations

42. A team lead has asked you to help with development process optimization. Developers spend a lot of time testing and building packages themselves. What would be your suggestion?

   A. Ask developers to install a newer IDE

   B. Implement a CI/CD pipeline

   C. Migrate applications to Kubernetes

   D. Migrate applications to large bare-metal servers

43. An old application cannot be easily containerized and must continue to run in a VM but be managed with Kubernetes. Which of the following projects allows us to extend Kubernetes beyond container orchestration to also manage VMs?

   A. KubeVirt

   B. Kubeless

   C. Swarm

   D. Istio

44. Which of the following formats is commonly used for writing Kubernetes spec files?

   A. CSV

   B. YAML

   C. HTML

   D. XML

45. Which of the following elements are a part of GitOps? Pick two:

   A. Kubernetes

   B. Infrastructure as Code (IaC)

   C. Jenkins

   D. Merge (pull) requests

46. Which of the following are valid telemetry signals?

   A. Logs, metrics, traces

   B. Logs, pings, tracks

   C. Logs, metadata, traces

   D. Logs, measurements, traces

47. What does cluster-level logging mean in the Kubernetes environment?

   A. When logs from each node in the cluster are stored on the control plane nodes at the `/var/log` path

   B. When logs from all containers are shipped to a separate backend independent from the K8s lifecycle

   C. When each Pod has its own logging configuration and individual log storage location

   D. When all cluster events are logged into a separate log file

48. You're troubleshooting an application that misbehaves and decide to enable maximum log verbosity to get as many details as possible. Which is the corresponding logging level?

   A. `CRITICAL`

   B. `WARNING`

   C. `INFO`

   D. `DEBUG`

49. You've been asked to configure autoscaling for a new application. Which class of telemetry signal is suitable?

   A. Metrics

   B. Application logs

   C. Kubernetes events

   D. Traces

50. Your organization has started a cost optimization initiative and is looking to reduce monthly cloud bills. Which of the following would you recommend?

    A. Switch critical workloads to spot instances

    B. Lower log level to save on storage

    C. Implement autoscaling based on the load

    D. Move from microservices to monoliths

51. What makes it possible to query Prometheus metrics from the past?

    A. Alertmanager

    B. Time Series Database (TSDB)

    C. PVC

    D. Graphite

52. Which of the following CNCF bodies is responsible for approving new CNCF projects and aligning existing ones?

    A. Board of Directors

    B. End User Community

    C. **Governing Board (GB)**

    D. **Technical Oversight Committee (TOC)**

53. Which of the following is the format of Prometheus metrics?

    A. Traces

    B. JSON

    C. Time series

    D. Spans

54. Which of the following should never be done in a team with an established GitOps process?

    A. Opening (pull) merge requests

    B. Manual changes in the live environment

    C. Reviewing teammate's code

    D. Monitoring the system state

55. Your team is operating a Kubernetes cluster with a containerd runtime. Why might this be a concern for a new application with strict security requirements?

    A. containerd is not the fastest runtime and can be a bottleneck

    B. containerd does not support network policies

    C. containerd relies on a shared kernel

    D. containerd does not support Pod security policies

56. What are the advantages of containers when compared to VMs? Pick two:

    A. Containers consume fewer resources than VMs

    B. Containers are more secure than VMs

    C. Containers take less time to start

    D. Containers don't need OS updates

57. How many times per year does a new Kubernetes release come out?

    A. 1

    B. 2

    C. 3

    D. 5

58. Which of the following allows us to use different container runtimes with Kubernetes?

    A. CSI

    B. CNI

    C. SMI

    D. CRI

59. It's been said that Kubernetes has a declarative API. What does that mean?

    A. We always need to declare a YAML spec file to use a K8s API

    B. We declare the desired state and K8s will reach it once

    C. We declare the desired state and K8s will constantly try to reach it

    D. We instruct Kubernetes exactly what to do with which resource

60. Which of the following container runtimes adds an intermediate kernel layer between the host kernel and containers that become sandboxed?

    A. containerd

    B. gVisor

    C. Kata

    D. dockerd

That's it! Have you managed to complete it under 90 minutes? Hopefully, you did. Now, check the correct answers and calculate your score based on the following simple formula:

$$\frac{\text{Number of correct answers}}{60} \times 100\% = \text{Your score as a percentage}$$

If you are not happy with the results or you'd like to get more confidence, read more on the topics where you've made mistakes and do another attempt with *Mock exam B*.

Make sure to take a break between the attempts. Sometimes, it is better to have a rest for a day or even two days to let everything sink in. Good luck!

Mock exam B

Correct answers can be found in the *Assessment* section of the *Appendix*.

1. Which of the following are valid telemetry signals?

    A. Measurements, traces, logs

    B. Pings, traces, logs

    C. Metadata, traces, logs

    D. Metrics, traces, logs

2. Your organization is running Kubernetes, and the development team asked whether it would be possible to run Serverless applications with it. Which of the following projects can be used to implement your own Serverless platform on top of Kubernetes? Pick two:

    A. Knative

    B. OpenFaaS

    C. KubeVirt

    D. KubeConf

3. You're planning a production deployment of a Kubernetes cluster in your organization. The control plane should be highly available. How many control plane nodes should be deployed?

   A. 2

   B. 4

   C. 3

   D. 1

4. Which of the following is the smallest, individually schedulable workload unit in Kubernetes?

   A. Pod

   B. Container

   C. Deployment

   D. Service

5. You have prepared a Kubernetes spec file for a new application. The file is named `kcna-microservice.yaml`. How would you deploy it to the cluster with `kubectl`?

   A. `kubectl deploy -f kcna-microservice.yaml`

   B. `kubectl apply -f kcna-microservice.yaml`

   C. `kubectl run -f kcna-microservice.yaml`

   D. `kubectl exec -f kcna-microservice.yaml`

6. Some applications in your organization cannot be easily containerized and must continue to run in a VM but be managed with Kubernetes. Which of the following projects allows us to extend Kubernetes to also manage VMs?

   A. KubeVirt

   B. Kubeless

   C. Swarm

   D. Knative

7. An application in Kubernetes runs under different loads depending on the time of the day. You've been asked to implement autoscaling for it to accommodate fluctuations. Which of the following tools can be helpful?

   A. CA

   B. HPA

   C. HNA

   D. DA

8. An application is misbehaving, and you've been asked to find the root cause. You decide to enable maximum log verbosity. Which of the following log levels provides the most details?

   A. INFO

   B. WARNING

   C. ERROR

   D. DEBUG

9. Which of the following are maturity levels for projects curated by the CNCF?

   A. Sandbox, Incubating, Finished

   B. Sandbox, Incubating, Graduated

   C. Sandboxed, Namespaced, Graduated

   D. Alpha, Beta, Release

10. Which of the following types of nodes does Kubernetes have?

    A. Minion and worker nodes

    B. Control plane and worker nodes

    C. Control plane and minion nodes

    D. Primary and secondary nodes

11. Which technology stands behind the default service discovery mechanism of Kubernetes?

    A. Iptables

    B. SSL

    C. DNS

    D. DHCP

12. You've been asked to deploy a tracing tool to analyze a distributed microservice-based application. Which of the following options can be considered? Pick two:

    A. Zipkin

    B. Traefik

    C. Prometheus

    D. Jaeger

13. You're debugging an application in Kubernetes and need to check the logs from a container named kcna of the microservice Pod. How to do that with kubectl?

    A. kubectl logs microservice

    B. kubectl get logs microservice -c kcna

    C. kubectl get logs microservice kcna

    D. kubectl logs microservice -c kcna

14. Which of the following are part of the OCI specifications? Select all that apply:

    A. Kubernetes specification

    B. Runtime specification

    C. Distribution specification

    D. Image specification

15. Your team is evaluating Kubernetes for container orchestration and would like to know which network-related features are available by default. Pick two:

    A. Request tracing

    B. IPAM

    C. Service discovery

    D. Full traffic encryption

16. Which of the following Kubernetes resources allow us to recover (self-heal) an application if the node it was running on has failed? Pick two:

    A. Deployment

    B. Pod

    C. StatefulSet

    D. Service

17. You've been asked to deploy a new application in Kubernetes. Which check feature helps to constantly ensure that the application is running and healthy?

    A. Deployment probe

    B. Container runtime check

    C. Reconciliation check

    D. Liveness and readiness probes

18. With `kubectl` version 1.24 installed, which Kubernetes cluster versions would you be able to manage? Select all that apply:

    A. 1.24

    B. 1.25

    C. 1.23

    D. 1.21

19. Which crucial element of service mesh must be a part of all workloads in Kubernetes?

    A. LoadBalancer service deployed in front of each Pod

    B. Proxy config injected to all Pods

    C. Service ConfigMap injected to all Pods

    D. Sidecar container injected to all Pods

20. Which of the following Kubernetes components is used to store information about the cluster and its state?

    A. `etcd`

    B. `kubelet`

    C. `kube-store`

    D. PVC

21. Which of the following CNCF bodies is responsible for approving new CNCF projects and aligning existing ones?

    A. TOC

    B. End User Community

    C. GB

    D. Board of Directors

22. You've received security requirements for a new microservice-based application that should not run on hosts with shared kernels. Which of the following could be a solution?

    A. Use Docker

    B. Use namespaced container runtime

    C. Use virtualized container runtime

    D. Use Pod security policies

23. You're operating a Kubernetes cluster in a cloud environment where worker nodes are spread across multiple AZs. You need to ensure that application Pods run across all AZs. Which K8s feature can be used?

   A. StatefulSet

   B. Pod topology spread constraints

   C. Pod network policies

   D. Pod availability policies

24. Which of the following `kubectl` commands can be used to get detailed information about a deployment called `microservice-kcna`?

   A. `kubectl get pod microservice-kcna`

   B. `kubectl describe pod microservice-kcna`

   C. `kubectl describe deployment microservice-kcna`

   D. `kubectl explain deployment microservice-kcna`

25. Which of the following is a valid container runtime? Select all correct answers:

   A. KVM

   B. Kubernetes

   C. gVisor (`runsc`)

   D. containerd

26. Which of the following best describes a highly resilient application and infrastructure?

   A. Ability to automatically shut down in case of issues

   B. Ability to automatically recover from most failures

   C. Ability to preserve the state in case of failure

   D. Ability to perform rolling updates

27. You are reviewing the release notes of a new Kubernetes version, and it turns out one of the resources you're using has been deprecated. How much time would it take for a deprecated resource to be removed?

   A. About 2 years

   B. 4 months

   C. 2 months

   D. 6 months

28. Your development team is adding Prometheus-compatible telemetry instrumentation to a new microservice it's working on. Which endpoint is scraped by Prometheus by default?

    A. `/metrics`

    B. `/metric`

    C. `/prometheus`

    D. `/collect`

29. You're working on the deployment of an application that is missing native support for exposing Prometheus metrics. Which of the following allows us to collect metrics in such a case?

    A. Running the application in Kubernetes

    B. Installing `Pushgateway`

    C. Installing `Alertmanager`

    D. Installing Prometheus Exporter for the application

30. What are the four Cs of Cloud Native security?

    A. Code, Commit, Compliance, Cloud

    B. Code, Container, Cluster, Collocation

    C. Code, Collaboration, Cluster, Cloud

    D. Code, Container, Cluster, Cloud

31. Which of the following Kubernetes components is used to download container images and start containers?

    A. `kubelet`

    B. Container runtime

    C. `etcd`

    D. `kube-scheduler`

32. Which of the following is true about Serverless?

    A. It is only available in the cloud

    B. It only works with Kubernetes

    C. It uses no server hardware at all

    D. It abstracts all server management operations away

33. Which of the following is the smallest part of a Serverless application?

    A. Gateway
    B. Function
    C. Commit
    D. Container

34. You have just received credentials to access a Kubernetes cluster and would like to find out which namespaces are there. Which of the following `kubectl` commands can be used to list all namespaces in the cluster?

    A. `kubectl list namespaces --all-namespaces`
    B. `kubectl show namespaces`
    C. `kubectl get namespaces`
    D. `kubectl list all namespaces`

35. What happens when the Kubernetes scheduler cannot assign a Pod to a node?

    A. It will be stuck in the `Pending` state
    B. It will be forcefully run on one of the control plane nodes
    C. It will be stuck in the `NotScheduled` state
    D. It will be gone after five scheduling attempts

36. You're working on a solution for a microservice-based application with strict security requirements. All network Pod-to-Pod communication has to be encrypted. Which of the following would be a suitable option?

    A. Deploy a service mesh
    B. Enforce K8s security policies
    C. Set up Kubernetes RBAC
    D. Use K8s network policies

37. Which of the following formats is normally used for application logs?

    A. CSV
    B. SSL
    C. YAML
    D. JSON

38. You've been asked to evaluate service mesh solutions. Which of the following projects can be used? Pick two:

    A. Linkerd

    B. Swarm

    C. Istio

    D. Traefik

39. You're managing a Kubernetes cluster and need to run a logging agent on each node to ship the log to a centralized logging system for storage and processing. Which Kubernetes resource controller fits best?

    A. DaemonSet

    B. Deployment

    C. StatefulSet

    D. ReplicaSet

40. You're debugging an application running in Kubernetes and you need to get the logs from a Pod called `microservice-kcna` that was just terminated. Which `kubectl` command allows you to do that?

    A. `kubectl get logs microservice-kcna -p`

    B. `kubectl logs microservice-kcna -p`

    C. `kubectl logs microservice-kcna`

    D. `kubectl get logs microservice-kcna –previous`

41. You're reading the best practices guide and it recommends setting up cluster-level logging on Kubernetes. What exactly does that mean for log storage?

    A. K8s needs separate log collection and aggregation systems

    B. K8s aggregates all cluster logs on control plane nodes

    C. K8s comes with a log storage and aggregation solution out of the box

    D. K8s has storage only for the most important cluster health logs

42. Which Kubernetes spec setting configures the number of Pods managed by a Deployment?

    A. podnum

    B. Replicas

    C. Containers

    D. Instances

43. You're evaluating different tools for building CI/CD pipelines to automate build-test-release processes for your development team. Which of the following can be considered? Pick two:

   A.   Prometheus

   B.   Jenkins

   C.   Linkerd

   D.   GitLab CI

44. A colleague has shared credentials to access a new Kubernetes cluster they just deployed. What do you need to do to access its API from your workstation?

   A.   Add new credentials to the `kubecon` file

   B.   Add new credentials to the `kubernetes-conf` file

   C.   Add new credentials to the `kube-proxy` file

   D.   Add new credentials to the `kubeconfig` file

45. You're preparing to deploy a new application in a Kubernetes cluster, and you need to provide non-default configuration files for it. Which of the following K8s resources is suitable for storing and injecting generic configuration into containers?

   A.   SettingMap

   B.   ConfigMap

   C.   PV

   D.   Ingress

46. You're evaluating options to deploy a microservice application into a Kubernetes cluster. The application must automatically recover from individual K8s node failures and should be updated via rolling updates. The application does not need to store data locally. Which K8s resource fits best for such a case?

   A.   StatelessSet

   B.   StatefulSet

   C.   ReplicaSet

   D.   Deployment

47. Your team runs Kubernetes in the public cloud, and due to fluctuating demand would like to dynamically add and remove cluster nodes depending on current demand. Which of the following would allow you to achieve that?

    A. K8s Node autoscaler

    B. K8s CA

    C. K8s HPA

    D. K8s VPA

48. Which of the following Kubernetes cluster configurations can be recommended for a highly available infrastructure setup?

    A. 3 control planes and 10 worker nodes

    B. 1 control plane and 10 worker nodes

    C. 2 control planes and 10 worker nodes

    D. 3 control planes and 1 worker node

49. Which of the following is true about containers and VMs? Pick two:

    A. Applications are easy to package in containers

    B. Applications are easy to package in VMs

    C. Container images are easy to share

    D. VM images are small in size

50. A development team has reached out, asking to help it improve its workflow and increase developer productivity. Which of the following can you recommend?

    A. Deploy a service mesh

    B. Switch to a different language such as Go or Python

    C. Build a CI/CD pipeline

    D. Migrate to a better cloud provider

51. Which of the following allows direct instrumentation for applications to provide metrics in Prometheus format?

    A. K8s service discovery

    B. Client libraries

    C. Exporters

    D. Pushgateway

52. Several departments have requested a partition with their own users and quotas on the corporate Kubernetes cluster. Which of the following can help?

    A. Namespaced runtime

    B. Shared runtime

    C. Pod quota policy

    D. Kubernetes namespaces

53. A development team is planning to deploy a new application soon, and you're asked to configure autoscaling for it. Which class of telemetry is the best source for autoscaling decisions?

    A. Metrics

    B. Traces

    C. Pings

    D. Logs

54. A new colleague has recently started in your team, which follows a GitOps workflow. Which of the following should they not do as it goes against established GitOps processes?

    A. Review any pull or merge requests

    B. Make manual changes to environments

    C. Deploy workloads to Kubernetes with declarative specifications

    D. Respond to any alerts raised across production environments

55. Which of the following best describes horizontal scaling?

    A. Adding more CPUs to the same service instance

    B. Adding more RAM to the same service instance

    C. Adding more replicas/instances of the same service

    D. Adding an extra load balancer in front of the service instance

56. The development team has asked to automate the testing, build, and release of the applications it is working on, but the software should not be automatically deployed to any environments. Which of the following can help? Pick two:

    A. GitOps

    B. Flux CD

    C. CI/CD pipelines

    D. Jenkins

57. Which of the following characterizes Serverless computing? Pick two:

    A. Servers are not needed anymore

    B. It supports all programming languages

    C. It is event-based

    D. The provider takes care of server management

58. Why is using Kubernetes resource controllers such as Deployments a preferred way of deploying workloads in Kubernetes?

    A. They make workloads run faster

    B. They add self-healing, scaling, and rolling update features

    C. They optimize CPU and RAM usage and consume fewer resources overall

    D. They allow changing container images without restarting the Pods

59. What is the main operational mechanism behind Kubernetes resource controllers?

    A. CI/CD

    B. Serverless

    C. Readiness probe

    D. Reconciliation loops

60. The development team is working on incorporating telemetry into all applications written in different programming languages. They are asking whether there are any open source projects that can help. Which would you suggest?

    A. Knative

    B. Istio

    C. OpenTelemetry

    D. Traefik

Congratulations and well done on finishing the second mock exam!

Hopefully, your score is 75% or higher, and that gives you more confidence in taking the real certification exam. As you can see, many questions are essentially small scenarios where you must find the best solution. Some questions are also easier compared to those at the end of the chapters as the intention of many chapters is to take you one step further than required for passing KCNA. In fact, for the scope of KCNA, you need to understand core concepts and be familiar with the tools and their purpose.

Don't expect very deep or super complex questions but expect broad questions from all domains of the KCNA curriculum with a lot of focus on Kubernetes.

Now, go ahead and schedule the KCNA exam. Wishing you the best of luck and hoping that you'll also read the next, and final, chapter where I share some tips on how to move forward and advance your career in the world of Cloud Native.

13
The Road Ahead

This is it! Congratulations on reaching the final chapter of the book! I hope this has been an exciting journey and you're eager to learn more and move forward.

In this chapter, we're going to cover a few final topics:

- Advancing a cloud-native career
- Contributing to open source
- Further reading

There is no prerequisite for passing the KCNA exam for this chapter, but the following information should give you some guidance on what your next career goals and milestones could be after becoming KCNA-certified.

Advancing a cloud-native career

Let's assume you've taken the exam and hopefully passed it. What's next?

First, take a moment to celebrate and be celebrated. Upload your certificate to LinkedIn and share a post about your achievement. Get connected and tag me; I'm always happy to give a thumbs-up and hear about your experience!

You'll find my LinkedIn profile at the following URL:

```
https://linkedin.com/in/dmitry-galkin
```

> **Note**
> If you don't have a LinkedIn profile yet, that is something to be addressed immediately. Go ahead and create one, and connect with your past and present colleagues. LinkedIn is the number one professional network, and it can help you to keep in touch, stay up to date with industry trends, and maybe even land your next dream job.

Wherever you are in your career, whether you're just starting in IT after graduating from college or maybe coming from a completely different field, remember that **practice and continuous learning are the keys to success**.

We covered many things in theory in this book because, essentially, KCNA is a theoretical exam (unlike CKA, CKAD, CKS, and so on). And it is not just Kubernetes and containers but also many other technologies that are essential to pursue a cloud-native career. CI/CD, monitoring, IaC, and automation all require practical experience for a deep understanding of the topics.

Obviously, you won't be asked to set up an actual Prometheus exporter or write an alert during a job interview, but knowing how to do that in theory is not enough. And of course, not every role would require you to write IaC and CI/CD pipelines, but if you're targeting DevOps, SRE, and other engineering roles, that would be a part of your regular responsibilities. So, go ahead and get hands-on experience with technologies we've covered in theory, check tutorials and quick start guides, and read another book if needed.

Next, I'd like to mention the usefulness of programming languages for engineering roles. Even basic knowledge of high-level programming languages such as Python helps a lot. As an engineer, you'll often encounter the need to automate small tasks and repetitive actions. Remember, doing manual changes, especially in production and live environments, is error-prone and often dangerous. Therefore, having some Python, Ruby, or Golang skills to do automation and scripting would allow you to be more efficient. And no, you're not required to have in-depth knowledge or write complex data structures. Basic skills and familiarity with some standard libraries would be sufficient.

If you've been in the industry for some time, you likely know that the Linux OS family massively dominates the world of cloud and IT infrastructure (more than 90% of servers run Linux). It has been a long time since Linux became the de facto standard OS for the majority of server workloads, especially for cloud and web applications. Today, Kubernetes is similarly becoming the standard platform to run and orchestrate modern applications in the cloud and on-premises.

By starting to learn about Kubernetes and a cloud-native approach, you took a big step in the right direction. Keep up the good work, stay curious, and stay up to date with trends and technologies. Continue learning even after you get your dream job! IT is one of the most rapidly changing industries and it requires constant development of skills to be among the top, most in-demand specialists. That's why I personally feel very excited about what will come next after the cloud, containers, serverless, Kubernetes, and service meshes.

Next, we will briefly discuss the importance of open source contributions.

Contributing to open source

As you know by now, Kubernetes, Prometheus, Helm, and all of the 120+ projects curated by CNCF are all open source. Contributing to open source projects can be challenging at first, yet it is a rewarding process that helps you to learn, build new skills, and sometimes even teach others.

Why is that? Here are some good reasons to consider:

- **Improving software**: It's not a secret that even the best and long-standing projects have bugs and regressions. If you encounter wrong, unexpected behavior or find a bug, the least you should do is the following:

  I.   Check whether the problem is already known in the project community.

  II.   If not, report it.

  III. Finally, if you're feeling comfortable enough, try to find the root cause and propose the patch to the source code.

  This ensures that the whole community benefits from it.

- **Improving your skills**: It is not always about coding and software development. User interfaces, design, documentation writing, and organizing can all be applied in open source projects, and your contributions are likely to be reviewed by other, often more experienced, community members and project maintainers. Their feedback might be very valuable for your growth.

- **Meeting people with similar interests**: You'll find many warm and welcoming open source communities, learn from others, and sometimes even find mentors while working on shared projects. Open source project summits and conferences that take place all over the world are a great way to share knowledge and have fun.

- **Strengthening your profile**: By definition, all contributions to the open source are public. Mentioning these on your CV lets you stand out from the crowd and serves as a demonstration of what you can do.

While it might be harder to start contributing if you're at the very beginning of your IT career, doing so will help to build skills, learn, and eventually, get support from the community.

> **Note**
> Remember, even small contributions matter!

In fact, during the past few years, I've met several university students who already had their contributions accepted to well-known open source projects. Thus, it is never too early to start contributing! Many projects have so-called *low-hanging fruits* – the issues or bugs that are easy to solve. This might be a great starting point to get familiar with the project and the contribution processes.

To wrap it up, I encourage you to go and explore open source projects and communities, contribute, and always keep learning. Once again, good luck with your exam and your cloud-native career! See you on the internet!

Further reading

- Contributing to CNCF: `https://contribute.cncf.io/`
- CNCF events: `https://www.cncf.io/events/`
- CNCF projects: `https://www.cncf.io/projects/`
- Projects trending on GitHub: `https://github.com/trending`

Here are a few more resources about Kubernetes for the future:

- Kubernetes Ingress: `https://kubernetes.io/docs/concepts/services-networking/ingress/`
- Kubernetes in a production environment: `https://kubernetes.io/docs/setup/production-environment/`
- Kubernetes common tasks: `https://kubernetes.io/docs/tasks/`

Assessments

In the following pages, we will review all the practice questions from each of the chapters in this book and provide the correct answers.

Chapter 1 – From Cloud to Cloud Native and Kubernetes

1. B, D
2. C
3. B, D
4. D
5. B, D
6. B, C, D
7. A
8. C
9. A, B, D
10. A
11. A, B
12. C
13. B, C, D
14. A, B, D
15. C

Chapter 2 – Overview of CNCF and Kubernetes Certifications

1. A, C, D
2. D
3. B, C, D
4. C
5. A, B, D
6. A, B

7. A, B, C
8. D
9. A, B
10. C
11. C, D
12. B, C
13. A
14. A, B
15. B, C, D

Chapter 3 – Getting Started with Containers

1. A, C
2. A, C
3. D
4. A, D
5. C, D
6. A, C
7. B, D
8. A, C
9. B, D
10. A

Chapter 4 – Exploring Container Runtimes, Interfaces, and Service Meshes

1. D
2. B, C, D
3. B
4. D
5. D
6. B
7. C

8. C
9. B
10. D
11. A, B, C
12. B
13. A, D
14. B, C
15. A, C
16. A, C
17. B
18. D

Chapter 5 – Orchestrating Containers with Kubernetes

1. C
2. B, C, D
3. B, C
4. C, D
5. D
6. D
7. B
8. C
9. B, D
10. D
11. B, D
12. B, D
13. A, D
14. D
15. B
16. C
17. C
18. B
19. C

20. C
21. C, D

Chapter 6 – Deploying and Scaling Applications with Kubernetes

1. C, D
2. B, C
3. B
4. D
5. D
6. B
7. C
8. C
9. B
10. D
11. C
12. B
13. D
14. B, C
15. A
16. C
17. B
18. D

Chapter 7 – Application Placement and Debugging with Kubernetes

1. C, D
2. B
3. B
4. B
5. C

6. D
7. C
8. C
9. B
10. D
11. B
12. B, D
13. A
14. C
15. A
16. C

Chapter 8 – Following Kubernetes Best Practices

1. C
2. D
3. B
4. C
5. B
6. C
7. B
8. A
9. D
10. D
11. B, D
12. B
13. A
14. C, D
15. B

Chapter 9 – Understanding Cloud Native Architectures

1. C
2. B
3. A
4. D
5. B
6. D
7. C, D
8. C, D
9. A
10. D
11. B
12. D
13. A
14. A, C
15. A
16. D

Chapter 10 – Implementing Telemetry and Observability in the Cloud

1. C, D
2. B
3. D
4. B
5. D
6. B
7. C
8. C, D
9. B
10. D
11. A

12. D
13. A
14. C
15. D
16. A, C, D
17. D
18. C

Chapter 11 – Automating Cloud Native Application Delivery

1. C
2. A, B
3. B, D
4. C
5. A, B, D
6. B, C, D
7. C
8. D
9. C
10. B, D
11. A, C
12. C, D
13. A
14. C
15. C
16. A, C
17. A, C, D

Chapter 12 – Practicing for the KCNA Exam

Mock exam A

1. C
2. B
3. D
4. D
5. B
6. D. Deployment is the best option because ReplicaSet does not allow rolling updates and StatefulSet is not required for stateless applications.
7. C
8. D
9. A
10. D
11. B
12. D
13. A. DaemonSet is the best option because it can ensure a replica is running on each Kubernetes node.
14. C
15. A, C
16. C
17. D. Containers in one pod can file system mounts and communicate over localhost. All containers of one pod will always run together on the same node.
18. D
19. B
20. D. CI/CD is the correct answer because we need build and test automation and we don't need automatic deployments. CD is Continuous Delivery in this case.
21. A, C
22. D
23. B. Using namespaces is the best option as it allows to further restrict access by implementing RBAC policies. A team can be restricted to only one namespace.
24. A
25. B

26. B

27. D

28. A, B, C

29. B

30. D

31. C, D

32. B

33. D. HPA is the correct answer because we need to scale an application in the context of the question. Obviously, a cluster autoscaler would be required eventually to adjust the number of nodes.

34. B

35. C, D

36. B, D

37. B

38. B, C

39. D

40. B

41. D

42. B

43. A

44. B

45. B, D

46. A

47. B

48. D

49. A

50. C. Other options might either impact the stability or make it harder to operate the applications.

51. B

52. D

53. C

54. B

55. C

56. A, C

57. C. At the time of writing this book, it is approximately 3 releases per year.

58. D

59. C

60. B

Mock exam B

1. D

2. A, B

3. C

4. A

5. B

6. A

7. B

8. D

9. B

10. B

11. C

12. A, D

13. D

14. B, C, D

15. B, C

16. A, C

17. D

18. A, B, C. By default, kubectl should work with one version above and one version below.

19. D

20. A

21. A

22. C

23. B

24. C

25. C, D

26. B
27. A
28. A
29. D
30. D
31. B
32. D
33. B
34. C
35. A
36. A
37. D
38. A, C
39. A
40. B
41. A
42. B
43. B, D
44. D
45. B
46. D. Deployment is the best option because it satisfies all the requirements, and the application is stateless.
47. B
48. A
49. A, C
50. C
51. B
52. D. Kubernetes namespaces allow configuration of resource quotas.
53. A
54. B
55. C

56. C, D. GitOps would be helpful for continuous deployment and FluxCD is a GitOps tool, so both A and B are incorrect answers.

57. C, D

58. B

59. D

60. C

Index

Packt.com

Subscribe to our online digital library for full access to over 7,000 books and videos, as well as industry leading tools to help you plan your personal development and advance your career. For more information, please visit our website.

Why subscribe?

- Spend less time learning and more time coding with practical eBooks and Videos from over 4,000 industry professionals

- Improve your learning with Skill Plans built especially for you

- Get a free eBook or video every month

- Fully searchable for easy access to vital information

- Copy and paste, print, and bookmark content

Did you know that Packt offers eBook versions of every book published, with PDF and ePub files available? You can upgrade to the eBook version at packt.com and as a print book customer, you are entitled to a discount on the eBook copy. Get in touch with us at customercare@packtpub.com for more details.

At www.packt.com, you can also read a collection of free technical articles, sign up for a range of free newsletters, and receive exclusive discounts and offers on Packt books and eBooks.

Other Books You May Enjoy

If you enjoyed this book, you may be interested in these other books by Packt:

The Kubernetes Bible

Nassim Kebbani, Piotr Tylenda, Russ McKendrick

ISBN: 9781838827694

- Manage containerized applications with Kubernetes
- Understand Kubernetes architecture and the responsibilities of each component
- Set up Kubernetes on Amazon Elastic Kubernetes Service, Google Kubernetes Engine, and Microsoft Azure Kubernetes Service
- Deploy cloud applications such as Prometheus and Elasticsearch using Helm charts
- Discover advanced techniques for Pod scheduling and auto-scaling the cluster
- Understand possible approaches to traffic routing in Kubernetes

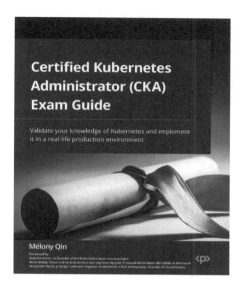

Certified Kubernetes Administrator (CKA) Exam Guide

Mélony Qin

ISBN: 9781803238265

- Understand the fundamentals of Kubernetes and its tools

- Get hands-on experience in installing and configuring Kubernetes clusters

- Manage Kubernetes clusters and deployed workloads with ease

- Get up and running with Kubernetes networking and storage

- Manage the security of applications deployed on Kubernetes

- Find out how to monitor, log, and troubleshoot Kubernetes clusters and apps among others

Packt is searching for authors like you

If you're interested in becoming an author for Packt, please visit authors.packtpub.com and apply today. We have worked with thousands of developers and tech professionals, just like you, to help them share their insight with the global tech community. You can make a general application, apply for a specific hot topic that we are recruiting an author for, or submit your own idea.

Share Your Thoughts

Now you've finished *Becoming KCNA Certified*, we'd love to hear your thoughts! Scan the QR code below to go straight to the Amazon review page for this book and share your feedback or leave a review on the site that you purchased it from.

https://packt.link/r/1804613398

Your review is important to us and the tech community and will help us make sure we're delivering excellent quality content.

Download a free PDF copy of this book

Thanks for purchasing this book!

Do you like to read on the go but are unable to carry your print books everywhere? Is your eBook purchase not compatible with the device of your choice?

Don't worry, now with every Packt book you get a DRM-free PDF version of that book at no cost.

Read anywhere, any place, on any device. Search, copy, and paste code from your favorite technical books directly into your application.

The perks don't stop there, you can get exclusive access to discounts, newsletters, and great free content in your inbox daily

Follow these simple steps to get the benefits:

1. Scan the QR code or visit the link below

https://packt.link/free-ebook/9781804613399

2. Submit your proof of purchase
3. That's it! We'll send your free PDF and other benefits to your email directly

Made in United States
Troutdale, OR
09/22/2023

13123118R00170